The Long Life of *Evangeline*

The Long Life of *Evangeline*

A History of the Longfellow Poem in Print, in Adaptation and in Popular Culture

Ron McFarland

McFarland & Company, Inc., Publishers
Jefferson, North Carolina, and London

ALSO BY RON MCFARLAND

The Rockies in First Person: A Critical Study of Recent American Memoirs from the Region (McFarland, 2009)

Frontispiece: Thomas Faed (1854) "The landscape,—the melancholy seashore,—the face and attitude of Evangeline, so full of sorrow and patience, tells the whole story with great power and truth." H.W. Longfellow, *Letters*, III, 490.

LIBRARY OF CONGRESS CATALOGUING-IN-PUBLICATION DATA

McFarland, Ronald E.
The long life of Evangeline : a history of the Longfellow poem in print, in adaptation and in popular culture / Ron McFarland.
p. cm.
Includes bibliographical references and index.

ISBN 978-0-7864-4217-1
softcover : 50# alkaline paper ♾

1. Longfellow, Henry Wadsworth, 1807–1882. Evangeline.
I. Title.
PS2263.M35 2010
811'.3—dc22 2009042188

British Library cataloguing data are available

On the front cover: Arthur Dixon illustration from *Evangeline: A Tale of Acadie* (London and New York: Ernest Nister and E.P. Dutton, n.d. [ca. 1907])

Manufactured in the United States of America

McFarland & Company, Inc., Publishers
Box 611, Jefferson, North Carolina 28640
www.mcfarlandpub.com

Acknowledgments

I am grateful to the University of Idaho for granting me a sabbatical about twelve years ago, during which I visited the *Evangeline* collection at the St. Martin Parish Library in St. Martinville, Louisiana, spent time in the stacks of the Library of Congress, and visited the Houghton Library at Harvard University. More recently I have contented myself with volumes from the Special Collections at the Suzzallo Library of the University of Washington and with imposing upon the good folks at the University of Idaho Interlibrary Loan department, to whom I am most grateful. Particular thanks to the editors of *American Drama*, where an early version, now much expanded, appeared in their fall 1998 issue (8.1, 26–49). I am also grateful to Georgia Tiffany, who has sustained my working environment and helped proofread the manuscript of this book. Any lingering errors or faulty locutions, however, are my responsibility.

Table of Contents

Acknowledgments v
Preface: Evangeline's Quiet Heroism 1
A Longfellow Chronology 17

1. *Evangeline* and the Popularity of Poetry in the United States 23
2. The Contexts of Longfellow's *Evangeline* 36
3. *Evangeline* Goes to School 61
4. *Evangeline* Illustrated 93
5. *Evangeline* on Stage, in Song, and on the Silver Screen 144
6. Reflecting on *Evangeline* 175

Bibliography 197
Index 203

Preface: Evangeline's Quiet Heroism

If not you, then perhaps your parents, and almost certainly your grandparents, encountered Henry Wadsworth Longfellow's 1,399-line narrative poem in unrhymed dactylic hexameters, *Evangeline* (1847), probably around the eighth grade. In all likelihood you, or at least they, were compelled to memorize all or part of the nineteen-line Prelude beginning with the short declaration: "This is the forest primeval." Evangeline represented for many generations the paradigmatic American woman, a model for adolescent girls and young women for at least a hundred years. Although she has become familiar as the avatar of patient, suffering endurance and self-abnegation, Evangeline's character evolves throughout the poem. She moves from the privileged but subordinate status of "daddy's girl" and "local small-town sweetheart" (the archetypal "girl next door") to mature womanhood; she never compromises her values or ideals; she asserts her autonomous identity or selfhood; she exhibits considerable courage; she commits herself to a life of service to others. For the most part, Evangeline possesses the "four cardinal virtues" of what Barbara Welter, in her historical study, *Dimity Convictions: The American Woman in the Nineteenth Century*, calls "True Womanhood": "piety, purity, submissiveness and domesticity" (21). Only in the fourth of these attributes, through no fault of her own, does she fall short. In a different context Welter addresses the issue of what might be called Evangeline's transferred domesticity: "To be a New England spinster was to be a kind of nun," and in maintaining her virginity, "woman was exercising a degree of autonomy" (164). As a Sister of Mercy, Evangeline provides the vocation by which she redefines herself, if not as what Welter calls a "New Woman," then at least as a woman unwilling to compromise her passion for the comforts of conventional domesticity. Curiously, Welter does not mention the poem in her book.

Evangeline exemplifies the virtuous character in action. As Judith Fryer's "faces of Eve" go, Evangeline represents one noteworthy type of the "American Princess" (Eve before the Fall). Moreover, Evangeline evolves as a character, maturing from the model obedient, passive daughter inclined to servility to the independent, active woman devoted to service. She remains loyal to her love for Gabriel, while undertaking a search for him that draws her to the borders of civilization, and when her life does not fall into the paradigmatic plotline one might have expected for a heroine in a mid–nineteenth-century romance, she transcends her conventional "limitations" as a woman, maintaining her independence in the process. This may be something of a best-possible-case scenario, but I suspect it comes close to the sort of reading Longfellow expected and received from the vast majority of his readers in the mid-and later nineteenth-century. In a letter dated just a week after the poem was published, Samuel G. Howe wrote, "I can understand and admire the instructive story, the sublime moral, the true poetry, which it contains. Patience, forbearance, longsuffering, love, faith,—these are the things which Evangeline teaches" (*Life* II, 98). Howe's conventional view conforms to Barbara Welter's description: "Woman's nature [...] transcended the grossness of the flesh and the grubbiness of the market place, in which man was so frequently mired by his passions and his greed" (71). In the process of acquiring her "high road of the heart" and her "higher spiritual plane," however, as Welter observes, woman was regarded as having a lesser intellect. In a journal entry for July 1, 1848, Longfellow notes, "Going to Mr. R's, the importer of shoes, he greeted me with beaming face, and praised with much feeling Evangeline, which his wife had read to him" (*Life* II, 124). Evangeline established herself early as an edifying character, as indicated by Longfellow's journal entry for February 14, 1852: "I have a letter from Laura Bridgman, the deaf, dumb, and blind, written with her own hand, on reading Evangeline. She closes by saying, 'I should love to meet her with my soul in heaven when I die on earth'" (*Life* II, 231).

It would be misleading to suggest that women have been universally attracted by Longfellow's poetry. Ironically, the poet who was to give American literature its first heroine of any consequence was himself the target of the most noted advocate of women's rights at the time. In a review published in the *New-York Daily Tribune* just two years before the publication of *Evangeline*, Margaret Fuller describes herself as one who "must confess a little coolness toward Mr. Longfellow, in consequence of the exaggerated praises that have been heaped upon him" (*Essays* 319). Specifically, she argues that Longfellow lacks originality, that "he has no style of his own" (*Essays* 320), and she concludes that in twenty years he will have dwindled to "a writer of elegant, if not always accurate taste, of great imitative power, and occasional felicity in an original way" (*Essays* 323). Fuller appears to have left no account of her reactions to *Evangeline*, if indeed she read the poem, which seems unlikely, as she was in Rome when it first appeared, was busy getting married and having her only child the next year, and died in a shipwreck on her way back to the States in the summer of 1850 with her husband and son.

We do, however, have a record of Longfellow's reaction to Fuller's "furious onslaught," which he characterizes in his journals as "bilious" (*Life* II, 27). One wonders how Fuller might have reacted to *Evangeline* in light of her vaunted "self-dependence" and her declaration of "faith" in *Woman in the Nineteenth Century* (1845), in woman's "feminine side, the side of love, of beauty, of holiness" (103). The qualities of love, beauty, and holiness are integral to Evangeline's character, and she may be the most "self-dependent" female character in American literature prior to James' Daisy Miller. I do *not* mean to imply here that Evangeline and Daisy are "sisters under the skin." For his part, Longfellow was not so small as to hold a grudge against his erstwhile critic, as his journal entry for July 23, 1850 attests: "The paper brings us news of the wreck of the 'Elizabeth' on Fire Island near Long Island, and the loss of Horace Sumner, and of Margaret Fuller, Marchioness Ossoli, with her husband and child. What a calamity! A singular woman for New England to produce; original and somewhat self-willed; but full of talent and work. A tragic end to a somewhat troubled and romantic life" (*Life* II, 185).

Margaret Fuller taught school for a couple of years in Providence, Rhode Island, beginning in the spring of 1837. Had she remained in that profession she might well have had the opportunity to teach *Evangeline*. But would she have chosen to do so? The poem sold well with Longfellow's Boston publisher, Ticknor & Fields, printing nineteen editions by 1865 (his London publisher, Bogue, issued six editions by 1862), but its later adaptation by the public schools established *Evangeline* in the canon. The notes, study questions and other apparatus provided for the school text editions from the 1880s through the 1960s provide particular evidence of how the poem was to be read and interpreted. In his introduction to the 1900 text edition for Macmillan, Lewis B. Semple, who taught high school in Brooklyn, New York, wrote: "One may safely say that Evangeline is the most read poem in American literature. The reason is clear: it is a story of love, ideal love, so simply told that the least imaginative can understand" (xxix). One might speculate that its simplicity accounts for the poem's virtual disappearance from the canon today. In one of the composition assignments prepared for the 1916 Riverside edition, Margaret Ashmun directs the student to

"Imagine that you are a little girl who wanted to see Longfellow" (109), a prologue that may suggest the difficulty of avoiding at least some gender bias. But that assignment is balanced by one in which the student is instructed to "Imagine that you are Gabriel" (111). Another composition topic directs students to describe Evangeline's kitchen in Grand-Pré "and show her at work in it churning, or getting dinner, or baking cookies. Try to show by what she does that she is a good housekeeper. Try to show her sweet, kindly nature" (110). That is, the poem was being appropriated, ironically *by* a woman, for support of the dominant, essentially patriarchal, ideology of the day: woman as sweet and kindly housewife—little wonder the poem has largely disappeared from the canon since the 1960s.

William Wasserstrom does not mention *Evangeline* in *Heiress of the Ages: Sex and Sentiment in the Genteel Tradition*, but the poem compellingly embodies his premise that "In literature, the chief result of this mystique of sex [which he later traces to the conclusion of Goethe's *Faust*]—women are better than men—is a preference for heroines rather than heroes" (3). If not his intellectual peer, woman, as Welter notes, was conceived during the nineteenth century to be man's spiritual superior: "When man spoke of something bigger than all of us, mysterious, sublime, and unresponsive to logic, the sea, the weather, the fates, he spoke of 'her'" (71). The initial descriptions of Evangeline (*ll.* 65–81) focus on her dark beauty (black eyes gleam beneath brown hair), on her role in the community (her carrying of "Flagons of home-brewed ale" to the reapers is one of the most frequent topics of illustration), and on her spiritual nature (eight of the seventeen lines in this passage, concern her "celestial brightness"). Throughout the poem she is associated symbolically with the lamp, which performs in the poem as what folklorists would call a "life index." The "brazen lamp" she lights on the night of her betrothal (*l.* 330) might be said to be extinguished only with the darkness that accompanies Gabriel's death (*l.* 1375), "As when a lamp is blown out by a gust of wind at a casement." The passage also indicates Evangeline's national dress: Norman cap, blue kirtle, and heirloom earrings. This associates her explicitly with her ethnic identity and helps establish her as symbol or emblem of her people. At the same time her "more ethereal beauty" hints at saintliness, and in nearly all illustrations of her walking home from confession "with God's benediction upon her" the community obviously regards her as something special: "When she had passed, it seemed like the ceasing of exquisite music." In her interpretive notes on this passage, Lucy Adella Sloan, head of the English department at Central State Normal School in Mount Pleasant, Michigan, wrote: "Three pictures are introduced from her daily life showing that she has also the beauty of usefulness, of spirit, and of personality" (61).

Later in the canto we are reminded that in this sunny, idyllic world seventeen-year-old Evangeline "governed his [her elderly father's] household." Not surprisingly, she has many suitors, and a close reader will note that their attraction borders on idolatry: "Happy was he who might touch her hand or the hem of her garment!" (ℓ. 107). Only Gabriel Lajeunesse, however, the son of Basil the blacksmith and her father's good friend, is welcome. In fact, they are childhood sweethearts, and Longfellow briefly surveys their youthful play at the end of the first canto. One might note that her preference for a man acceptable to her father might be predicted of the character who would be recognized as American literature's premiere Daddy's Girl. We are told that she is "a woman now, with the heart and hopes of a woman!" (ℓ. 143), but Longfellow continues to suspend her character between the human and the saint. The Acadians call her the "Sunshine of Saint Eulalie," the saint associated with fruitful harvest (particularly of apples); at the same time, as a woman, she will quite conventionally be expected to bring "love and the ruddy faces of children" (ℓ. 147) to her husband's house.

Evangeline does not appear on stage, so to speak, until about sixty lines into the second canto, and when she does, we find her seated at her father's side on the evening of her betrothal contract "Spinning flax for the loom" (ℓ. 211). The patriarchal nature of Acadian society manifests itself nowhere more clearly than in this portion of the poem, in which the angry Basil announces the arrival of the British fleet and points to the imminent danger to their community, while the old farmer smokes his pipe and temporizes. Although the canto ends with her blushing and holding hands with Gabriel at the window, Evangeline's only other role is to bring her father Benedict's pipe. This may imply that political matters lie outside the realm of a woman's concern, as Longfellow does not indicate her reaction to the men's debate. On the other hand, young Gabriel is also preoccupied, so one could surmise that such issues are not of concern to the young in general, or at least not to young people in love.

In the third canto the old notary, René Leblanc, father of twenty children, enters to draw up the marriage contract, and the debate continues with Leblanc supporting Benedict's moderate views on the British against the fiery words of "the hasty and somewhat irascible blacksmith" (ℓ. 297). Noted as the village storyteller, Leblanc offers a fable of divine justice, but Basil the blacksmith remains unconvinced. Evangeline's role in the matter remains as in the previous canto: she lights the lamp and pours ale, and after the contract is sealed, she brings out the checkerboard. Longfellow gives over the last thirty or so lines of the canto, however, to a description of Evangeline in her moonlit room, associating her with the moonlight, silence, and simplicity as she dreams of her lover, who watches her from outside. The emphasis falls on the simple dowry she brings to the marriage, "Linen and woolen stuffs, by the hand of Evangeline woven [...] Better than flocks and herds, being proofs of her skill as a housewife" (*ll.* 1. 366, 368). Presumably, however, Gabriel would be heir to the Bellefontaine farm (the "flocks and herd"), a point made quite explicit in the 1929 film version starring Dolores Del Rio (page 172). Two important foreshadowing passages occur at the end of the canto when Evangeline experiences "a feeling of sadness" (*l.* 376) and, more subtly but more ominously, when Longfellow compares a star following the footsteps of the moon with "young Ishmael" wandering from Abraham's tent with Hagar, his mother. The passage from Genesis 21:9–21 refers to the expulsion of the Israelites and their ordeal in the desert.

In the fourth canto the betrothal feast opens with Evangeline smiling and serving ale, but Colonel Winslow soon disrupts the merriment with the expulsion orders. In the furor that follows Basil is struck down and Father Felician restores order by preaching "lessons of love and forgiveness" (*l.* 471), but Evangeline's reactions are again muted. In fact, she responds as does Father Felician, and in keeping with her own moral character:

> Ah! on her spirit within a deeper shadow had fallen,
> And from the fields of her soul a fragrance celestial ascended,—
> Charity, meekness, love, and hope, and forgiveness, and patience!
> Then, all-forgetful of self, she wandered into the village,
> Cheering with looks and words the disconsolate hearts of the women
> [*ll.* 499–503].

The qualities listed in the third line of the passage above not only define Evangeline's character, but also move toward the climactic culmination in "patience," which will prove to be her cardinal virtue and which, one might note, connects her with Penelope, the other major symbol of woman's domestic virtue in western literature. Significantly, however, Longfellow also associates her with the spirit of self-abnegation and with the welfare of the community.

At the end of the fourth canto Longfellow deceives or misleads Evangeline and the reader, or perhaps it is more accurate to say that in the process of showing how the unhappy Evangeline is reassured by the "voice of the echoing thunder" that "God was in heaven, and governed the world He created" (*l.* 521), the reader is at least temporarily set up. The thunder reminds her of Leblanc's tale of "the justice of heaven," so her "troubled soul" is "soothed" and she sleeps peacefully. From much of what happens thereafter in the poem, most readers will detect no reason to assume "God's in heaven—/ All's right with the world!" (Browning's "Pippa Passes" had been published in 1841.) Only at the end, against all evidence to the contrary, will Evangeline insist on the assertion of divine justice. As is usually the case in narratives that concern tests of faith, the triumph comes through the hero's willingness to embrace paradox.

In the fifth canto the deportation occurs and Evangeline is separated from Gabriel. Predictably by now for the reader who knows her, Evangeline waits silently, "Not overcome with grief, but strong in the hour of affliction" (ℓ. 554). To her stricken lover she speaks "words of endearment where words of comfort availed not" (ℓ. 566), thus taking over what is regarded conventionally as the man's role. Significantly, in fact, the first words Evangeline utters in the poem occur at this moment: "'Gabriel! be of good cheer! for if we love one another, / Nothing, in truth, can harm us, whatever mischances may happen!'" (ℓℓ. 559–560). In his "Suggestive Questions" on this passage W. F. Conover, a public school teacher from San Diego who edited the poem for an 1899 text published in Chicago, asked, "What characteristic of woman is shown in these lines?" (130). Conover's question does not imply that Evangeline's strength, optimism, and grace under pressure are aspects of her individual character, but universal "characteristics of woman."

Only after Gabriel has been transported and she has failed to get her elderly father to eat or even to speak does Evangeline yield to the tears that filled her eyes when she saw "the face of Gabriel pale with emotion" (ℓ. 556) at the shore. The image Longfellow draws of her and Father Felician weeping "together in silence" (ℓ. 612) anticipates not only their companionship in the search for Gabriel that occurs in Part Two, but also their stoic acceptance of adversity and disappointment. When old Benedict dies, Evangeline wails "aloud in her terror," faints, and then falls into a "deep, oblivious slumber" (ℓ. 644). Here and elsewhere in the poem, sleep for the innocent Evangeline represents the gentle nurse "that knits up the sleeve of ravel'd care." Her sleep, uninterrupted by dreams, is the "Balm of hurt minds" (*Macbeth* II, ii, 37). The first part ends with the burial of Benedict near the sea and the embarkation of the rest of the Acadians as their village lies in ruins, torched by the British.

Although Longfellow does not specify how many "weary" years have passed when Part Two of the poem begins, editors Maud Elma Kingsley and Frank Herbert Palmer declare that, based upon historical evidence, ten years have gone by (56). The diaspora occurred in September of 1755, when Evangeline was seventeen, and presumably the second part of the poem, which runs sixty-nine lines longer than the first, opens in May of 1765 ("Outline Study" 9). Sloan, however, suggests that "probably not more than seven or eight years" have elapsed, "perhaps not more than five" (90). Scholars are generally agreed that the closing scene in Philadelphia coincides with the yellow fever epidemic of 1793 (Evangeline would have been about fifty-five years old). We first encounter her in the second part of the poem surveying tombstones, "a maiden who waited and wandered, / Lowly and meek in spirit, and patiently suffering all things" (ℓℓ. 681–682).

Despite the passage of as many as ten years, Longfellow describes her still with the epithet, "Fair was she and young," but she has changed from the ebullient teenager she was in the first part of the poem. The cheerful, composed, spiritually serene, and domesticated self is now "urged by the fever within her, / Urged by a restless longing, the hunger and thirst of the spirit" (ℓℓ. 693–694). Something in her life remains "incomplete, imperfect, unfinished" (ℓ. 689), so that whereas at the age of seventeen she seemed on the verge of "completion," of "being" a woman, we find her now, ironically, some five to ten years later, in the midst of becoming. In textbook terms she has moved from being a "static" to a "dynamic" character. She could, presumably, fall into a malaise that would prove fatal, and although her searching through graveyards serves a practical function, at the same time this sort of morbid behavior could signify chronic depression.

When other displaced Acadians remind her that Baptiste Leblanc, the notary's son, has long been in love with her, Evangeline responds "serenely but sadly,—I cannot!" (ℓ. 174). In one of her lengthier speeches, she explains,

> Whither my heart has gone, there follows my hand, and not elsewhere.
> For when the heart goes before, like a lamp, and illumines the pathway,
> Many things are made clear, that else lie hidden in darkness [ℓℓ. 715–717].

Her reference to the lamp may remind readers of her associations with light in the first part of the poem, notably in the third canto, after the signing of the betrothal papers; and Father Felician, who has at least figuratively replaced her biological father for what will prove to be the trial of her spiritual character, promptly commends her metaphor: "O daughter! thy God thus speaketh within thee!" (ℓ. 719). This leads to his most frequently quoted sermon, in which he preaches, first, that "affection never was wasted" and that if it does not enrich others, it has the capacity to return and renew the self: "That which the fountain sends forth returns again to the fountain" (ℓ. 723). Second, he counsels "Patience" and accomplishing the "work of affection" or the "labor of love" in what amounts to a theology of good works. Finally, he offers a maxim that anticipates her eventual lesson: "Sorrow and silence are strong, and patient endurance is godlike" (ℓ. 725).

Against the fairly bland imagery of the domestic scenes from Grand-Pré, Longfellow indulges his palette in the second canto of Part Two, when he enters the subtropics of the Louisiana bayous. A vision sustains Evangeline as she pursues her beloved, "the thought of her brain that assumed the shape of a phantom" (ℓ. 787), but as phantoms tend to be, Gabriel proves elusive, and amid the swampy islands, his boat of fellow hunters and trappers passes hers unsighted. Significantly, Evangeline's quest or search for the beloved situates the woman in the role of the pursuer. While not unique in literature—consider, for example Una's pursuit of the Red Cross Knight in the first book of Spenser's *Faerie Queene*—the circumstances are at least unusual. Gabriel, in fact, "thoughtful and careworn," with "Dark and neglected locks" overshadowing his brow, has become "weary with waiting, unhappy and restless" (ℓℓ. 831–832). He succumbs to a Byronic sort of flight from self reminiscent of Manfred's as, with "a sadness / Somewhat beyond his years" he "Sought in the Western wilds oblivion of self and of sorrow" (ℓℓ. 852, 954). In short, Evangeline is made of sterner stuff than her melancholy lover.

When Evangeline awakens with the presentiment that Gabriel has been near, Father Felician encourages her, arguing that "feeling is deep and still" and urging her to "trust to thy heart, and to what the world calls illusions!" (ℓℓ. 852, 854). Longfellow continues to lure (and to mislead) the reader just as he deceives Evangeline. Subtle deception, in fact, appears to be the modus operandi of Longfellow throughout most of the poem. "'Gabriel is truly near thee,'" Father Felician promises, and he is a priest, after all. At St.Martin[ville], he says, echoing the most famous bridal verse in western culture, the *Song of Songs*, "There the long-wandering bride shall be given her bridegroom, / There the long-absent pastor regain his flock and his sheepfold" (ℓℓ. 858–859). Buoyed with exotic images and promises of "the Eden of Louisiana," Evangeline's heart is filled with "inexpressible sweetness" and is "Touched by the magic spell, the sacred fountains of feeling" (ℓ. 871). When a welcoming bird sings out from a "neighboring thicket," wary readers will take note that it is a "mocking-bird, wildest of singers" (ℓ. 872). In fact, Longfellow promptly conceals this foreshadowing by extending the description over the next nine lines. Yet the purple passage is itself as deceptive as the mockingbird's song. The reader will suspect the party should be entering the bayou with very mixed emotions.

The third canto, however, opens with a domestic scene in the bayous that might be regarded as the antithetical counterpart to the opening scene of the poem. We have moved from the pleasures of Hard Primitivism in Nova Scotia to the comforts of Soft Primitivism in Louisiana. Although readers are well aware that Gabriel is not at his father's ranch, they may have assumed (back in 1847, before the poem and its legend became almost universally familiar) that a reunion was at hand. After all, the last lines of the Prelude have implicitly assured us as readers that if we believe in "affection that hopes, and endures, and is patient" and "the beauty and strength of woman's devotion," all will be well. Basil confidently assures Evangeline they will set out after the "fugitive lover" who left home only that day, and in the whirl of social activity and celebration that follows, we temporarily lose sight of the sorrowing Evangeline.

When we encounter her alone in the evening as the party goes on in the house, Evangeline remembers the sound of the sea and is seized with "an irrepressible sadness" (ℓ. 1025). The moonlight which bathed her room at the end of the third canto of Part One with luminous promise now falls "here and there through the branches" as a "tremulous gleam [...] / Like the sweet thoughts of love on a darkened and devious spirit!" (ℓ. 1030). The "indefinable Longing" that "inundate [s]" her soul may remind us of the odd "feeling of sadness" she felt almost seven hundred lines earlier. The "oracular" oaks answer her impassioned lament for Gabriel with the whisper of "Patience!" (ℓ. 1057), but like so many optimistic hints scattered through the second half of the poem, the prophecy is not to be fulfilled, or at least not as the reader might suppose. Readers may, or may not, recall Longfellow's use of the word "devious" in II.2 (ℓ. 767) with respect to how both the river and the Acadians in their "cumbrous boat" have "swerved from their course" and entered the Bayou of Plaquemine where they are "lost in a maze of sluggish and devious waters."

At this point in the poem Father Felician stays behind and Evangeline continues her journey accompanied by Basil. Presumably, the first stage of her spiritual education has been completed, and from one perspective, at least, she has changed father figures. As she enters the "desert land" and mountains of the West, where she will manage to avoid "the scattered tribes of Ishmael's children, / Staining the desert with blood" (ℓℓ. 1095–1096), Evangeline requires a more physically fit companion. Longfellow opens the fourth canto with references to bears, wolves, and "savage marauders," and at a Shawnee camp an Indian woman tells of her Canadian husband being murdered by "the cruel Camanches [sic]" (ℓ. 1120), but in fact she encounters no threat of bodily harm in her subsequent wanderings. Unlike Spenser's Una, Longfellow never portrays Evangeline as the heroine of a romance in danger of rape or seduction.

Throughout the poem, however, Evangeline faces psychological and spiritual perils. The question is not whether she will be murdered or raped, but whether her devotion to Gabriel and to God will remain intact. If these do remain intact, she will have sustained her matured sense of self and proven her character. The greatest threat to her heroic status, after all, is not physical, but lies in the stories the Shawnee woman tells "as if a mysterious horror / Passed through her brain" (ℓℓ. 1138–1139). The first concerns Mowis, "the bridegroom of snow" who "wedded a maiden" and then vanished, "melting away and dissolving into the sunshine" (ℓ. 1141), leaving the woman to follow him eternally into the forest. The second tells of "the fair Lilinau, who was wooed by a phantom" (ℓ. 1145) and who followed him into the forest, never to be seen again.

Although these stories fill Evangeline with "thoughts of love," she is stricken with a subtle sense "of pain and indefinite terror, / As the cold, poisonous snake creeps into the nest of a Swallow" (ℓℓ. 1158–1160). Although Longfellow separates the allusions by more than a thousand lines, the swallow's nest he mentions at the end of the opening canto (ℓ. 139) surely is echoed with ominous irony here: "Lucky was he who found the stone in the nest of the swallow!" Footnotes explain that an old French fable tells of how a mother swallow will seek out a pebble to restore the sight of a blind fledgling, and anyone finding such a stone in the bird's nest will have good luck (10n). Evangeline has experienced a broad range of emotions during her search, including sadness, longing, and doubt, but this is the first time Evangeline has felt fear, and it is described as "no earthly fear." She fears that "like the Indian maiden, she, too, is pursuing a phantom" (ℓ. 1163). If Gabriel is dead, her quest has been in vain and her definition of herself is meaningless. With this thought, however, she falls into a healing sleep reminiscent of the "oblivious slumber" into which she fell after the death of her father, and both her fear and the phantom vanish. The next morning, accompanied by the Shawnee woman, they resume their search and go to a Jesuit mission among the Indians, where they learn that Gabriel has been dwelling there within the past six days. Once again Longfellow lures Evangeline and the reader into assuming that a happy discovery scene and romantic ending are at hand.

Longfellow returns to the metaphor of the bird's nest when the priest's news falls "as in winter the snow-flakes / Fall into some lone nest from which the birds have departed" (ℓℓ. 1198–1199). But again Longfellow offers her (and us) hope, as the Jesuit priest expects Gabriel to return after the hunting expedition. Basil now returns to the bayous, leaving Evangeline to be healed by the message that has echoed throughout the poem (patience will be rewarded) and by the lesson of the compass flower of faith, the "delicate plant" on its "fragile stock" that directs the traveler "Over the sea-like, pathless, limitless waste of the desert" (ℓ. 1221). The priest explains that the "blossoms of passion, / Gay and luxuriant flowers [...] beguile us, and lead us astray [...] / Only this humble plant can guide us here, and hereafter / Crown us with asphodel flowers, that are wet with the dews of nepenthe" (ℓℓ. 1222–1226). The "blossoms of passion" presumably relate to the showy passion flower (*Passiflora*), as opposed to the more common compass flower (*Silphium*). Annotators who point out the association of the asphodel with Greek mythology (the flower is sacred to Persephone), where it is connected with the shades of heroes, have made the allegorical message clear enough, but some readers might wonder whether the Jesuit priest's message here doesn't conflict with the earlier advice of Father Felician (*ll*. 851–854, page) to the effect that Evangeline should trust her heart and "to what the world calls illusions" (presumably the "illusions" of feeling and passion).

In the remaining lines of the fourth canto Longfellow summarizes Evangeline's year-long wait at the mission and her subsequent search, apparently unaccompanied, into the north woods of Michigan, where she finds the hunters' lodge "deserted and fallen to ruin" (*l*. 1238). She turns her search eastward during the period of the Revolutionary War, moving through battlefields, towns, and cities "Like a phantom," recalling the phantom of the Shawnee woman's story (*l*. 1244). No longer young and fair, but faded and old, with "faint streaks of gray o'er her forehead" (*l*. 1249), Evangeline appears in danger of becoming herself the very phantom she fears she is pursuing.

What saves her from despair or madness or the fate of the undead is not the end of her "fruitless search," but her capacity to transform the object of that search into an image, "Clothed in the beauty of love and youth, as last she beheld him, / Only more beautiful made by his deathlike silence and absence" (*ll*. 1277–1278). In effect, one might say she is saved by the imagination, or by art; she becomes a de facto poet. "Into her thoughts of him time entered not"; we are told: "he was not changed, but transfigured" (*ll*. 1279–1280). The word choice is obviously charged. Paradoxically, Gabriel has "become to her heart as one who is dead, and not absent." The lessons taught her by her life of "trial and sorrow" by now have become predictable: "Patience and abnegation of self, and devotion to others" (*l*. 1282) She becomes a beloved Sister of Mercy, ministering to the dying at the almshouse in Philadelphia during the yellow fever epidemic. The "celestial light" that announced her beauty in the first canto of the poem still encircle[s] her forehead with splendor" (*l*. 1315), but her physical beauty has been transformed or "transfigured."

When she encounters the dying Gabriel, we meet with one of the most memorable scenes in all of the literature of sentiment, a scene that was at least the equal in its day of the death in *Uncle Tom's Cabin* of Little Eva, who was likely named after Longfellow's heroine. The cry of "terrible anguish" she utters upon recognizing Gabriel recalls her wailing "aloud in her terror" at the death of her father in the last canto of Part One, and echoes of earlier portions of the poem are scattered throughout the last lines, culminating in the light from Gabriel's eyes that is extinguished "As when a lamp is blown out by a gust of wind at a casement" (*l*. 1375), which draws the reader back to the end of the third canto of Part One, where Gabriel sees Evangeline through a window holding a lamp.

Evangeline emerges as a symbol of patient endurance of suffering and of loyal devotion to genuine love, piety, and chastity. She exemplifies courage and determination in the face of great odds, and when her Odyssean quest fails of its goal, she does not simply acquiesce to fate by pining away, on the one hand, or by accepting the best available domestic option (marriage, as offered, with Baptiste Leblanc, the notary's son) on the other. After a life devoted to service, as opposed to an empty or a self-indulgent spinsterhood, Evangeline, worn out by "All the aching of heart, the restless, unsatisfied longing, / All the dull, deep pain, and constant anguish of patience!" (*ll.* 1377–1378), still has the faith to bow her head "meekly" and murmur, "Father, I thank thee!" (*l.* 1380). Whether this ending is more, or less, "sentimental" than that of *Uncle Tom's Cabin*, or than such scenes therein as the death of Little Eva, may be debated (I would suggest "more"), but surely Evangeline merits some notice from those following in the wake of Ann Douglas's *The Feminization of America* (1977). Male scholars have often neglected the domestic and sentimental novel, the novel of feeling, as the product of Hawthorne's "damned mob of scribbling women," but recent scholars have attended to that oversight (or prejudice). Although it was not a product of a "scribbling" woman, *Evangeline* has been another casualty of the anti-sentimental trend in American literary criticism, and as a result its significance has been all too casually disregarded.

The fact that over the past forty years most readers, teachers, and scholars interested in women's issues or feminist agendas have ignored *Evangeline* may simply indicate how far Longfellow himself and this poem in particular have fallen from canonical grace. If, as Roland Barthes is supposed to have said, literature is "what gets taught," then perhaps *Evangeline* was but is no longer "literature," a prospect that leads to the question of whether, after all, a text's literary identity is determined whimsically. When I visited the St. Martin Parish Library in St. Martinville, Louisiana, a dozen years ago to examine their extensive collection of Evangeline[iana] I found that the librarian had never read the poem and that it was no longer taught in the local public schools. Once the most popular and perhaps the "best-loved" poet in America, Longfellow was honored and read throughout the world, and *Evangeline* was translated into languages ranging from Basque and Danish to Polish and Portuguese. But today the poem is neither taught nor anthologized, as even college texts stay with shorter, and I think both less impressive and less important, poems like "A Psalm of Life," "Hymn to the Night," and "The Jewish Cemetery at Newport."

Longfellow's decline in status, it could also be maintained, does not entail simply a matter of changing tastes, for he had influential detractors from the start, with Edgar Allan Poe being only the most vociferous among them. Without rehearsing here the grim litany of charges, suffice it to say that as early as 1885, just three years after Longfellow's death, poet, banker, and literary critic E.C. Stedman (1833–1908), while a sympathetic reader, could write that Longfellow failed the "higher tests of poetic genius,—spontaneity, sweep, intellect, imaginative power" (191) and that his "admirers may form no longer a critical majority" (180).

But it may be that a certain poetic justice has been served in the case of *Evangeline*, for if it is valid, for reasons implicit in my observations hereafter on the text of the poem, that women as readers, teachers, and commentators first established it in the canon, it may well be that another generation of women as readers, teachers, and commentators have expelled it. As Robyn R. Warhol and Diane Price Herndl assert in their introductory essay to *Feminisms*, "Its overtly political nature is perhaps the single most distinguishing feature of feminist scholarly work" (x). The diminished reputation of *Evangeline* may be as much a matter of politics as of taste. After all, a teacher today would not be likely to ask a thirteen year-old girl to imagine herself in Evangeline's position (though Harriett Tippett does precisely that in her Suggestions for Writing in the 1962 text edition).

One may as easily read *Evangeline* as a subtly, if not overtly, anti-feminist text as one may read it as a celebration of woman as hero. First, lacking a sexual dimension to her identity, Evangeline never becomes a complete woman, never realizes her own sexuality or becomes a mother (nor is she even a sister). Second, her philosophy (or theology, and implicitly even her politics) remains typically passive. Her "patient endurance of suffering" is precisely what patriarchal society demands, elicits or procures from women (and from the proletariat as well), and religion can be a primary tool of procurement. Indeed, in her meek acquiescence to God the Father at the end of the poem, Evangeline might be said to have surrendered symbolically to western patriarchal culture. Moreover, one might note that the words of wisdom—"Sorrow and silence are strong, and patient endurance is godlike" (ℓ. 725)—are spoken by a male, which may suggest that Evangeline is not capable of discovering such truths (or truisms) on her own; that is, she seems to require a man to give voice to her predicament. Presumably, one patriarchal figure (her father) is replaced by another in Father Felician and by yet another in Basil the blacksmith/herdsman. Finally, Evangeline may appear all too willing to accept that "wisdom" cheerfully, which is to say uncritically, unthinkingly, passively. In short, while it may have been Longfellow's intent to empower women in some ways through his portrayal of Evangeline, he may actually have swept the rug out from under their feet.

Moreover, what we know of Longfellow's attitudes toward women and the women's rights movement suggests that he was very much a man of his moment and, as one of his biographers argues, an "American Victorian" if not in fact America's equivalent of Victoria herself in his propriety (Gorman, ix). Even Ralph Waldo Emerson, in his "Address to the Woman's Rights Convention" of 1855, which he repeated in 1860 and with revisions in 1869 for the New England Woman's Suffrage Association, while he advocated offering women the vote, asserts their conventional, Evangeline-like strength, that "women are strong by sentiment": "The life of the affections is primary to them, so that there is usually no employment or career which they will not, with their own applause and that of society, quit for a suitable marriage" (215). Longfellow's brother and biographer Samuel cites a companion's letter: "You were ever an admirer of the sex; but they seemed to you something enshrined and holy,—to be gazed at and talked with, nothing further." Gorman concludes that Longfellow's "chivalrous attitude" was what "made him in later years to have less sympathy with the movements for women's enfranchisement from homage and privilege to equal standing with men" (*Life* I, 39). In his journal for March 21, 1848, Longfellow writes: "Mr. [Henry L.] Giles lectured on 'Womanhood.' Not so good a lecture as the last [on Don Quixote]. I do not like to have woman discussed in public. Something within me rebels at the profanation" (*Life* II, 118).

Regarding the poem from a feminist perspective raises questions worth considering. Perhaps there is more to the poem, and to Evangeline herself, than has met the eye over the hundred sixty years that have elapsed since its appearance. Such readings cut against the grain of a conventional response to the poem, which is, I believe, overtly honorific with respect to women, or at least it would have been considered so in Longfellow's day.

* * *

This book would probably never have happened if my eighth-grade English teacher, Mr. Philip I. Eschbach, had not compelled me to memorize some of those lines from the Prelude to *Evangeline* and if I had not come across an 1892 illustrated edition of the poem featuring the 1850 designs of Jane Benham, Birket Foster, and John Gilbert years ago in an antique shop. My collection now includes more than forty different editions of the poem, a dozen of them illustrated versions. The book reflects various aspects of what I call my "Evangeline obsession," or more accurately, "infatuation." In addition to making some reflections on Longfellow's poem and the state of poetry today, I devote a chapter to its early reception and its current status in the literary world. The third chapter concerns *Evangeline* as it was studied in the public schools, the source of its canonicity, and the next chapter focuses on the myriad illustrated editions of the poem. Both of these approaches open up different avenues to appreciation and interpretation of the poem while at the same time reflecting on pedagogical trends and on the art of book illustration. In perhaps my most self-indulgent chapter, the fifth, I undertake a survey of the poem as it has been adapted for theatrical and musical performance over the generations, from musical comedy to the movies, and yes, including a passing observation on the popular Emmylou Harris song.

In the final chapter I have attempted a fairly close commentary on *Evangeline*, moving away from the feminist slant I have adopted above. Here and elsewhere readers will discover redundancies—reiterations both of factual details and of textual citations and interpretive comments. I prefer to think of these as "emphatic," but some readers might find them simply irksome. I hope not. In lieu of a biographical sketch I have provided a chronology of Longfellow's life which I hope readers will find useful.

Throughout the text I have commented on the connections between *Evangeline* and popular culture. While the poem has played various important and indeed unique historical roles over eight generations, Longfellow inadvertently created something of a commercial monster, and I suppose he might have gotten a kick out of that, but perhaps not. The website of the McCord Museum of Canadian History in Montreal accounts for many varieties of commercial appropriation.* From Evangeline candy to Evangeline soaps and candles, his heroine has been thoroughly commodified: a newspaper in Nova Scotia, a state park in Louisiana. The Maine Memory Network, the state's online museum, features an Evangeline calendar dated 1904. She might be said to have transcended her own poem, as many who seem to know a great deal about Evangeline have apparently never read the poem.

* *http://www.museemccord.qc.ca/scripts/viewobject.php?section=162&Lang=1&tourID=GE_P2_1_EN&seqNumber=32&carrousel=true*

A Longfellow Chronology

Because this study focuses on a single text, I have elected not to present a conventional biographical chapter, but realizing that some readers might appreciate having immediate access to certain details of Longfellow's life and work (his marriages, dates of his children's births and wives' deaths, publication dates of his most important books), I have opted for what I hope will be a more useful chronology featuring selected cultural and political events that coincide with important dates in the biography. In deciding which parallel events to include, I confess to having occasionally indulged my whims.

1807 Henry Wadsworth Longfellow born (February 27) in Portland, District of Maine (state of Massachusetts) to Stephen, an attorney and seven-term Federalist representative to Congress, and Zilpah, whose prosperous father had served as a general in the Revolutionary War. HWL had an older brother (Stephen, Jr.), two younger brothers, and four sisters. Robert Fulton's steamboat *Clermont* makes its first successful run, initiating a new era in transportation and river commerce.

1814 HWL turns seven. In August British troops burn down the Library of Congress, destroying 3,000 volumes as President James Madison and wife Dolly flee Washington; in September Francis Scott Key writes "The Star Spangled Banner"; in December the Treat of Ghent ends the War of 1812. George Gordon, Lord Byron's narrative poem, *The Corsair*, sells 10,000 copies the first day of publication, 25,000 copies in the first month.

1822 HWL enters Bowdoin College at age 15, to graduate fourth in a class of 28 in 1825; among his classmates were Nathaniel Hawthorne and future president Franklin Pierce. Revolutionary leaders/liberators José de San Martín and Simón Bolívar meet at Guayaquil, Ecuador. Franz

Schubert's *Symphony #8* ("The Unfinished"). Percy Bysshe Shelley drowns in Italy.

1826–1829 HWL studies in France, Spain, Italy, and Germany (at his father's expense) in preparation for a teaching position in modern foreign languages at Bowdoin. Internal combustion engine patented (1826); Baltimore & Ohio Railroad incorporated, the first to haul both people and freight commercially (1827); Andrew Jackson elected president (1828); Goethe's *Faust*, written mostly between 1806 and 1808, premieres on stage (1829)—Goethe is generally regarded as Longfellow's favorite writer.

1831 HWL marries the reputedly beautiful Mary Storer Potter, daughter of a judge in Portland. HWL prepares texts in various languages for his students, translates texts including a Spanish version of Washington Irving's "Rip Van Winkle," and writes scholarly essays. Nat Turner leads an unsuccessful slave rebellion in Virginia, where more than fifty whites are killed. In the aftermath 55 blacks are executed, including Turner, and as many as 200 are killed in the ensuing mob violence.

1835 HWL travels to Germany and Scandinavian countries in order to prepare himself for the Smith Professorship of Modern Languages and Belles-Lettres at Harvard. His prose travel memoirs, *Outre-Mer* (beyond the sea), is well received. HWL's wife Mary dies in childbirth in Rotterdam. Charles Dickens' *Pickwick Papers* published serially (1836–1837).

1837 HWL turns thirty, reviews Nathaniel Hawthorne's *Twice-Told Tales*. Victoria is crowned queen of England. HWL begins courting Frances "Fanny" Appleton but is rejected. Abolitionist editor Elijah Lovejoy is killed by pro-slavery mob in Alton, Illinois.

1839 *Voices of the Night*, HWL's first slender book of poetry, featuring "Hymn to the Night" and "A Psalm of Life," appears along with his autobiographical and philosophical travel novel, *Hyperion*. Reviews of the poems are exceptionally positive, setting aside that of Edgar Allan Poe, who is to be a lifelong literary adversary. Journalist John L. O'Sullivan coins the phrase "Manifest Destiny." Louis Daguerre patents his camera—beginning of commercial photography.

1841 *Ballads and Other Poems* is published, featuring "The Village Blacksmith" and "The Wreck of the Hesperus," which achieve immediate popular acclaim. Robert Schumann's *Symphony #4* premieres. Thomas Carlyle's *Heroes and Hero Worship* published (HWL met Carlyle in 1835).

1842 HWL spends several months in Germany for his health. *Poems on Slavery* published in December and praised by abolitionists, including

John Greenleaf Whittier. Treaty of Nanking ends the First Opium War in China.

1843 HWL marries Fanny Appleton; they receive Craigie House in Cambridge, Massachusetts, formerly General Washington's headquarters, as a wedding gift from her father. Publication of the closet drama, *The Spanish Student*, which Poe claims on improbable grounds was plagiarized from one of his own unpublished plays. Dickens' *A Christmas Carol* first published. Britain declares Natal, in South Africa, a colony.

1844 Charles "Charley" Appleton Longfellow born. Samuel Morse sends first telegraphic message. Charles Goodyear patents vulcanization process for rubber. Karl Marx and Friedrich Engels meet in Paris (their *Communist Manifesto* is published in 1848). Ralph Waldo Emerson's *Essays. Second Series*, including "Nature" and "The Poet," published.

1845 Ernest Wadsworth Longfellow born. HWL's *The Belfry of Bruges and Other Poems* is published, including "The Arrow and the Song" ("I shot an arrow into the air, / It fell to the earth, I knew not where [...]"). Poe's "The Raven" first published. Margaret Fuller's *Woman in the Nineteenth Century* published. Florida admitted to the union as the 27th state and Texas as the 28th. The rubber band invented in England. *Scientific American* begins publication.

1847 Frances "Fanny" Longfellow born (dies 1848). HWL turns forty. *Evangeline* published (November 1). First American postage stamp issued. Brigham Young and his Mormon followers settle at the Great Salt Lake. Charlotte Brontë's *Jane Eyre* published under the pseudonym Currer Bell—an immediate success. American Medical Association founded. John C. Frémont named first governor of the California Territory.

1849 HWL's prose fiction, *Kavanagh*, is published, said to depict the first lesbian relationship in American fiction. Potato famine in Ireland. Gold discovered at Sutter's Mill in California. Francis Parkman's *The Oregon Trail* published.

1850 Alice Mary ("grave Alice" of "The Children's Hour") Longfellow born. HWL's *The Seaside and the Fireside* published. Nathaniel Hawthorne's *The Scarlet Letter* and Alfred, Lord Tennyson's *In Memoriam* published. Henry Clay's Compromise of 1850 postpones the secession crisis, but the Fugitive Slave Act strengthens the status quo with respect to slavery in the South.

1853 Edith ("Edith with golden hair" of "The Children's Hour") Longfellow born. Sales of Harriet Beecher Stowe's *Uncle Tom's Cabin* (1852) surpass 300,000 copies in its first year—commercially the most successful American novel of the nineteenth century.

1855 Anne Allegra ("laughing Allegra" of "The Children's Hour") Longfellow born. HWL's—*The Song of Hiawatha* published—an extraordinary success (he had resigned his position at Harvard the previous year). First edition of Walt Whitman's *Leaves of Grass* published—*not* a success. *Bartlett's Familiar Quotations* first published. Sevastopol falls to Britain and its allies, ending the Crimean War. Leo Tolstoy's *Sevastopol Sketches*, part reportage and part fiction, is published. Isaac Singer patents his sewing machine motor. P.T. Barnum's *The Life of P.T. Barnum, Written by Himself* published. British explorer David Livingstone names Victoria Falls on the Zambezi River.

1858 HWL's *The Courtship of Miles Standish and Other Poems* published, featuring the courtship of Longfellow's maternal ancestors Priscilla Mullen and John Alden. HWL's "First Flight" of *Birds of Passage* published, including "The Jewish Cemetery at Newport" and "My Lost Youth." Trans-Atlantic cable begins operation. Pikes Peak gold rush begins; city of Denver, Colorado, founded. Oliver Wendell Holmes' *Autocrat of the Breakfast Table* published.

1861 Frances (Fanny) Appleton Longfellow dies in a fire. HWL grows a beard to hide his scars. Outbreak of the Civil War. Serfdom abolished in Russia. Longfellow resumes translation of Dante's *Divine Comedy*. George Eliot's *Silas Marner* published.

1863 First part of HWL's *Tales of a Wayside Inn*, including "Paul Revere's Ride," published. Charley Longfellow, serving as a Union cavalry officer, is wounded in action near Culpeper, Virginia. President Lincoln signs the Emancipation Proclamation. West Virginia admitted to the Union as the 35th state. Death of the British novelist William Makepeace Thackery.

1867 HWL turns sixty; collection of a dozen poems published as *Flower-de-Luce*, including "Christmas Bells" ("I heard the bells on Christmas Day / Their old, familiar carols play [...]"). Publication of HWL's translation of Dante's *Divine Comedy* begins (through 1870). First ship passes through the Suez Canal. "Seward's Folly"—Alaska purchased from Russia for a little over seven million dollars. First elevated railroad begins service in New York. Harvard establishes first dental school in the U.S. Alfred Nobel invents dynamite.

1868 HWL makes his last trip to Europe where he is received by Queen Victoria at Windsor Castle and is granted honorary degrees by Oxford and Cambridge. *The New England Tragedies*, five-act plays in blank verse on John Endicott and Giles Corey, are published. These were to form the third section of an elaborate project, never completed, to be entitled *Christus: A Mystery* (published in partial form in 1872). Louisa May Alcott's *Little Women* published.

1874 John Cheever Goodwin and Edward Everett Rice's musical comedy version of *Evangeline* premieres in New York City (July 27). Claude Monet's *Impression, Sunrise* in a Paris exhibition gives identity to the Impressionist Movement in painting. Levi Strauss and Jacob Davis receive a patent for making blue jeans using copper rivets. Philadelphia Zoo opens, first public zoo in the U.S. Premiere in Vienna of Johann Strauss, Sr.'s *Die Fledermaus.*

1875 HWL's *The Masque of Pandora and Other Poems* published—including "Morituri Salutamus," a 285-line poem to commemorate the fiftieth anniversary of the Bowdoin College class of 1825. First performance of Georges Bizet's *Carmen.* Tufts plays Harvard in what may be the first American college football game. The running of the first Kentucky Derby. Publication of *Roderick Hudson*, Henry James' first important novel.

1876 HWL visits Walt Whitman (briefly) in Camden, New Jersey. The U.S. celebrates its centennial. Custer's Seventh Cavalry is massacred at the Battle of the Little Bighorn in Montana. Mark Twain's *Tom Sawyer* published.

1878 HWL's *Kéramos and Other Poems* published (the title poem, an ode to art, is the Greek word for pottery). Thomas A. Edison patents the phonograph. First commercial telephone exchange opens in New Haven, Connecticut. Thomas Hardy's *Return of the Native* published.

1880 HWL's *Ultima Thule* published, including a short, haunting poem entitled "Jugurtha." A street in Wabash, Indiana, becomes the first to be lighted by electricity. Deaths of French novelist Gustave Flaubert and English novelist George Eliot.

1882 HWL's last book, *In the Harbor*, is published; *Michael Angelo: A Fragment* published posthumously in 1883 and 1886. Oscar Wilde visits. HWL dies on March 24. Rockefeller's Standard Oil Trust becomes the first industrial monopoly in the U.S. The outlaw Jesse James is killed by Robert Ford. Tchaikovsky's *1812 Overture* debuts in Moscow. William Dean Howells' novel, *A Modern Instance*, published.

1883 George Lowell Austin's *Henry Wadsworth Longfellow. His Life, His Works, His Friendships* is published—first full-length biography. Krakatoa volcano erupts in Indonesia. *Ladies Home Journal* begins publication. First Vaudeville theater opens. Brooklyn Bridge opens to traffic. Buffalo Bill Cody's first Wild West show. Johannes Brahms' *Symphony #3* premieres. Robert Louis Stevenson's *Treasure Island* published.

1886 HWL's brother Samuel Longfellow's two-volume *Life of Henry Wadsworth Longfellow* published; a third volume is added in 1891, including selections from the journals and letters. Death of Emily Dickinson. William Butler Yeats is studying art in Dublin and getting his first poems published.

1

Evangeline and the Popularity of Poetry in the United States

Christoph Irmscher begins his introduction to *Longfellow Redux* (2006) with some reflections on the ostensible "death of poetry." One might speculate that if, as Nietzsche's madman so memorably declared in 1882, coincidentally the year of Longfellow's death, that "God is dead," then poetry's days are also numbered. Irmscher comments perhaps too briefly on such essays as Joseph Epstein's "Who Killed Poetry?" and Dana Gioia's "Can Poetry Matter?" Literary critic, poet (often connected with the so-called New Formalism), and former Vice President of General Foods, Gioia (pronounced *joy*-ah) was named chairman of the National Endowment for the Arts in 2003. His controversial essay, published in the May 1991 issue of *Atlantic Monthly*, begins as follows: "American poetry now belongs to a subculture. No longer part of the mainstream of artistic and intellectual life, it has become the specialized occupation of a relatively small and isolated group" (94). Gioia likens poets to "priests in a town of agnostics," and he argues that, in effect, poetry has been remanded to the custody of Academe, particularly to creative writing programs, which he projects will "produce about 20,000 accredited professional poets over the next decade" (95). This prospect Gioia finds alarming, whereas Longfellow, as Irmscher demonstrates in his first chapter, would likely have welcomed it.

Gioia registers particular concern over the apparent abandonment of "the hard work of evaluation" (98) that has followed the decline of poetry reviews in newspapers and other periodicals. At the same time, he notes, "journals that love poetry not wisely but too well," particularly those that publish poetry only, often without providing reviews, tend to lose the "radiant poem among the many lackluster ones" (97). Gioia also laments the fact that poets "now occupy niches at every level of academia," resulting in conditions that have made poetry "a modestly upwardly mobile, middle-class profession—not as lucrative as waste management or dermatology but several big steps above the squalor of bohemia" (102). He proposes that fifty years prior, around 1940, few poets haunted the college campus, people widely bought and read ("with curiosity and attention") well-edited anthologies, and poetry "mattered outside the classroom" (104). Presumably Robert Frost's long association with Amherst College, the Bread Loaf School, which he helped to establish at Middlebury College, and several other universities would be an exception, as would the careers of such poets as John Crow Ransom and Randall Jarrell. Novelist William Van O'Connor, writing in 1960, reflected no such skepticism toward the academy, declaring in "The Writer and the University," that "English departments nowadays look at literature pretty much as writers do" (56). "The creative act and the critical act," he asserted, "are inseparable."

Happily, however, Gioia has come not to bury poetry but to praise it.* He cites the familiar passage from William Carlos Williams' "Asphodel, That Greeny Flower" to the effect that "It is difficult / to get the news from poems / yet men die miserably every day / for lack / of what is found there" (318). Poetry "matters to the entire intellectual community," Gioia writes, because it is "the art of using words charged with their utmost meaning," and "one is hard pressed to imagine a country's citizens improving the health of its language while abandoning poetry" (105). These observations recall Ezra Pound's pronouncements in *The ABC of Reading* (1934): "Literature is language charged with meaning" (28); "If a nation's literature declines, the nation atrophies and decays" (32); "A people that grows accustomed to sloppy writing is a people in the process of losing grips on its empire and on itself" (34). Gioia concludes his essay by offering half a dozen "modest proposals" for the stimulation of interest in poetry, the first of which is that poets giving public readings "should spend part of every program reciting other people's work." He also urges poets to "write prose about poetry more often, more candidly, and more effectively" and in doing so to "avoid the jargon of contemporary academic criticism and write in a public idiom" (106).†

The next year, 1992, *Harper's Magazine* ran a brief "jeremiad" entitled "Poetry's Decay" by poet August Kleinzahler, complaining that "these days the better animals in the jungle are not drawn to poetry" (35). Presumably, Mr.

* *I am appropriating Eric L. Haralson's appropriation of Shakespeare employed in a slightly different context in his essay on Longfellow (328).*

† *Poet, critic, and biographer Jay Parini offers a sort of rebuttal in his recently published* Why Poetry Matters *(New Haven: Yale University, 2008): "Plato did not manage to sink the art of poetry, but the light of suspicion has continued to shine on poets ever since he raised these objections [in* The Republic*]" (4).*

Kleinzahler, a long-time resident of San Francisco and the author of ten books of poetry, regards himself as an exception among the beasts of that jungle. He lashes out against misunderstanding and misuse of line and detects among other "symptoms of decay" the "academization" of the avant-garde and "the ascendancy of the arts administrator and the grant writer" (36). Curiously, on the website operated by the Academy of American Poets, Kleinzahler is credited with having received a fellowship from the Guggenheim Foundation and with teaching stints at Brown University, the University of California at Berkeley, and the University of Iowa Writers' Workshop. Perhaps the most significant symptom of decay he detects, tongue-in-cheek perhaps but with some point, is the dearth of parties after the readings, "or at least none worth attending" (36). This is so much as to say that the poetry reading has dwindled into a pro forma event, not so much a celebration of poetry or even of one poet's poems, as an obligation to attend and perhaps, if one is receiving extra credit in an English course, to take notes. Kleinzahler implies that the fun, the joy of poetry, is being extracted from the event. Obviously the setting or "happening" of the so-called Poetry Slam might constitute an exception.

Such interrogations of the decline of poetry and of the status of poet in the United States did not start with Dana Gioia's essay. In 1988 Joseph Epstein, writer and quondam editor of *The American Scholar*, the Phi Beta Kappa magazine, inquired in an essay published in *Commentary*, "Who Killed Poetry?" Not surprisingly, he pointed his finger at "the professionalization of poetry" by the academy, which has threatened "the entire enterprise of poetic creation," taken it "out of the world," and "chilled [it] in the classroom." Poetry, Epstein asserts, is "vastly overproduced by men and women who are licensed to write it by degree if not necessarily by talent or spirit" (20). Citing the "more than 250 universities with creative-writing programs" for complicity in having created the "vacuum" in which "contemporary poetry in United States flourishes," he seems almost to be complaining that this unfortunate state of affairs "has made it possible for a large number of poets [...] to earn their living in work closely connected with their craft" (14). But the vacuum he regrets is that despite the "honors, publication possibilities, and opportunities to gather public adulation," poetry is, "outside a very small circle, scarcely read" (15). The number of undergraduate and graduate creative writing programs in the United States has increased considerably in the twenty years that have elapsed since Gioia's essay appeared. According to its website, the Associated Writing Programs now supports "over 400 member colleges and universities."*

Epstein cites Delmore Schwartz's essay, "The Isolation of Modern Poetry," in a 1941 issue of *Kenyon Review*, to the effect that poetry has become

* *http://www.awpwriter.org/*

too difficult and also Randall Jarrell's 1950 Harvard lecture entitled "The Obscurity of the Poet." T.S. Eliot's assertion in his essay "The Metaphysical Poets" (1921) that "poets in our civilization, as it exists at present, must be *difficult*" because of the increased "variety and complexity" of this civilization (65), is often taken as the point of departure for the Modernist decision to oust poetry from the easy confines of the parlor and thrust it into the arcane and esoteric carrels of academic libraries and (presumably) sterile classrooms. Schwartz concludes "there is no genuine place for the poet in modern life," and consequently, "The modern poet has had nothing to do, no serious activity other than the cultivation of his own sensibility" (9–10). From this "isolation," Schwartz observes, the obscurity of modern poetry also arises" (11). Other titles in Schwartz's *Selected Essays* include "The Vocation of the Poet in the Modern World" (1951), "The Present State of Poetry" (1958), and more than a dozen on individual poets like Ezra Pound, T.S. Eliot, and Wallace Stevens.

One suspects that Gioia's call for poets to write more prose about poetry may be unnecessary. As if, one is inclined to add, the tradition extending in English poetry at least to Sidney's "A Defence of Poesy" were not enough. Beginning with Wordsworth's "Preface to the Lyrical Ballads" at the end of the eighteenth century, poets have proven themselves to be anything but reluctant to speak out on poetry in general and on their own poems and those of their contemporaries in particular. Reflecting on the role of poets as teachers (mostly of literature in this case), Schwartz expresses contradictory feelings: "Today since so many poets are teachers, it is no longer true that the poet is regarded by most other human beings as a strange and exotic being" (36). Poets and other artists, then, are not so isolated from society as they once were. On the other hand, Schwartz notes, among the things he was asked to do over some twenty years as a teacher, "the one thing I was *not* asked to do very often was to write poetry" (38, emphasis mine). He concludes that although "the present state of poetry in America is not in an unquestionably flourishing state in any full sense," it is "superior to what it has ever been in the past" (42).

Randall Jarrell began his lecture delivered at Harvard by saying he was "delighted" to address the problem of the poet's "obscurity," but then realized he "was being asked to talk not about the fact that people don't read poetry, but about the fact that most of them wouldn't understand it if they did." He was being asked to reflect not upon the "neglect" of contemporary poetry but on its "difficulty." Implicit in such issues is whether "difficult" or "complex" poems are ipso facto "good" or "better than" poems that are "easy" or "accessible." Standards of taste and judgment change. Another generation admired the comfortable verse of Robert Herrick and considered John

Donne's "metaphysical" verse of lesser worth. Jarrell asserts, however, that "it is not just modern poetry, but poetry, that is today obscure" (3). He rather wittily sums up the situation thus: "If we were in the habit of reading poets their obscurity would not matter; and, once we are out of the habit, their clarity does not help" (4). What will become of poetry, or what is becoming of it? The enthusiasm for the comfortable Longfellow appears to have given way, perhaps decisively, to the greater challenges and divergent voices of Walt Whitman and Emily Dickinson. Is the more difficult Wallace Stevens "better" than the easier Robert Frost? Do the recent terms of Billy Collins and Ted Kooser as U.S. poets laureate indicate a change of direction in American poetry away from the abstruse? Jarrell writes hopefully, or perhaps threatens, "Human life without some form of poetry is not human life but animal existence" (16). Sooner or later one asks—if no one else then at least oneself—whether poetry, like the play that Hamlet comments on in the second scene of Act Two, is in its nature "caviar to the general."

At that point, though, one is inclined to step back from the precipice. Perhaps, as Joseph Harrington has suggested in his provocative essay, "Why American Poetry is Not American Literature," published in the fall 1996 issue of *American Literary History*, the indifference toward or disesteem for poetry (the choice of adjectives here *does* matter) is peculiar to the United States. An English professor at the University of Kansas, Harrington takes issue with Modernists like Eliot and Allen Tate, "who distanced themselves from the market in order to accrue cultural legitimacy" (500). Focusing on the "social form" of the genre of poetry, Harrington argues that the "poet-critic's textual formalism presumes the decline of the audience: disciplined craftsmanship and popularity are implicitly at odds. Writers who championed high modernism typically asserted the death of the audience (as, indeed, they still do)" (502). "Lovers of poetry" in the early years of the twentieth century, he observes, "hailed its ability to beget spiritual sensibility, to build character, and to refine one's sense of beauty, truth, or morality" (497). Harrington associates the repudiation of the public function of poetry with the New Critics whose "goal" was "the privatization of poetry" (503). Modernist poetics was then "installed as the Party of the Institutional Revolution, with the academy, not the commercial publishing industry, as its home" (505). The "side" of Ezra Pound, then, "won in the academy," but Robert Frost's "side" did not actually lose "in terms of general readership or popular esteem" (506).

The result for poetry's status in "American literature," Harrington suggests, has been unfortunate: "Today, Americanists of all methodological and political stripes allow this conception [the separation of poetry from historical and social contingencies] to remain unchallenged, and as a result poetry is on the outs" (506), while fiction (particularly the novel), and increasingly the emergent subgenre of "creative nonfiction," one might add, has risen in favor. Creative nonfiction, encompassing the ever-popular memoir, tends to favor narration over more discursive (expository or meditative) modes. Delmore Schwartz notes in his essay on isolation in modern poetry that "Nothing could be more peculiar than the fact that modern poetry is lyric poetry. Almost without exception there is a failure or an absence of narrative or dramatic writing in verse" (4). Harrington concludes "there is no reason for critics to take popular tastes in poetry less seriously than popular tastes in novels or other media" (510), and he finds indications "that the poetry scene of the 1990s, far from being the last bastion of pure transcendent literariness, is the scene of an impure assortment of different types of values for different sizes, types, and sites of audiences"; moreover, "In this light American poetry shows itself to be paradigmatic of new social forms American literature is taking at the turn of the twentieth century" (511).

In the context of this more pluralistic view of the nature of poetry in the United States, a perspective which, as Harrington puts it, "like the country itself, encompasses multiple, difficult negotiations between normative standards, equality, community, subjectivity, and competing conceptions of and reactions to the public" (511), Longfellow's place in American literature has been undergoing some reconsideration over the past twenty or so years. The dilemma of those who have been revisiting the poems of Henry Wadsworth Longfellow over these years is implicit in John Seeley's essay published in the *Virginia Quarterly Review* in 1984, "Attic Shape: Dusting Off *Evangeline.*" Currently Professor of English at the University of Florida, Seelye has authored such books as *The True Adventures of Huckleberry Finn* (1970, now in a second edition) and *Memory's Nation: The Place of Plymouth Rock* (1998); he serves as General Editor of the Penguin American Library. Seelye begins his essay as follows: "Longfellow survives largely as a bad example, not a *poete maudit* but a maudlin poet, afloat on the lachrymose seas of a sentimental age" (21). Describing the poem as a "kitsch epic," Seelye appears to delight in his portrayal of *Evangeline* as "a dated demonstration of misguided metric virtuosity" that, "like Unguentine, seems a patent producer of a slow-fading past, an oleaginous balm with a sweet smell, reminiscent of the sickroom, or, worse, the schoolroom" in its "unpleasant redolence" (22). Some twenty pages later, however, Seelye finds himself, after considerable seesawing, concluding that "Longfellow's West is a wilderness sanctuary and preserve sacred to the national memory, a territory of the mind through which a great river flows, an American Alph emblematic of the national imagination and darkly prophetic of the national fate" (44). Like other reluctant admirers, Seelye is disturbed by the poet's "retreat from the world of affairs to poetry and dreams" (40), by his "armchairism and fireside poetics" (41), but he defends Longfellow as a "sensitive and perceptive" poet who was touched by "the issues of his day."

Similarly, Dana Gioia, whose substantial essay in *The Columbia History of American Poetry* (1993) may be said to have initiated the revival of interest in Longfellow's poetry, feels obliged, about halfway through, to break for some apologies:

> Longfellow's faults as a lyric poet are too well known to belabor. His work often lacks intellectual depth. It strays into sentimentality. [...] He rarely passes up the opportunity to moralize. He is often derivative of foreign models. He sometimes becomes so engrossed in his metrical scheme that he loses the intensity of his poetic impulse. He rarely looks into the harsher side of reality [81].

As with others who defend Longfellow's poetry and his place in American literature, Gioia perceives that because the poems are representative of "the traditional aesthetic Modernism defined itself against," they have been "doubly damned": "In a critical culture where literary merit is a function of how much discourse (in classrooms or learned journals) a poetic text can generate, their expansive and lucid poems have little to offer" (80).

One might reflect along these lines that the renaissance of enthusiasm for the poetry of John Donne spurred by T.S. Eliot's review in 1921 of Herbert J. Grierson's anthology, *Metaphysical Lyrics and Poems of the Seventeenth Century,* did little to kindle renewed interest in the poetry of the so-called Tribe of Ben (Jonson). Modernist poets and New Critics could find much to probe and dissect in Donne and George Herbert, but little in need of explication in the poems of Ben Jonson or Robert Herrick. Perhaps we should ask whether we expect *all* poets to challenge only the best minds or to speak to the highest common denominator. Or should we expect or demand that only of our *best* poets? Implicit in what might be called The Case for Longfellow, may be a premise to the effect that he intended to raise the intellectual prospects of the lowest brows while at the same time lowering the pretensions of the highest. Poets of the greatness of Shakespeare and Pablo Neruda, most readers would agree, provide ample sustenance for both extremes of the mental spectrum.

Gioia celebrates Longfellow's oeuvre broadly in the opening pages of his essay, which opens with the assertion that he was "not merely the most popular American poet who ever lived but enjoyed a type of fame almost impossible to imagine by contemporary standards" (64). With other commentators, Gioia notes the appeal of Longfellow's poems to "every social class from laborers to royalty, from professors to politicians." As Indiana University English professor Christoph Irmscher phrases it in his introduction to *Longfellow Redux,* "In his own day, Longfellow's works appealed to bespectacled university professors and servant girls alike" (3). One might readily develop various premises from such assertions, at least one of which is that the serious study of Longfellow's writing and its influence belongs as much to "pop culture" as it does to "American literature." Gioia illustrates in passing how lines from the poems, like "Ships that pass in the night" and "The patter of little feet," have entered the public consciousness (or perhaps its sub-consciousness) as surely as quotes not-necessarily-"remembered" from Shakespeare like "my kingdom for a horse." To speak blithely of "libido energy" or of the "superego," after all, is *not* necessarily to have read Freud.

Longfellow, Gioia reminds the reader, "was the first American poet to achieve an international reputation" (64), and he remains the only American poet to have had his bust "unveiled in the Poet's Corner of Westminster Abbey" (65). Gioia observes that the poems "became subjects for songs, choral work, operas, musicals, plays, paintings, symphonies, pageants, and eventually films": "'The Village Blacksmith' became a film at least eight times, if one counts cartoons and parodies, including John Ford's 1922 adaptation, which updated the protagonist into an auto mechanic" (65). Anticipating such Modernist poets as his distant relative Ezra Pound and such contemporaries as Robert Bly, Longfellow succeeded as a translator in several languages, including his translation of Dante's *Divine Comedy* completed in 1867. In his recent biography, *Longfellow: A Rediscovered Life,* Charles C. Calhoun briefly notes Michael Pearl's construction of an "ingenious literary detective story," *The Dante Club* (2003), based on the informal club Longfellow formed in the 1860s while working on his translation. Gioia points out that Longfellow's first book of poems, *Voices of the Night,* published at the end of 1839 when the poet was 32 years old, features twenty translations from the Italian, Spanish, French, German, Danish, and Anglo-Saxon. By that time Longfellow had made extended visits to Europe and had taught foreign languages at Bowdoin College and Harvard for ten years. While he was introducing the world to American poetry, Longfellow was representing the world's poetry (or at least Europe's) to America. Poets as varied as Eliot and Pound and as Bly and James Wright, Gioia suggests, "continued a poetic tradition pioneered by Longfellow" (77). Calhoun goes so far as to posit that "Longfellow more or less invented the discipline of comparative literature in the American college" (81).

After briefly tracing the decline of Longfellow's critical reputation as measured by the dwindling appearance of his poems in anthologies (usually short lyrics like "A Psalm of Life," "The Village Blacksmith," "My Lost Youth," and "The Jewish Cemetery at Newport"), Gioia argues that "Longfellow's status as a major poet ultimately rests on the critical assessment of his four booklength poems" (85), starting with *Evangeline* (1847).

Gioia is well aware that "Most American long poems [like William Carlos Williams' *Paterson*] have been epics of self-discovery [...] sprawling, discontinuous, idiosyncratic, and obscure," while Longfellow's "extended poems are distressingly neat and lucid: they are polished, linear, autobiographical narratives." Moreover, "They are conceived as serious but popular entertainments, stories meant to enlarge the reader's humanity without deconstructing his or her moral universe" (86). Gioia's declaration in favor of the long narrative poems, therefore, constitutes something of a risk and at the same time a challenge to current trends. He regards *Evangeline* as "the most poetically impressive of the longer poems" (86–7).

As to the "moral element" or content of Longfellow's poems, Gioia does not attempt to avoid its apparently "old-fashioned" nature, but insists that "the poems remain surprisingly contemporary in their concerns," ranging from the "personal tragedies of a displaced ethnic and religious minority driven from its homeland by an imperial power" in *Evangeline* to the *Tales of a Wayside Inn* (1863–1873) "whose very framework celebrates multiculturalism" and whose stories concern "environmental sensitivity, religious tolerance, political freedom, and charity" (86). Longfellow, Gioia asserts, "helped articulate the New England liberal consciousness that eventually became mainstream American public opinion." Whatever its inconsistencies, he adds, Longfellow's ideology "represented the most enlightened viewpoint of its era" (86).

Author and columnist for the conservative *National Review Online*, John Derbyshire, whose books include *Seeing Calvin Coolidge in a Dream* (1997) and *Unknown Quantity: A Real and Imaginary History of Algebra* (2007), opens his celebration of Longfellow, oddly enough, by reflecting on a visit to Disneyland. His intention, however, is not to diminish Longfellow's literary contribution by association with trivial entertainment, but to connect it with "fruits of the imagination" that he finds "have proved far more durable than those of any bohemian counterculture you can name" (12). Actually a lengthy review essay of J.D. McClatchy's edition of the poems for The Library of America, Derbyshire's observations appeared in the December 2000 issue of *New Criterion,* and like John Seelye he concedes early on that "So far as the literary authorities of our time are concerned, Longfellow is not merely a dead poet, he is a *dead* dead poet." But he quickly counters that "whatever our literary clerisy may feel," no other American poet "has so penetrated the general consciousness of the entire English-speaking world" (13). Longfellow himself, as Derbyshire presents him, "never broke the law, never got drunk, never discharged a firearm or socked anybody on the jaw in anger, never played at cards for money or speculated on the stock market, never betrayed a friend or made a pass at another man's wife" (12).

What can be made, one might ask, of a writer so non-"transgressive" that he must come across either as merely "passive," or, in the parlance of counseling psychology, as dangerously "passive-aggressive"? Opposite Henry Wadsworth Longfellow on the spectrum of writers whose lives offer grist for the biographical mills one might place Ernest Miller Hemingway, whose life indeed has been ground exceedingly fine over the past sixty or so years. Whether the socked jaw that Derbyshire has in mind was that of poet Wallace Stevens, as memorably punched in Key West by Papa in 1936, is debatable, but certainly Derbyshire's representation of Longfellow appears tepid in admiration. He describes Longfellow as "the very opposite of an intellectual" and as "an idiot savant" as a "creator of verse," a poet with "no real theory of poetic composition" (14). Although he does not list Derbyshire's commentary in his index, Charles C. Calhoun does account for the piece in his selected bibliography, and certainly his biography responds to some of the assertions, or accusations, stated above.

The ultimate thrust of Derbyshire's essay, however, aims at "one of the great conundrums of our time: whatever happened to popular poetry?" (16). Predictably, he declares that "free verse did not work very well" (17), concluding that although he can "applaud" what such poets are attempting, "I can't remember a line of their stuff, though I have sincerely tried" (18). He laments the passing of narrative poetry, and vis-à-vis modern poets, Derbyshire writes, "poets like Longfellow attained a breadth and durability of appeal that modern poets, for all their writer-in-residence sinecures and Pulitzer Prizes, can only dream of" (19).

In his introductory chapter Calhoun turns out a paragraph quite reminiscent in its tenor of one cited above. He begins, "The problem, of course, is that Longfellow was so very nice a man" (x). Longfellow's "days in general were so placid," Calhoun continues, "his livelihood so secure, his contemporary fame so universal, that in time he came to be seen as a symbol of everything that a writer should not be." Calhoun carefully details Longfellow's considerable intellectual accomplishments and among other things draws attention to an essay in the January 1832 issue of *North American Review* that proves "Longfellow has a poetics before he has a poetry" (81). Christoph Irmscher proceeds from a similar viewpoint in *Longfellow Redux* (2006), opening with a lengthy chapter on the close, even intimate, relationship Longfellow *enjoyed* (the verb applies well) with his readers. He entitles the first section of that chapter "Liking to Be Liked" (7). At the end of that chapter he concludes, "More than anything else, it has been this emphasis on pleasing his readers [...] that has turned Longfellow into the pariah of the modern pantheon of American literature" (70). Gioia admires the poems for being "lucid"; Irmscher goes so far as to describe them as "relentlessly accessible texts" (67).

While Calhoun's book focuses primarily on biographical matters, Irmscher tends to delve more deeply into individual texts, providing, for example, a very close reading of "The Children's Hour" at the beginning of his second chapter, which offers an engaging and intimate portrait of Longfellow as a father. Irmscher claims to "like to think" he has produced "more of an essay in four parts than a traditional monograph," and his "primary purpose" with the book "was to take the discussion of Longfellow's importance beyond the conversation of specialists and to see what he has to say about the business of literature in general" (5). Irmscher's choice of the Latin "redux" for his title (as opposed for example to "redivivus," which would imply "renewed" or "revived") is suggestive, indicating his intent in some way to "bring back" or "restore" Longfellow and his lost or strayed reputation as a poet. Calhoun concludes that "Longfellow's power to endure is very much rooted in place" (260), and he submits that while it might be an "exaggeration to say that Longfellow invented America," that he "imagined and perfected and made memorable so many aspects of how America is conceived remains his most enduring Achievement" (262).

Calhoun devotes a chapter of a little more than a dozen pages to *Evangeline,* observing that "Recent scholarship on gender relations in nineteenth-century American culture has revealed *Evangeline* as a much more fruitful and complex achievement than it had seemed in the heyday of purely formalist criticism" (188). Calculating his sales in 1857, the market-conscious Longfellow indicated that *Evangeline,* in its tenth year, had sold some 35,850 copies, a number which would then have ranked it sixth among his titles, led by *Hiawatha* at 50,000 (199; Irmscher 53). Irmscher comments on the poem primarily as it was translated by two amateur French Canadian and German American writers. In his essay, "Mars in Petticoats: Longfellow and Sentimental Masculinity," published in 1996, Eric L. Haralson, English professor at Stony Brook University and author of *Henry James and Queer Modernity* (2003), argues that in poems like *Evangeline* "the psychological posture of selfless working and waiting recommended by Longfellow conformed more to period stereotypes of femininity and owed more to domestic ideology than to rugged-male discourse of steam power, commercial enterprise, and 'action'" (330). Accordingly, Longfellow's "rise to authority" in that "'feminizing' age" precipitated his "subsequent fall from grace" later in that century and on into the twentieth, although, as Haralson notes, the "demotion did not occur overnight" (355).

The challenge to Longfellow's hegemony over American poetry is implicit in the lengthy chapter (nearly fifty pages) devoted to him in *American Literature, 1607–1885* (1888) by Charles F. Richardson (1851–1913), Professor of English at Dartmouth University. Although he represents

Longfellow as "beloved" and "honored for his poetic evangel" (51), Richardson notes that his "position as leader of the American choir" has not been "unquestioned" and "is not likely to escape sharp challenge in the future" (52). Richardson, preferring Emerson's poetry for its "clearness of vision" and "profundity of thought" (50), was to be among many who would damn, or perhaps simply demote, Longfellow with faint albeit apparently sincere praise: "What he misses in intellectual greatness he possesses in heartfulness" (93). By the time University of Washington English professor Vernon Louis Parrington was preparing the second of his influential three-volume *Main Currents of American Thought* (1927), he could dismiss if not outright disparage the "gentle, lovable soul" that was Longfellow in about two and a half pages: "In his work the romantic, the sentimental, and the moralistic, blended in such just proportions, and expressed themselves with such homely simplicity as to hit exactly the current taste and establish a reputation that later generations have difficulty in understanding. [...] There was little intellect in Longfellow, little creative originality" (439). Here, wrote Parrington, was "the poet of an uncritical and unsophisticated generation." He consigns Longfellow to a chapter he entitles "The Reign of the Genteel."

Although Parrington does not cite the philosopher George Santayana's important essay, "The Genteel Tradition in American Philosophy," originally delivered as a lecture at the University of California in 1911, he appears to have shared some of Santayana's views. Describing the "two mentalities" (187) of the United States, Santayana asserts "The American Will inhabits the sky-scraper; the American Intellect inhabits the colonial mansion. The one is the sphere of the American man; the other, at least predominantly, of the American woman. The one is all aggressive enterprise; the other is all genteel tradition" (188). He takes Emerson to task, more as philosopher or thinker than as poet, but he does not mention Longfellow. "The one American writer who has left the genteel tradition entirely behind," Santayana speculates, "is perhaps Walt Whitman" (202). The philosophical opponent of that tradition, he proposes, is the "Father of Pragmatism," William James.

What *Evangeline* might mean in these post-genteel days and the ways in which it might be read and interrogated are of course the subjects of the remainder of this book. Haralson speaks of the poem's "long slow slide from canonical shrine to antiquary shop" (328). *Can* the poem be read today? Having timed his reading out loud of the 1,018 lines of *The Courtship of Miles Standish* (1858), composed like the 1,399 lines of *Evangeline* (1847) in dactylic hexameter, John Derbyshire speculates that "anyone who cared to" might read silently through *Evangeline* "in an hour and a quarter" (19). If time were money, then, the investment would not be very great. But *should* the poem be read today, and if so, *why?* What might 21st-century readers take from the experience? What, for that matter, were readers in the latter half of the nineteenth through the first half of the twentieth century supposed to take from reading and studying the poem? May one legitimately infer the failure of poetry—notably of a *popular* readership for poetry—from the fact that *Evangeline* has apparently faded from the canon? And as Gioia, Derbyshire, and others involved in the so-called New Formalist or "Expansivist" movement (if it may properly be called that) seem to suggest, would a return to meter and rhyme, or at least to narrative poetry, return us to the days when Byron, writing for a far smaller audience than poets vie for today considering both the population figures and the literacy rate, could sell 10,000 copies of a poem on the day of publication (*The Corsair,* 1814) and 25,000 in the first month (Day 296)

2

The Contexts of Longfellow's *Evangeline*

The Poem's Composition and Early Reception

This "shabby and to us disgraceful war with Mexico" is how Longfellow expressed it in his journal entry on the twenty-seventh of May in 1846, just a week after writing, curtly, "Tried to work at Evangeline. Unsuccessful" (29). General Zachary Taylor had taken Matamoros on the eighteenth. Longfellow had started work on his "idyll in hexameter," in earnest on the twenty-eighth of November, 1845, when he declared, "I do not mean to let a day go by without adding something to it, if it be but a single line" (26). It was not to prove so easy a task. By the twelfth of January in 1846, however, Longfellow had completed two "cantos," as he called them, of what was to be a poem of nearly fourteen hundred lines divided into two parts of five cantos each. On September tenth of that year Elias Howe patented his sewing machine, an invention, some argue, that rivals the steam locomotive in its historical impact. In early December 1846, Longfellow encountered John Charles Frémont's *Report of the Exploring Expedition to the Rocky Mountains in the Year 1842*, an event that may have prompted his decision to expand Evangeline's search for the lost Gabriel from New England to the western frontier (Seelye 28).

On the tenth of December Longfellow reports being "Laid up with a cold," but despite feeling "wretched," he "commenced the second part of Evangeline" (66). At a site then known as Truckee Lake, near what was later to be called Donner Pass in California, a band of eighty-seven pioneers, thirty-nine of them children, was trapped in a snowstorm. Forty were to die, and the survivors were to resort to cannibalism. Gold had not yet been found at Sutter's Mill, so their motives for westering were more domestic. Longfellow was attending lectures at the Lyceum and reading Chapman's translation of Homer and being visited by Ralph Waldo Emerson. He would attend several lecturers by noted naturalist Louis Agassiz in the early months of 1847, while still at work on *Evangeline.* James K. Polk, a North Carolina Democrat avid for westward expansion, was in the White House. On the fifteenth of December Longfellow stayed home, "working a little on Evangeline; planning out the second part, which fascinates me. [...] Of materials for this part there is superabundance" (67).

On the nineteenth of December Longfellow viewed John Banvard's "moving diorama of the Mississippi. One seems to be sailing down the great stream, and sees the boats and the sandbanks crested with cottonwood, and the bayous by moonlight. Three miles of canvas, and a great deal of merit" (68). This experience was to direct his descriptive passages in the second part of *Evangeline.* The next day "poor Mr. Sales" came into his study, "with his bald head gashed and bleeding. He had been run over by a sleigh" (68). So it happens that the composition of a poem and the momentous historical concerns of the poet's life can be at any moment fused with personal concerns, "the quotidian," Wallace Stevens might have said. On the fourteenth of January, chafing over being "cribbed and shut up in college" (73), his head aching, his eyesight bothering him, Longfellow "finished the last canto of Evangeline," but there were still "three intermediate cantos to be written" (75). By February 23, 1847, Longfellow was feeling optimistic: "Evangeline is nearly finished. I shall complete it this week, together with my fortieth year" (80). On April third he wrote, "The first canto of Evangeline in proofs. Some of the lines need pounding; nails are to be driven and clinched" (85). On the evening of July twenty-sixth Longfellow "corrected proofsheets of Evangeline, and then played billiards" (90). The next day, some 2,400 miles to the west, Brigham Young led the Mormon emigrants into the land of milk and honey, the New Zion in Utah, and declared, "This is the place." The second half of Longfellow's poem would play well to a nation becoming infatuated with its Manifest Destiny (the term appears to have been coined by journalist John L. O'Sullivan in 1839) as it was being played out in the exotic West. On the second of February, 1848, the Treaty of Guadalupe Hidalgo was signed, ending that "shabby" and "disgraceful" war with Mexico and providing the United States title to California, Nevada, and Utah along with portions of Arizona, Colorado, New Mexico, and Wyoming.

In September of 1847, Longfellow was playing host to his good friend Charles Sumner, leader of the "Radical" Republicans, whose outspoken opposition to slavery would lead to his brutal beating on the floor of the Senate in 1856. "A dull day," Longfellow writes on Sunday, September 19, "and a duller sermon" (94). On October 30, 1847, his daughter Fanny was christened ("She looked charming, and behaved well throughout") and, he added almost as an afterthought, "Evangeline published" (96). Although he wrote on the eighth of November that "The public takes more kindly to hexameters than I could have imagined," Longfellow received a letter composed on that same date by Dr. Samuel G. Howe, a noted Boston philanthropist who established schools for the blind and who was to edit the anti-slavery periodical, *Commonwealth,* commending the poem but objecting to "the hybrid character of the measure" (98). Longfellow would hear more such objections, but he would also receive more plaudits like the following, also from Howe's letter: "A book! a book that pleases, instructs, improves people, what a gift to the world! [...] You feed five times five thousand souls with spiritual food which makes them forever stronger and better" (97–98). On the thirteenth of November, with the poem in print for just two weeks, Longfellow remarks simply, "The third thousand of Evangeline" (100).

A few days later Longfellow received a congratulatory letter from Nathaniel Hawthorne, who had passed on to him the story from which *Evangeline* evolved, as it had been told to him by the Rev. H. L. Conolly, who in return had received it from a parishioner. In his response, dated November 29, Longfellow thanked his old friend "for being willing to forego the pleasure of writing a prose tale which many people would have taken for poetry, that I might write a poem which many people take for prose" (100). On the eighteenth of December the minor novelist John Lothrop Motley, who was later to write a history of the Netherlands, sent a letter praising the poem but regretting the hexameters, "for which I suppose you will think me a blockhead." Although conceding that Longfellow's were as good if not better than any other hexameters in English, Motley wrote they will not make music in my ear, nor can I carry them in my memory" (104).* Nevertheless, on the third of Januarym, 1848, Longfellow wrote, "I am more than ever glad that I chose this metre for my poem" (107). Indeed, it is only with the present generation that school children have escaped memorizing the incantatory lines of the prologue:

> This is the forest primeval. The murmuring pines and the hemlocks,
> Bearded with moss, and in garments green, indistinct in the twilight,
> Stand like Druids of eld, with voices sad and prophetic,
> Stand like harpers hoar, with beards that rest on their bosoms.

"We are reading a very interesting novel, Jane Eyre," Longfellow notes on February tenth. "Who wrote it? Nobody knows" (110). The immensely

* *Nine years later, however, Motley wrote (13 May 1856) that he found himself "more and more fascinated with Evangeline. I never before could abide English hexameters; but these seem to me 'musical as is Apollo's lute'"* (Samuel Longfellow, Life II, 313).

popular novel was of course the work of Charlotte Brontë, published under the pseudonym Currer Bell. As is often the case in his journal entries, Longfellow complains about the burden of teaching: "[March 9th] Gave the whole muddy day to college. Evening, finished Mme. de Sevigners Memoirs" (115). On the twenty-first of that month he attended a lecture on "Womanhood" delivered by Henry L. Giles (118, see page 15). Perhaps one might expect, given his portrayal of Evangeline, that Longfellow might find public discussion of womanhood to be a "profanation." Certainly, his comment squares with conventional notions about Victorian male attitudes toward gender; nevertheless, by most accounts Longfellow was considered a liberal and progressive thinker in his day. The next week his entries celebrate the newly established republic in France. On the eighth of April he notes the printing of "the sixth thousand of Evangeline, making one thousand a month since its publication" (120).

These are only a few of the immediate contexts of Longfellow's first important poem of any considerable length on a distinctively American subject. In fact, as Edward Wagenknecht wrote in 1955, *Evangeline* is often credited with being "the first important long poem in American literature," period (6). Champions of Michael Wigglesworth's *Day of Doom* (1662) might beg to differ. Other events might be said to bear even more directly on the composition of *Evangeline* and its reception. For example, the decades between 1840 and 1860 saw the population soar from 17,069,453 to 31,433,321. This population was increasingly and even alarmingly urban. Within two years of the publication of *Evangeline* Longfellow would have been able to travel from Boston to New York by rail, and by 1856 the Illinois Central connected Chicago and New Orleans. Industrialization and the expansion of capitalism were at their height in the United States, and labor in the mills and factories, with attendant exploitation and labor agitation, was just beginning to draw people from the farms, or perhaps it would be more accurate to say that fewer people were being attracted to the farms, particularly among the burgeoning immigrant population. Longfellow was working on the poem in the midst of the devastating Potato Famine in Ireland. The poem's idealization of rural life would exercise a particular, and growing, appeal—the powerful lure of nostalgia—on its readers throughout the century. For some readers Longfellow's Grand-Pré would become the American version of Oliver Goldsmith's cautionary tale of Auburn in "The Deserted Village" (1770): "Ill fares the land, to hastening ills a prey, / Where wealth accumulates, and men decay" (2878).

In those same two decades prior to the Civil War, 1,694,838 Irish immigrants swelled urban enclaves in the United States, and these people tended to be unskilled, poor, and Roman Catholic. According to the *New Catholic*

Encyclopedia, "Between 1840 and 1900 [...] approximately 40 religious orders of women of European origin took up the teaching apostolate in the U.S." (V, 137). Evangeline's identity as a Roman Catholic is certainly one of her distinguishing features as an American heroine, as is her eventual taking of orders as a Sister of Mercy. Here, in fact, Longfellow made an error that has gone generally unnoticed, as that order was not founded until 1831 in Dublin, moving to the United States in 1841, while Evangeline is supposedly a member of that nursing order in 1793. Not surprisingly, given the burgeoning immigrant population from Catholic nations in Europe, "the largest growth of religious hospital nursing in the U.S. came after 1820 (*NCE,* X, 584).

Historical contexts tend to be interwoven. Synchronicity. Evangeline is a displaced farm girl, an immigrant, and a Roman Catholic, but what also distinguishes her as a literary heroine is her eventual commitment to a life of service. She is a woman whose story was being read during the infancy of the woman's movement in the United States, marked by such events as the publication of Margaret Fuller's *Woman in the Nineteenth Century* in 1845 and the Seneca Falls convention of 1848. With the Crimean War in 1854, Florence Nightingale was to define the role of women in nursing for generations to come, and Clara Barton was to follow her lead during the Civil War. Amid the popular sentimental novels being written by women, on the one hand, and Hawthorne's portrayal of Hester Prynne in 1850, on the other, Evangeline emerges as one embodiment of the Victorian "new woman," increasingly independent and occupied with activities outside the home, as opposed, one should hastily add, to the Victorian "traditional woman," devoted housewife, mother, and homemaker. The Victorian traditional or conventional woman is almost certainly what Evangeline was on track to become before the expulsion of the Acadians at the end of Part One.

Women were also becoming teachers in the public schools for the first time in significant numbers, following the opening of Oberlin College as a coeducational institution in 1833 and the spread of women's seminaries like Mount Holyoke, founded in 1837, and normal schools, the first of which was established in Lexington, Massachusetts, in 1839. Horace Mann's Antioch College went coeducational in 1853. The fact that the publication of *Evangeline* coincides fairly well with the expansion of "common" or public schools and with the sudden need for large numbers of poorly paid teachers is not especially significant when it comes to the immediate context of the poem's publication, but it is integral to its acceptance into the canon. Although virtually no women were teaching in the public schools in 1830, by 1902 only 27.8 percent of public school teachers were men (Dexter 628). By the turn of the century *Evangeline* was firmly entrenched in the public school curriculum, and it is hard to imagine that would have been the case if the women teaching in those schools had not welcomed it.

The expanding context of *Evangeline's* provenance no doubt involves the death of America's most popular poet in 1882. The next year, Houghton Mifflin inaugurated its inexpensive (fifteen cents) Riverside Literature Series with the poem, complete with a biographical essay by Horace E. Scudder that ran more than thirty pages and read in places like a saint's life. Alice Longfellow's four-page sketch, "Longfellow in Home Life," added to the evolving mythopoeia: "With Mr. Longfellow, there was complete unity and harmony between his life and character and the outward manifestation of this in his poetry. It was not worked out from his brain, but was the blossoming of his inward life" (xxxvii). Writing within a year after the publication of the poem in "A Fable for Critics," satirist James Russell Lowell admired "that rare, tender, virgin-like pastoral Evangeline" and concluded in a vein reminiscent of Alice Longfellow's observation about the relationship between her father's life and his art:

> That's not ancient nor modern, its place is apart
> Where time has no sway, in the realm of pure Art,
> 'Tis a shrine of retreat from Earth's hubbub and strife
> As quiet and chaste as the author's own life [140].

The postmodern ironic sensibility might incline us to read this praise today as two-edged. Although critic and literary scholar E. C. Stedman declared in 1885 that Longfellow's "admirers may form no longer a critical majority" (180, see page 14), he himself contributed to the myth: "His life and works together were an edifice fairly built,—the House Beautiful, whose air is peace" (183).

In fact, a survey run in the Philadelphia *Weekly Press* the same year that Stedman's *Poets of America* appeared suggests that his estimate of the "critical majority" was erroneous. A poll of readers on their favorite story-teller and favorite poem placed *Evangeline* at the top with 125 votes. Of course such polls lack statistical reliability, but respondents voted for no fewer than 178 poems, with Thomas Gray's "Elegy Written in a Country Churchyard" placing second at 113 votes. Rounding out the top five were William Cullen Bryant's "Thanatopsis" (80 votes), Milton's *Paradise Lost* (40), and Longfellow's *Song of Hiawatha* (20). For the record, the favorite story-teller was Harriet Beecher Stowe, whose *Uncle Tom's Cabin* had sold in the millions since its publication in 1852. One might note in passing the considerable edge of *Evangeline* over *Song of Hiawatha,* which was published just eight years later. This sort of poll suggests that both Longfellow and *Evangeline* had passed into the realm of popular culture, perhaps as icons of Victorian sentimentality, or perhaps as something greater than that.

Of course the fact that the poll was taken in Philadelphia and that *Evangeline* draws to its sad close in that city may well have skewed the results.

Critical Contexts

To become a popular icon is not an unmixed blessing. In 1887 Acadia's leading French language newspaper was established using Evangeline's name (*L'Évangéline* ceased publication in 1982), and by the end of the nineteenth century the poem had provided a focus for Acadian ethnic identity in the fictional Evangeline's homeland. A church and monument were erected where she once "lived," and in 1919 the Canadian Pacific Railway boosted tourism in Nova Scotia in her name. James Allen Evans has traced the tourist development of Grand-Pré (French for "great meadow") to an Acadian jeweler named John Frederic Herbin who in 1907 "bought the land where local tradition placed the Church of Saint-Charles" and "erected a cross there" (104; see the Société Promotion Grand-Pré website).* The park was designated a Canadian national historic site in 1961. The statue of Evangeline, erected in 1920 by the Daughters of the American Revolution, is a prominent feature of the park. Evans indicates a certain irony is involved in the DAR's role, inasmuch as it was Americans (in the form of the colonial governor of Massachusetts) who had pressed for the *déportation* and *le grand dérangement* of 1755. According to a film clip provided by the Evangeline Trail Tourism Association, "Evangeline Beach is a short distance from Grand-Pré." I suspect the children pictured in the video are unlikely ever to read the poem, but who knows?

In St. Martinville, Louisiana, where the parish library houses a strong collection of *Evangeline* editions, one may spend the night at the Old Castillo Bed & Breakfast, formerly the Place D'Évangéline, which dates from 1827, stroll along the Têche Bayou and stand under the Evangeline Oak, visit a new museum at the Longfellow-Evangeline State Park, and buy Gabriel and Evangeline memorabilia. Cajun kitsch. What one cannot do so easily is locate people under the age of sixty who have read the poem. Acadian/Cajun cuisine, however, has managed to sustain its popularity in the culinary canon. The website for St. Martinville† features a photograph of the Evangeline statue outside the St. Martin de Tours church. In 1907 Felix Voorhies published *Acadian Reminiscences, with the True Story of Evangeline,* offering one Emmeline Labiche as the historical Evangeline, but she appears likely to be as fictional as Longfellow's heroine. Cajun historian Carl A. Brasseaux offers a thorough account of the efforts to discover an historical counterpart to

* *http//:www.grand-pre.com/Histoireen.html*
† *http://mitchellspublications.com/guides/lalstm*

Longfellow's heroine in his monograph, *In Search of Evangeline* (1988), along with details pertaining to the establishment of Evangeline's presence in St. Martinville, particularly through the "evangelical zeal" (44) of "self-styled local authority" André Olivier, who operated an Evangeline Museum during the 1920s (32). "The passing years," Brasseaux notes, "endowed this *fakelore* with a mantle of authenticity" (48).

The academy may, or may not, prove less fickle than the public. Commentators have been divided from the outset about both Longfellow as a poet and about *Evangeline* as a poem. Those who probe such matters are likely to detect some sort of inverse ratio: As the popularity of the poet increases, the critical and scholarly praise decreases. One could argue the issue in quite contradictory fashion: 1. If children (as in the phrase "mere children") enjoy Longfellow's poems, then there must not be much to them. 2. If children (as in the phrase "even children") enjoy Longfellow's poems, then there must be at least something to them. One context in which *Evangeline* will be almost inevitably read is that of its critical reception, but as my observations imply, this context suggests at least two scenarios.

First, the worst-possible-case scenario. Critics and scholars were not slow to assail Longfellow even when he was at the peak of his popularity, and his *Evangeline* was not exempt. Edgar Allan Poe and Margaret Fuller were only the best known of his detractors, and whether one credits Poe's charge of plagiarism against Longfellow pertaining to other works, notably the verse drama *The Spanish Student* (1843), is perhaps less important than the more general accusation of imitativeness or lack of originality. Yet even those charges today, in light of Postmodernist appropriations, reconstructions, and pastiches like those of Kathy Acker, sound dated, and Poe's lengthy rebuttal of a letter in support of Longfellow by "Outis" (Greek for "no one") smacks of manic defensiveness. Charles C. Calhoun goes so far as to suggest that his response to the Outis letter was in some ways "a projection of Poe's own creative anxieties onto a well-established literary figure" (160). Longfellow himself did not dignify Poe's attacks with a response. But Poe could also be complimentary, upon occasion, and to a point. For instance, in an 1849 review of James Russell Lowell's "A Fable for Critics" Poe takes exception to Margaret Fuller's assault on Longfellow and Lowell, arguing that "so pointedly picked out for abuse as the worst of our poets, [they] are, upon the whole, perhaps, our best."

His satiric "trifle" or "*jeu d'esprit*," as Lowell described it, remains among his most frequently read poems, at least in edited portions that almost always include his description of Poe as follows: "There comes Poe, with his raven, like Barnaby Rudge, / Three fifths of him genius and two fifths sheer fudge" (140). It may well be that today's student of literature, at least in the United

States, is more likely to have stumbled across this passage than to have read Dickens' novel. Lowell almost certainly relished placing his tribute to Longfellow immediately after his dig at Poe. Charles Richardson's conclusion that Longfellow possessed a "sweet and sympathetic and strong and self-reliant soul" (93) is reflected in Lowell's playful warning to Poe not to "fling mud-balls at Longfellow so," after which he asks, "Does it make a man worse that his character's such / As to make his friends love him (as you think) too much?" (140). As I have suggested above, Longfellow's personal congeniality, the fact that, as Lowell puts it, "there is not a bard at this moment alive / More willing than he that his fellows should thrive," made him strangely vulnerable to attack.

In addition to charging Longfellow with lack of originality, a caveat that was to be repeated throughout his career and after, Poe, in his lengthy review of *Ballads and Other Poems* in 1842, reflected on "the too obtrusive nature of their didacticism" (683). In that essay Poe formulated his famous definition of poetry as "the Rhythmical Creation of Beauty. Beyond the limits of Beauty its province does not extend. Its sole arbiter is Taste" (688–689). Poe's perceptions themselves, in fact, are derivative of Goethe's in *Dichtung und Wahrheit*. While Poe commends several poems in the volume, including "The Village Blacksmith," his overall assessment of Longfellow as overly didactic and moralizing has stuck. For whatever reasons, Poe did not review *Evangeline*, but he and Margaret Fuller helped set the tenor of an important critical faction that is not likely to alter.

Even a cursory perusal of the comments by Fuller and Poe reveals traces of the sort of envy that for some readers at least might compromise the value of their judgments. Warning that "so much adulation is dangerous," Margaret Fuller confesses to feeling some "coolness toward Mr. Longfellow, in consequence of the exaggerated praises that have been bestowed upon him" (319). While allowing that "some measure" of Longfellow's poetical reputation may be "well-deserved," Poe opens his lengthy omnibus review of four of Longfellow's books with the observation that "it may be questioned whether, without the adventitious influence of his social position as Professor of Modern Languages and Belles Lettres at HARVARD, and an access of this influence by marriage with an heiress, he would have acquired his present celebrity—such as it is" (759–760). Such modern poets as Robert Lowell and James Merrill, connected with the Merrill-Lynch brokerage, have suffered occasionally from similar critical assaults.

A better, if not best-possible-case scenario is implicit in Nathaniel Hawthorne's letter to Longfellow dated the eleventh of November, 1847, and beginning, "I have read Evangeline with more pleasure than it would be decorous to express" (215). In his anonymous review published in the Salem

Advertiser on November 13, 1847, Hawthorne notes that "an ordinary writer" might have brought out "only gloom and wretchedness" in the theme, but this "true poet's deeper insight" brings out "its pathos all illuminated with beauty" (234). Anonymous reviews were common enough during the nineteenth century, but Hawthorne's reluctance to sign his name to this review stems most likely from the fact that he suspected readers would recognize him as a good friend of the poet. Few would have known that he actually led Longfellow to the narrative source for the poem itself. "The story is told with the utmost simplicity," Hawthorne continues, "with the simplicity of high and exquisite art, which causes it to flow onward as naturally as the current of a stream":

> Beautiful thoughts spring up like roses, and gush forth like violets as along a wood-land path; but never in an entanglement or confusion; and it is chiefly because beauty is kept from jostling with beauty, that we recognize the severe intellectual toil, which must have been bestowed upon this sweet and noble poem.

This passage reflects the shift in sensibility and taste—away from the "genteel tradition"—that makes it difficult for some readers to appreciate Longfellow's poems, or even to comprehend the nature of their enthusiastic reception. Hawthorne, as if anticipating the responses of Poe and Fuller, asserts that Longfellow "has placed himself on an eminence higher than he had yet attained, and beyond the reach of envy" (234). In that respect he was obviously quite wrong.

John Greenleaf Whittier famously greeted the poem in his review for *The National Era,* an abolitionist newspaper: "Eureka!—Here, then, we have it at last! An American poem, with the lack of which British reviewers have so long reproached us" (Calhoun 190). The praise of fellow writers is always welcome, so Longfellow doubtless felt gratified to receive German poet Ferdinand Freiligrath's letter of March 11, 1848, commending the poem as a "masterpiece" (Samuel Longfellow, *Life* II, 117). But perhaps he was equally pleased with more casual responses of the sort recorded in his journal entry for July 1, 1848, in which he mentions a young man "quite hilarious with wine" and "a lover of Evangeline" who claimed that "'his ladylove always quoted to him the lines about the compass-flower'" (124). The widow of Andrews Norton, a theologian and friend of Longfellow, told Charles Sumner when he was in Scotland that she had read the poem "some twenty times," and thought it "the most perfect poem in the language" (342).

Predictably, perhaps, *Evangeline* met with its greatest critical challenge when it came to the meter. Longfellow's experiment with unrhymed dactylic hexameters aroused an array of negative comments even from friends who otherwise esteemed the poem. Despite Longfellow's confidence in the hexameters, his friend Samuel G. Howe objected that the poem "would perhaps have pleased me better in ordinary verse, or in plain prose" (98). School text editors felt obligated to include a special section on the meter, usually balancing positive and negative comments. In his lengthy review essay for the *American Review* of February 1848, George Washington Peck opened his assault with comments on the "doleful decadence" of the meter that "in a short time carries the reader's courage along with it" (6). Later, he refers to them as "pile-driving hexameters" (12). In "A Fable for Critics" James Russell Lowell admires Longfellow's "smooth" rhythm and reminds the reader that "elegance also is force," but he confesses that he is "not over-fond of Greek metres in English," including the "modern hexameters" of *Evangeline* (140). Although conceding that at their best they had "an idyllic sweetness and grace," Charles F. Richardson concluded in the 1880s that "at their worst, the clumsy dactyls sounded like hoof-beats on a muddy road" (74).

Against such meter-bashing, commentators like Horace E. Scudder hastened to cite the words of Oliver Wendell Holmes: "From the first line of the poem, from its first words, we read as we would float down a broad and placid river, murmuring softly against its banks, heaven over it, and the glory of the unspoiled wilderness all around. [...] I do not believe any other measure could have told that lovely story with such effect as we feel when carried along the tranquil current of these brimming, slow-moving, soul-satisfying lines" (9). Scudder's own comments in 1883 on the "lingering melancholy" of the meter were also frequently cited: "a little practice will enable one to acquire that habit of reading the hexameter, which we may liken, roughly, to the climbing of a hill, resting a moment on the summit, and then descending the other side" (8). And when it came to metaphoric commendation of the dactylic hexameters, Longfellow was not above celebrating and singing himself: "Like the flight of the swallow the hexameter soars and sinks at will; now grazing the ground in its long sweep, now losing itself in the clouds" *(Letters,* III, 180).

At the conclusion of his unsigned review of *Evangeline* Hawthorne conceded that the "first impressions" of many readers when it comes to Longfellow's metrical "experiment" would likely be "adverse," but

> when it is perceived how beautifully plastic this cumbrous measure becomes in his hands—how thought and emotion incorporate and identify themselves with it—how it can compass great ideas, or pick up familiar ones—how it swells and subsides with the nature and necessities of the theme—and, finally, how musical it is, whether it imitate a forest-wind or the violin of an Acadian fiddler—we fully believe that the final judgment will be in its favor. Indeed, we cannot conceive of the poem as existing in any other measure [235].

As he finished the second canto of Part II of the poem, however, Longfellow appears to have had some second thoughts himself about his hexameters, as he records in his journal for January 26, 1847 an experiment with the mockingbird's song in rhymed pentameter couplets. The first four of the ten lines read as follows:

> Upon a spray that overhung the stream,
> The mocking-bird, awaking from his dream,
> Poured such delirious music from his throat
> That all the air seemed listening to his note [*Life* II, 77].

The lines as they appear in the poem read very differently indeed:

> Then from a neighboring thicket the mockingbird, wildest of singers,
> Swinging aloft on a willowy spray that hung o'er the water,
> Shook from his little throat such floods of delirious music,
> That the whole air and the woods and the waves seemed silent to listen
> [*ll.* 873–876].

I will not undertake to argue in any detail the superiority, as I see it, of the hexameters to the pentameter couplets here, and it would likely prove an exercise in futility in any event, as Longfellow composed both versions, but surely the energy of the passage, "Swinging aloft on a willowy spray" has something to recommend it against the rather static "Upon a spray."

In his lead essay in the *American Review*, however, Peck went well beyond meter in his attack on *Evangeline*, as a few selected comments will attest: "The figures and comparisons seldom come in naturally, but are the offspring of conscious choice" (9). Peck provides three double-column pages of examples of "strained" metaphors, similes, and images, and he takes on Longfellow's fashioning of character as well, asserting that Evangeline is an "insipid creature. [...] There is no soul in her. For seventeen she is so childish as to be silly. [...] There is no character-drawing in the piece; the hero and heroine are not alive" (12). As to the story element, "If we consider the bare plot and the naked thread of the description, there is nothing in them to be condemned. This is but negative praise, yet it is all they deserve" (14). Peck concludes that *Evangeline* is "radically defective as a great poem, in that it lacks a pervading tone. [...] The piece does not display the depth of emotion, nor the height of rapture, necessary to a great poem. It does not burn or glow with heat, but only congeals and coldly glitters" (15).

One might be surprised to find that the poem survived even its own moment, let alone its own century, given Peck's harsh treatment, and if his had been the majority voice, *Evangeline* would not likely have outlived Longfellow. But as Brander Matthews noted in 1896, like John Greenleaf Whittier's *Snowbound, Evangeline* "charmed alike the farmhand and the college Professor" (230). Something of a best-possible-case scenario may also be found in the *History of American Verse (1610–1897),* in which James L. Onderdonk argues that the instant popularity of the poem "demonstrated that the form commended itself to the masses as well as to the cultured few" (219). He praises the poem as "thoroughly American" and comments on its "broad humanity, its spirit of toleration, and its pictures of democratic simplicity," though he allows that "to idealize the genius of democracy" was alien to Longfellow's intents (221). In his introduction to the Macmillan Pocket Classic edition of the poem in 1900, Lewis B. Semple declared, "One may safely say that *Evangeline* is the most read poem in American literature" (xxix).

Of course one might counter with Ludwig Lewisohn, writing in 1932: "Who, except wretched schoolchildren, now reads Longfellow?" (65). The gap between popular and academic tastes has remained. As Richard Dilworth Rust's survey of the critical reception of Longfellow attests, the 1920s and 1930s, with the advent of New Criticism, was not hospitable to Longfellow or *Evangeline.* Alfred Kreymborg refers to Longfellow as "The Fallen Prince of Popularity" and takes no small pleasure in announcing that, "Of all the poets of the New England renascence, Longfellow is held in the greatest derision" (97). Like others, Kreymborg, operating from critical premises that must have been untenable even in the 1930s, excoriates Longfellow for having written *Evangeline* without having visited Nova Scotia or the Mississippi. Coleridge, by way of comparison, has not been assailed, but implicitly praised in such works as Lowes' classic study *Road to Xanadu,* for having written "The Rime of the Ancient Mariner" without having sailed past the South Pole. On the other hand, Wordsworth's familiarity with the locale has not prompted critics and scholars to celebrate his River Duddin sonnets.

Describing Longfellow as "distinctly a poet of the library" (440), Vernon Louis Parrington dismisses him in just three pages in *The Romantic Revolution in America* (1927), and although VanWyck Brooks was to treat Longfellow more generously with respect to space in *The Flowering of New England, 1815–1865* (1936), he is hardly more laudatory: "His mind was like a music-box, charged with all the poetry of the world" (153). Moreover, Brooks declared, "Twenty other poets and orators were saying the same things" (154). Also writing in 1936, Walter Fuller Taylor concluded, "It is in some restful cathedral of the mind, of some imaginary escape from the sordidness of reality, that the principal lifework of Longfellow consists" (195). And "Fundamentally, Longfellow lacked the highest type of imagination; he lacked greatness, profundity, and power of soul. He is winsome, without being majestic" (195). It might justly be argued that no poet in

America has ever had to stand up to such a metaphysically, or at least rhetorically, stacked critical deck.

Surely some readers will be surprised if they should come upon Walt Whitman's much more generous reflections on Longfellow's contributions to American poetry in his *Specimen Days,* recorded on the event of Longfellow's death and dated "April 3, '82":

> Longfellow in his voluminous works seems to me not only to be eminent in the style and forms of poetical expression that mark the present age, (an idiosyncrasy, almost a sickness, of verbal melody), but to bring what is always dearest to poetry to the general human heart and taste, and probably must be so in the nature of things. He is certainly the sort of bard and counteractant most needed for our materialistic, self-assertive, money-worshipping, Anglo-Saxon races, and especially for the present age in America—an age tyrannically regulated with reference to the manufacturer, the merchant, the financier, the politician and the day workman—for whom and among whom he comes as the poet of melody, courtesy, deference [...] [285].

At this point I have broken off the quotation on the verge of the place at which Longfellow's detractors are most likely to pick it up. Whitman, still in an apparently complimentary vein, calls Longfellow the "poet of the mellow twilight of the past," "poet of all sympathetic gentleness," and "universal poet of women and young people." Those passages tend to be quoted out of context. Some reflection on the critical mass of the passage above, however, may be in order.

Obviously Whitman was not taken with Longfellow's "verbal melody," but he does perceive that Longfellow appeals to "the general human heart"; moreover, he detects in Longfellow a strong voice against the excesses of the Gilded Age: "I should have to think long if I were ask'd to name the man who has done more, and in more valuable directions, for America."

Longfellow and his *Evangeline* have faded from the canon gradually, so that only in the past forty or so years has Lewisohn's compassion for "wretched schoolchildren" been unnecessary. Probably because of his historical position in American letters, Longfellow has managed to sustain some credibility among the scholars. Rust surveys the criticism through the 1950s and 1960s, accounting for Edward Wagenknecht's *Longfellow: A Full-Length Portrait* in 1955, Newton Arvin's *Longfellow: His Life and Work* (1963), Edward L. Hirsh's booklet in the University of Minnesota American Writers series and Cecil B. Williams' book in the Twayne series, both published in 1964. No scholar has taken up the cause of Longfellow more devotedly than Wagenknecht, who followed his 1955 study with *Henry Wadsworth Longfellow: Portrait of an American Humanist* in 1966 and *Henry Wadsworth Longfellow: His Poetry and Prose* in 1986. The most important work on *Evan-*

geline between its publication and John Seelye's essay (published in 1984 and discussed in Chapter 1) has been the essay by Manning Hawthorne and Henry Wadsworth Longfellow Dana, "The Origin of Longfellow's *Evangeline*" (1947). The latest item listed in Rust's survey is the Longfellow symposium issue of *ESQ* published in 1970.

Recent Critical Contexts

Rust notes that between 1959 and 1968 just 47 articles, five books, four scholarly editions, and two doctoral dissertations were listed in the *PMLA* bibliographies on Longfellow, "hardly an average year's output on Longfellow's friend Hawthorne" (263). Quantitatively, matters have changed little in the years since Rust's survey. The *PMLA* bibliographies between 1970 and the summer of 2008 list some 300 items of various types, including books, editions, full-length articles, notes, translations, announcements of letters or poems discovered, and doctoral dissertations. If one were to go simply by the raw number listed on the EBSCO site, the results would be misleading, including as they do, for example, several titles by Canadian film theorist Brenda Longfellow. A little over 200 items turn out to be of potential interest. The simple mathematics of the situation suggests that the number of verifiably substantial items, including those published in numerous languages other than English, has been sustained at the rate of five or six per year. I intend here to account quickly for the more important publications on Longfellow over the past 37 years with particular attention to items pertaining to *Evangeline.*

The most significant editions of Longfellow's poems post–1970 are George Monteiro's *Complete Poetical Works of Henry Wadsworth Longfellow,* published by Houghton Mifflin in 1975, and the Library of America edition, *Henry Wadsworth Longfellow: Poems and Other Writings,* selected and annotated by J.D. McClatchy and published in 2000. The general accessibility of Longfellow's writings, however, is implicit in other forms of publication. The University of Michigan's Historical Reprint Series has been republishing the writings since December of 2005, and Kessinger Publishing has been reprinting the works, including Samuel Longfellow's *Life,* first published in 1886 with extracts from the journals and letters, since 2003. Large-print editions of such titles as *Kavanagh* and *Hyperion* are now available. NuVision Publications reprinted Longfellow's translations of *The Divine Comedy* in the spring of 2007, and BiblioBazaar turned out a one-volume *Collected Works* that same summer. A Dover Thrift Edition of *Evangeline and Other Poems* (1995) can be had for just two dollars. Horace Gregory's 1964 Signet edition of *Evangeline and Selected Tales and Poems,* including *The Courtship of Miles Standish,* remains in print and readily available. Never, one might say, was Longfellow's writing more available, and according to Christoph Irmscher, the venerable poet, with his "emphasis on pleasing his readers" (70) would have been delighted: "[H]is savvy dealings with publishers show how he gradually refashioned himself as a poet who would appeal also to readers with smaller purses" (54). The Poetry for Young People series includes a 48-page selection of poems published in 1998 and intended for ages nine through twelve, the cover of which features an illustration from "The Wreck of the Hesperus." Readers with access to a computer may easily acquire on-line text of virtually all of the published work.

Of particular interest to enthusiasts is the Special Commemorative Edition of *Evangeline* prepared by Françoise Paradis from Buxton, Maine, and published in 2004 by Llumina Press. A psychologist and counselor of French Canadian ancestry, Paradis regards her long-term passion for the poem and her production of the illustrated volume, with foreword and biographical sketch by the poet's ancestor, Layne Longfellow, as her "destiny" (11). The 8" × 11" hardbound book includes Paradis' 23-page historical essay, "Acadia: From '*Le Grand Dérangement*' to '*The Great Upheaval*,'" with a map and black-and-white reproductions of Don Cyr's paintings of Nova Scotia in the seventeenth and eighteenth centuries. Most of the illustrations are the work of E[dwin] A[usten] Abbey (1852–1911) whose work was featured in Houghton Mifflin's Household Edition of Longfellow's *Complete Poetical Works* at the turn of the nineteenth century (see Chapter 4). Paradis has also published a coloring book of *Evangeline* and prepared a traveling exhibit *http://www.francoiseparadis.com/exhibition.html.*

Andrew Hilen's edition of the letters published by the Harvard University Press, the first volume of which appeared in 1966, had reached Volume 6 (1866–1874) by 1983. Hilen died in 1982, coincidentally the centennial year of Longfellow's death, leaving the project incomplete. Three important book-length studies of the life and work have appeared during the past twenty years, give or take a year: Edward Wagenknecht's *Henry Wadsworth Longfellow: His Poetry and Prose* (1986) in Ungar's Literature and Life: American Writers series, Charles C. Calhoun's *Longfellow: A Rediscovered Life* (2004), and Christoph Irmscher's *Longfellow Redux* (2006). To these should be added Robert L. Gale's encyclopedic volume, *A Henry Wadsworth Longfellow Companion* (2003). A young adult biography, *American Genius: Henry Wadsworth Longfellow,* by Libby Hughes and Marian R. Carlson, appeared in December of 2006. A collection of papers presented at the Longfellow Commemorative Conference held in Washington, DC, in April of 1982 incorporates eight items, published by the U.S. Government Printing Office.

The most valuable recent, sweeping reassessment of Longfellow's reputation aside from those offered in the books cited above is Dana Gioia's "Longfellow in the Aftermath of Modernism," published in the *Columbia History of American Poetry* (1993) and described in my first chapter. Unlike others who have indexed Longfellow's popular reputation simply to sneer at it, Gioia writes, "I offer this welter of anecdote not to argue the intrinsic worth of Longfellow's poetry, which I believe is considerable, but to make a simple point. There is something singularly odd in Longfellow's case that makes him extraordinarily difficult for contemporary critics to discuss: he is as much a part of our history as of our literature" (66). To which one might add, "a part of our history of popular culture in particular." Critics and scholars are notable for, on the one hand, bewailing such phenomena as "the death of poetry" and for decrying the disinclination of their students to read poems (even as those same students readily confess to an eagerness for writing them), and on the other hand for repudiating any poet who manages to establish something of a popular reputation.

While he observes that "Longfellow remains the one poet the average, nonbookish American still knows by heart—not whole poems but memorable snatches" (67), Gioia traces his decline in literature anthologies. Had he inquired into Longfellow's status in anthologies of American literature commonly taught in the nation's universities he would have detected a similar trend of "downsizing." The seventh edition (2007) of the Norton anthology of American literature includes eight poems (about ten pages), the longest of which is "My Lost Youth" (ninety lines). Only the prologue is offered from *Evangeline.* The 2004 Pearson-Prentice Hall anthology devotes just eight pages to Longfellow, enough for six poems including "The Jewish Cemetery at Newport" and "My Lost Youth." Even Whittier fares better at ten pages, and William Cullen Bryant is represented with eight poems, while the nine poems of Colonial poet Philip Freneau fill a dozen pages of text. The Heath anthology of 2005 whittles Longfellow to a mere half dozen poems in five pages, while the 2008 edition of the Bedford anthology reduces Longfellow to only two poems, half the number included for Poe and the same number listed for the likes of Elizabeth Oakes Smith and Frances E.W. Harper. The most generous among the recent college American literature anthologies is the McGraw-Hill tenth edition (2002), which devotes nearly forty pages to Longfellow's poems, partly because a major portion of *The Song of Hiawatha* is included, perhaps due to the increasing interest in Native American literature. Longfellow is all but absent from texts commonly used these days in public schools.

Gioia proposes Longfellow's first book of poems, *Voices of the Night* (1839), inaugurated the "archetype" in America of the "poet professor." He suggests that the other three "stereotypes for the American poet that permeate both high and popular culture" are the bohemian vagabond, the reclusive outsider, and the self-destructive fiery genius (76). Although he does not, Gioia might have added that the poets of those types (whether arche- or stereo-) are often at loggerheads with each other. One example Gioia offers of the "self-destructive fiery genius," is Longfellow's nemesis, Edgar Allan Poe. He might also have noted that because of the academy's almost uncanny capacity for containment, the types could place their feet in more than one camp. Another "self-destructive fiery genius" on Gioia's list, poet/professor John Berryman, is a prime example.

Whereas critics of the nineteenth century were inclined to regard Longfellow's enthusiasm for European poetry skeptically, insisting that it led to imitativeness (even plagiarism) and the curtailment of any "individual genius," affecting even the meter of *Evangeline,* which he apparently derived from Goethe's *Hermann und Dorothea* (1797), Gioia commends Longfellow's uses of European literature and notes the kinship with Ezra Pound's projects for uprooting the American public from its cultural isolation. Gioia goes so far as to defend the oft ridiculed "Psalm of Life," observing that "despite repeated assassination attempts by some of the best hit men in modern letters, this menacingly upbeat poem refuses to die" (78). While he relates the litany of Longfellow's "faults as a lyric poet" (lack of intellectual depth, sentimentality, propensity to moralize, unrealistically optimistic attitude, etc.), Gioia argues that Longfellow's advocates over the past half century have made the mistake of "attempting to justify his work by Modernism's standards rather than insisting it be approached—as one would other poets separated by a significant historical gap—on its own terms" (81).

Setting aside for the moment John Seelye's "Attic Shape: Dusting Off *Evangeline,*" a title that doubtless reflects the author's ambivalence, a hasty survey of some selected titles of the two dozen articles dealing with *Evangeline* over the past thirty-odd years will give some sense of how literary scholars have dealt with the poem: "Elements of Folklore, History, and Literature in Longfellow's *Evangeline*" (1982), "The Poetry and Prose of History: Evangeline and the Historians of Nova Scotia" (1988), "Mars in Petticoats: Longfellow and Sentimental Masculinity" (1996, see Chapter 1), "In Search of the Canadian Evangeline" (1997), "Images of Evangeline: Continuity of the Iconographic Tradition" (1997), "Dramatic Transformations of *Evangeline*" (1998, see Chapter 4), "Longfellow's Evangeline and the Cult of Acadia" (2002, mentioned above), "'Multitudinous Echoes': The Derisive Music of Longfellow's *Evangeline*" (2003), "Évangéline multimedia: Un Mythe acadien entre americanité et americanisation"(2004), "Longfellow's Long Line" (2006), "The Ghostly Presence of Evangeline: Faulkner's Exorcism and Revision of the Feminine Ideal (2006), "A Correction Between Henry Wadsworth Longefellow's Family and Acadian History" (2008).

Given the increasing popularity of the short story during the nineteenth century, one might argue that the narrative poem was doomed as a subgenre, but the short story was in the early stages of its definition when *Evangeline* appeared in 1847, and the narrative poem then wielded considerable clout. For example, "The Demon" (1841), by Pushkin's disciple, Mikhail Lermontov an heir to Byron's Romantic narratives (closer to "The Giaour" or "The Corsair" than to "Manfred" or *Childe Harold*), although it may seem flawed to a modern reader, was enormously popular in its time and remains one of Russia's literary classics. *Evangeline* might be best appreciated, then, in the context of the long narrative poem. Gioia goes so far as to assert that some passages of *Evangeline* are "both breathtakingly beautiful and, as Longinus understood the term, sublime" (87).

John Seelye's reconsideration of *Evangeline* comes off as a mélange of criticism from the past and fresh insights. Like past critics of Longfellow's "artificial" landscapes, Seelye seems at first not to perceive that *all* literary "landscapes" are artificial. The great house celebrated in Ben Jonson's "To Penshurst" is as artificial, despite its historical existence, as Spenser's Bower of Bliss, and ditto for Yeats' "Lake Isle of Innisfree" and Theodore Roethke's Far Field. But Seelye suggests several attractive contexts in his essay. "As an Acadian Ruth, a personification of alienation," he writes, "the embowered yet accursed American Eve is a projection of the poet himself" (22). While Seelye submits that "the poem is a thoroughly derivative work" (31) and that "the boisterous, ebullient spirit of Young America is entirely missing" (32), he notes in the transformation of Basil the blacksmith "a characteristic American metamorphosis, an atavistic return to preindustrial pastoralism" (37). In fact, he detects in Basil "a prefiguration of that agrarian avatar, the cowboy."

Committed to demonstrating Longfellow's "removal from the contemporary American scene," Seelye goes so far as to complain of his failure to deal with "the fate of the black man" in Louisiana (40), apparently failing to note how anachronistic such commentary might have been in a poem set there in the 1750s and 1760s, when Louisiana was a Spanish possession, as Longfellow makes clear when he has Basil and Evangeline travel to the town of Adayes in search of Gabriel. But Seelye also suggests that "Evangeline, whitely and quietly, serves as a vicarious vehicle for emotions aroused by the plight of enslaved black people," and he surmises, as others have, that she is "the inspiration for Little Eva's name and saintly character" (43) in Stowe's *Uncle Tom's Cabin*. If Evangeline's West is a "purely literary zone," Seelye concludes, after all, so too is the New England of Hester Prynne and the Pacific Ocean of Ishmael.

Evangeline may also be read, however, as a text that transcends such directly geographical and historical limits. Jacques M. Chevalier, currently Professor of Social Anthropology and Political Economy at Carleton University in Ottawa, has examined the myth of *Evangeline* as a type of lost paradise in considerable detail, devoting a book of more than three hundred pages to a reading of just the prologue and the first canto of the romance "against a backdrop of scriptural images of the model of the woman of the Old and New Testaments" (1). Probably because of its title, *Semiotics, Romanticism and the Scriptures*, and its publication in the Approach to Semiotics Series (1990), this text has been sometimes overlooked by Longfellow scholars. While of interest, the book is not particularly readable; it comes across as an odd blend of semiotics with attention to symbols and archetypes combined with intense biblical typology.

Re-Reading Evangeline

If *Evangeline* is to be read anew it will most likely be from perspectives of the sort that Dana Gioia, John Seelye, and Jacques M. Chevalier have outlined. Implicitly, certain questions have been asked and answered about this poem over the years, but other questions have never been posed. In the long years of its establishment in the canon, particularly in the public schools, certain contexts were established and generations of schoolchildren and others read the poem with those contexts in mind. One of these contexts from the outset was biographical. In her introduction for an edition published in 1911, Jane M. Cutts advises the teacher to "Acquire for yourself, as of prime importance, a thorough acquaintance with the events of Longfellow's life. [...] Thus equipped, proceed to interest your class in the poet." The study of *Evangeline* and other poems will then, Cutts writes, be "embodiments of the author's genius and attainments" (xxi–xxii). H.E. Scudder's substantial biographical commentary for the Riverside Literature Series doubtless contributed to the notion that the biographical context was essential. The so-called New Criticism of the 1930s and onward generally repudiated such an approach in favor of the text itself, the poem qua poem. "You can spot the bad critic," Ezra Pound wrote in *ABC of Reading* (1934), "when he starts by discussing the poet and not the poem" (84). Pound's assertion does not mean the deletion or "death" of the author *(pace* Roland Barthes), but rather the subordination of the poet's life to the life of the poem. Aspects of the writer's life that bear on the writing ought not to be ignored so much as they should be subordinated to the text at hand. In short, Cutts' advice requires some modification to the effect that "the events of Longfellow's life" are not of "prime importance," but of "secondary" importance.

Students and readers of the earliest annotated texts of *Evangeline* going back to an unauthorized London edition of 1848, were also advised to read the poem from an historical context, not necessarily as reflective of the American experience, as implied in Seelye's essay, but as a document, of sorts, in the history of French and English relations during colonial times. For some Canadians today, and particularly for modern Acadians, the poem remains alive as a tragedy of the Grand Deportation, as is evident in the play *Évangéline Deusse* (1976) by New Brunswick playwright Antonine Maillet (translated as *Evangeline the Second).* Nearly all of the school text editions of the poem were accompanied with historical backgrounds and accounts of Anglo-French relations. Maps were usually provided, and many editions included the text of Colonel Winslow's deportation orders. Presumably, the poem embodied both cross-cultural and cross-disciplinary lessons. In more recent years, as the selection of article titles listed above demonstrates, historical contexts remain important to the poem, and James Allan Evans' essay, "Longfellow's Evangeline and the Cult of Acadia," suggests that certain aspects of historical revisionism are involved, particularly with respect to the British and Colonial roles in what happened at Grand-Pré.

The unusual meter also occasioned, again in nearly every one of the many school text editions, an entry on "The Measure," which proved to have mnemonic qualities in those days of almost universal oral recitation. Some of these are quite sophisticated, especially if one assumes that the readers are eighth graders. In this respect, as noted above, the critical response to the poem, even when it was negative, contributed to the context of formalism. Critics and scholars in subsequent generations have sustained the controversy over the meter to such an extent that at least some formalist reflections seem inevitable. And even if the meter had not been an issue, the genre probably would have been. Early readers were inclined to emphasize the epic traits of the poem, which includes extended similes of Homeric or Miltonic design, at least one apostrophe in which the muse is invoked (Part II, Canto 1, lines 732–740), and such epic features as a narrative connected with cultural values and a protagonist of, in some ways, superhuman qualities. Of course Longfellow's selection of the epic meter contributed to that generic identification. By Longfellow's death, however, the poem had come to be almost universally regarded as an "idyll," a generic demotion of sorts, although Longfellow himself employed that term, but that also remains grist for the formalist's mill.

These three contexts—biographical, historical, and formalist—might be regarded as secondary to what Longfellow himself would likely have considered the most important one: the moral or conceptual context of the poem. Preeminently, *Evangeline* is a straightforward (the term "simple" is often used in the commentaries, and not pejoratively but in the sense of "lucid"), didactic poem in which the reader is offered explicit moral and ethical lessons: affection or love is never wasted, no matter how hopeless circumstances may seem; one should endure suffering silently and patiently (that is, stoically); the good (upright, virtuous) life requires self-abnegation and devotion to the welfare of others; justice does not necessarily equate with a happy ending. If these values seem quaint or outmoded, perhaps one might consider the alternatives: love is only a fine name for lust; avoid pain and suffering and seek pleasure at all costs (neo–Epicureanism); the good life involves self-indulgence and disregard for others; justice implies that everyone lives happily ever after. Longfellow's values, of course, are conventionally Christian and bourgeois, and from a 21st-century perspective they may seem naïve, but it may well be that we are haunted not just by the image of Evangeline as "a vague ghost adrift on the Mississippi in company with Uncle Tom and Huck Finn," as Seelye suggests, but by our own lingering love-hate relationship with the specters of these moral and ethical values.

What has intervened over the century and a half since the poem was published is what might be called a shift in sensibility. The context of emotional tonality has changed from one that tends to celebrate pathos, nostalgia and sentiment (or sentimentality) to one that prefers, on the one hand, hard-edged realism, or on the other, bitterly ironic (even sarcastic) fantasy. The former impulse, still alive today, may be said to have reached a crescendo among the literary Naturalists, so-called, whose numbers include such diverse talents as Émile Zola, Stephen Crane, Thomas Hardy, Willa Cather, Theodore Dreiser, and more recently Norman Mailer. The latter impulse lies at the heart of the "triumph of irony" connected with Postmodernism, evident among such writers as Thomas Pynchon, Don DeLillo, T.C. Boyle, Kathy Acker, and David Foster Wallace. Sentimentalism has been defined as "An indulgence in pity and tears to enjoy one's benevolence or self-pity without paying the psychic debt exacted by Aristotle's tragic terror" (Frye et al., 426). In his entry on sentimentality in the *Princeton Encyclopedia of Poetry and Poetics* Paul Fussell associates the term with excess emotion or "excessively direct poetic expression of pathos without a sufficient poetic correlative" (763). Sentimentality occurs when the emotions remain "vague and oversimplified" or when the poet indulges in self-pity. Fussell concludes by reminding the reader that strong pathos is not in itself a poetic vice, but how or exactly where to draw the line between acceptable expression of pathos and objectionable sentimentality is difficult to ascertain. Presumably, however, sentiment, nostalgia and pathos are now passé. At least, one might hastily add, in the realms of what passes for serious writing. But have we in fact reached a state of emotional necrosis, of the death of feeling? And if we have attained such a state, what does that condition indicate about the psychic health of our culture?

John Seelye proceeds from the assertion that Longfellow is a "maudlin poet" writing in a "sentimental age," and he detects in his work "a stale magic of remembrance," or nostalgia. Yet he discovers in *Evangeline* a national "icon" that exists in defiance of the "history and the conditions of real life" (33). Writing just a couple of years after Longfellow's death, E.C. Stedman described him as from the first "a poet of sentiment" and conceded that some of the poems are "little sermons in rhyme that are sure to catch the ear and to become hackneyed as a sidewalk song" (190). Others among Longfellow's lyrics Stedman pillories as "poems of sentiment and brooding twilight," and still others he finds merely "picturesque." Stedman appears to anticipate modern disesteem for sentimentality when he notes that "Tragedy went no deeper with him than its pathos; it was another element of the beautiful. Death was a luminous transition" (193). In effect, Stedman seeks to defend the sentimental vision of death, or at least to argue that the tragic vision of death is not the only viable one in serious literature. In recognizing *Evangeline* as Longfellow's personal favorite, Stedman treats the poem in a perhaps reluctantly respectful manner: "There are rooms in every house where one treads with softened footfall" (201). In short, both period and contemporary readers of *Evangeline* are compelled either to embrace the sentimental tonality (context and texture) of the poem, or else avoid reading it altogether. Among the earliest book-length critical studies of Longfellow and his work is that of Thomas Wentworth Higginson published in the American Men of Letters series in 1902. Best known among students of American poetry today as Emily Dickinson's major "preceptor," Higginson asserts that "every test continues to prove that the hold taken on the average human *heart* by Longfellow is far greater than that held, for instance, by Poe or Whitman" (10, emphasis mine).

Although the charge of sentimentality has always been a stigma and may remain so, *Evangeline* has not been rediscovered, curiously enough, by scholars like Nina Baym, who have asked important questions about sentimentality in American literature and culture. The reason for this is probably the understandable interest of Baym and other feminists or "gynocritics" in the women who wrote popular sentimental fiction and who have been pointedly ignored by the male-dominated critical establishment. But Evangeline as a heroine is very much among the "celibate women" who are "untrue to the imperatives of their gender, which require marriage, childbearing, domesticity" (14). She does not act in the role Baym describes of "entrapper" or "impediment" to men in the "melodrama of beset manhood," nor is she like James Fenimore Cooper's Alice, a cheerful, incompetent, thoughtless, and passive woman. Baym does not mention *Evangeline* in *Feminism and American Literary History,* but her views on Longfellow as a poet of domesticity (the ultimate poet of the fireside) are implicit in her comparison of his career and reception with Walt Whitman's (82–83). But the United States is not exactly overwhelmed with images of heroic women, either historical or literary, and surely one context from which to read the poem is in some sense of the term "feminist." Newton Arvin briefly associates Evangeline with such symbolic figures as Ruth and Penelope, but notes that she had "deep personal value, too, for Longfellow, with his dependence on the devotion of woman," and he comments that the poem "had a value, too, for his woman-oriented culture" (100).

With that potentially political context in mind at one extreme of the spectrum, however, one might reflect on a context that at least seems to be apolitical in nature—the pictorial or iconographic. Probably no American poem has been so widely and variously illustrated as *Evangeline,* and the reason is doubtless that Longfellow excelled at descriptive writing, particularly of landscape. In an era famous for "purple patches" of affectively charged scenery, Longfellow was a master. As various critics have noted over the years, *Evangeline* is not a poem noted for its dramatic action. It is a poem of scenes, of tableaux, and it is not much concerned with photographic reality. Longfellow's description of the "forest primeval" has little to do with the actual flora of Nova Scotia, and various readers have noted that the lotus which he places in the Louisiana bayous is more at home in Tennyson's "The Lotus-Eaters" than it is in the American South. As Arvin demonstrates, Longfellow defines a prevailing atmosphere of moonlight and inertia, avoiding the "fierce hostility of nature" in favor of "its painterly beauty, its picturesque charm" (105).

Clearly, *Evangeline* no longer has the status it once enjoyed as a privileged text, and whatever contexts one might propose as points of departure for reading it, or any other text for that matter, readers will proceed independently. One wonders, for example, how much success teachers in the early decades of this century had motivating their students by interesting them in Longfellow's life or in "the author's genius and attainment." Jane Cutts retells as an instance of "a teacher's infectious enthusiasm for this author" the story of one from the state of Washington who in 1910 "so impressed a class with the attractive qualities of the poet and with the marvel of what he did that one of her boys journeyed across the continent [...] to enroll himself in Longfellow's alma mater" (xxii). One suspects that the attractive qualities of Harvard, or possibly of Bowdoin (the college is not clearly indicated), had something to do with that decision.

What is it about *Evangeline* that has so fascinated readers that it has been translated into nearly every major language? (Richard Dilworth Rust notes ten Russian translators prior to 1900 and seven editions of Longfellow's poems between 1918 and 1935 in the Soviet Union.) Why was the poem so long a standard in American public schools? What was taught? Why is *Evangeline* no longer taught? What interpretations of the poem and its characters are implicit in the illustrated versions? Are the values around which the poem is constructed, whether conceived as moral or ethical, universal in some way, or not? Has *Evangeline,* in losing its status as a privileged text, ceased to become "literature"? Is the poem simply the victim of a cycle of taste, another revolution of which will bring it back to prominence? Is Evangeline a viable heroine? What is there in the poem for the male reader? Is *Evangeline* still worth talking about?

3

Evangeline Goes to School

An "introduction, historical and explanatory" to *Evangeline* appeared within just one year of the poem's publication. The sixteen-page essay, dated June 1848 in the London edition by Kent and Richards, purports to be written "by H.W. Longfellow," but it begins, "Mr. Longfellow's beautiful poem, 'Evangeline,' has given a celebrity to the unfortunate village of Grand Pre" (i); in short, it certainly appears to have been written by someone other than the poet. Whatever the case, this early work set the pattern for subsequent commentaries, as it traces the historical events surrounding the expulsion of the Acadians, going back to the cession of Nova Scotia to Great Britain by France in the Peace of Utrecht (1713). The anonymous commentator cites Abbé Reynal's idealized descriptions of Acadian life, Colonel Winslow's speech, and Thomas C. Haliburton's *History of Nova Scotia,* Longfellow's primary source for historical details in the poem. Implicit in this commentary is the perception of *Evangeline* as significantly, if not preeminently, an historical poem. That is, as it would be subsequently offered in the public schools, an important key to understanding and appreciating the poem would be its historical context. In fact, in some commentaries intended for public schools one gets the impression that the poem is valuable primarily because it concerns historic events, and that one should use the poem mostly in order to teach history lessons. In his 1882 limited edition essay on the poem, with illustrations by Frank Dicksee, Noah Porter (1811–1892), then president of Yale University, and noted author of books on moral philosophy, observed, "To understand and appreciate the poem of Evangeline, one needs not only to be made acquainted with the geographical features of the country in which it is placed [that is, Nova Scotia; like most commentators, Porter takes Louisiana for granted], but to trace the growth of the people it depicts to the imagination" (13).

Also published in London in 1848 was an unauthorized printing by H.G. Clarke with an anonymous eight-page introduction, perhaps by Eliza Robins, who inscribed the book to Longfellow on June 10, 1849 and whose initials appear in pencil at the end of the commentary in the edition at the Houghton Library. While she does cite Haliburton, Robins' comments focus on the characterization rather than the historical context of the poem: "So much of the charm of Evangeline is derived from the very foundation of the narrative—the simple dignity and earnestness of the characters." She also praises "the deep religious tone" of the work (v). "These unfortunate people," Robins observes, "were the victims of their own integrity."

As early as the 1870s, selections from *Evangeline* appeared in William Holmes McGuffey's influential eclectic readers (namely, the sixth, which was intended for use at the high school or even college level), but it was not until 1883 that the first important annotated textbook edition of the complete poem was published as #1 in the inexpensive Riverside Editions by Houghton Mifflin with an introduction and notes by author and editor of the *Atlantic Monthly*, Horace E. Scudder, known as a writer and editor of children's books. Between that date and 1916, when Eva March Tappan and Margaret Ashmun collaborated on a new edition for the Riverside series, at least sixteen other scholars and teachers of widely varying credentials, capacities and motives provided a plethora of introductions, prefaces, plot analyses, explanatory notes, guidelines, study plans, composition topics, exam questions, vocabulary lists, and advice to both students and teachers of the poem.

Occasionally one gets the impression that the more enthusiastic proponents of *Evangeline* believed it could, at the very least, make the world safe for democracy. In her "Study Helps," Ashmun poses a question that is all but rhetorical: "Do you see why it has always been so well liked and so much admired?" (105). The clear implication is "*don't* you see?" And the questions I am posing here are: Why *don't* "we" like and admire that poem so much? What has become of its purportedly universal appeal? Why does it no longer occupy a revered place in the canon of American literature? In his introduction to the 1900 edition of one of the most frequently reprinted texts of the poem (Macmillan's Pocket English Classics), Lewis B. Semple writes, "One may safely say that *Evangeline* is the most read poem in American literature" (xxix). Is it simply a matter of changing tastes that we may no longer "safely say" that, or is it the shift away from the literature of sentiment, or is it something more profound? As I see it, *Evangeline* has been repudiated and de-canonized as a literary text demoted, in effect; to the status of literary and cultural artifact: a poem important to know about, but not necessarily to read.

The answers to such questions are inevitably speculative, but they involve some consideration of the apparent rationale for the inclusion of the poem in the public school curriculum. By examining the introductions and other collateral materials, we should be able to derive some appreciation of what concepts and values were considered essential a hundred or so years ago. Somewhat more than coincidentally, we should also acquire some insight into pedagogical practices in the public schools of the generation that came of age between the 1880s and the 1920s.

The social, political, economic, and educational climate of the United States had changed drastically since the publication of *Evangeline* in 1847, so much so that a few observations are in order by way of resetting the context. In the three decades following the Civil War, the U.S. emerged as a leading industrial power, one aspect of which was the evolution of corporate America. John D. Rockefeller set up the Standard Oil Trust in 1882, the year of Longfellow's death, and by 1887 Congress had passed the Interstate Commerce Act to regulate the railroads, followed in 1890 by the Sherman Antitrust Act. By 1890 some 30 percent of the population, fed by immigration that exceeded five million in the decade between 1881 and 1890, lived in cities.

Following the post–Civil War settlement of the West, North and South Dakota and Montana became states in 1889, followed by Idaho and Wyoming, the first state to grant full equality for women, in 1890.

Although John Dewey's early books, like *My Pedagogic Creed* and *The School and Society,* are products of the late 1890s, signs of what one might call Progressivism in American education do occasionally appear in early study guides for *Evangeline.* The poem itself, however, may seem little short of an anachronism in the curriculums of public schools in a modern, industrial, post–Darwinian society. In his useful opening chapter of *How Teachers Taught: Constancy and Change in American Classrooms, 1880–1990,* Larry Cuban concludes that "Teacher-centered practices continued to prevail in most classrooms" (45), which meant, among other things, considerable emphasis on recitation: "Students recited passages from textbooks, worked at their desks on assignments, or listened to the teacher and classmates during the time set aside for instruction. Teachers assigned work and expected uniformity from students both in behavior and in classwork" (25). Memorizing at least the nineteen-line prologue to *Evangeline* was to be a common exercise for students for several generations.

Although I will comment on other collateral materials in passing, I will focus my remarks on annotated editions by Horace E. Scudder, Claude Towne Benjamin, Edward Everett Hale, Agnes Lathe, F.M. Muhlig, W. F. Conover, E.O. Vaile, Maud Elma Kingsley and Frank Herbert Palmer, Lewis

B. Semple, Eva March Tappan and Margaret Ashmun, and Jay Earle Thomson. Scudder's rather elaborate apparatus appeared with the first Riverside Edition of the poem in 1883, the year after Longfellow's death, and was reprinted at least half a dozen times before Tappan and Ashmun's new Riverside edition appeared in 1916. Scudder's 34-page "Sketch of the Life and Writings of Henry Wadsworth Longfellow," illustrated with wood engravings of the poet's birthplace and Craigie House, is a tribute divided into six sections tracing his ancestry and boyhood, his European travels and early years as a professor at Bowdoin College, his first years at Harvard (highly anecdotal), his remarriage and growing literary reputation (1839–1849), the period of Longfellow's international recognition (to about 1869), and the last years, those of gray hair and laurels.

Horace E. Scudder

Following Scudder's biography, the poet's daughter, Alice ("grave Alice" of "The Children's Hour"), provided a four-page sketch entitled "Longfellow in Home Life." Although she praises her father's "consideration and thoughtfulness for others" and his "quick sense of humor," Alice M. Longfellow offers the portrait of a perfectionist who was "a great foe to procrastination" (xxxviii). "There was really no line of demarcation between his life and his poetry," Alice writes: "anything out of place distressed him, as did a faulty rhyme or defective metre." Not surprisingly, "An unpaid bill weighed on him like a nightmare" (xxxvii). Referring to her father with the distant formality of the age as "Mr. Longfellow," Alice concludes, he "was always full of reserve, and never talked much about himself or his work, even to his family" (xl). For the reader of that era, particularly for the twelve or thirteen-year-old most likely finishing his or her formal schooling with the eighth grade, the message was clear: from the pen of an admirable person is likely to come a worthy poem; that is, the character of the poet determines in most ways the quality of the poems.

Next follows an eight-page historical introduction to the poem, a map of Nova Scotia, and a brief comment on the meter. Scudder appends a brief bibliography of historical accounts of the Acadian expulsion in 1755, including Thomas C. Haliburton's *An Historical and Statistical Account of Nova Scotia* (1829). One feature that distinguishes Scudder's comments on the historical context from earlier and succeeding ones is his relatively benign treatment of the British: "It must also be remembered that to many men at this time the English power seemed trembling before France, and that the colony at Halifax regarded the act as one of self preservation" (4). He also departs from earlier commentators (and some later ones) who celebrate the

Acadians as virtually prelapsarian in their virtues: "Most of the Acadians were probably simple-minded and peaceful people, who desired only to live undisturbed on their farms." But Scudder goes beyond that with some rather typically Protestant speculation: "but there were some restless spirits, especially among the young men, who compromised the reputation of the community, and all were very much under the influence of their priests, some of whom made no secret of their bitter hostility to the English" (2). Clearly, Scudder's view of the historical event is at odds with that of Eliza Robins (presumed editor of the unauthorized London edition cited above).

In effect, such prefatory comments constitute readings and interpretations of the text that follows. The signals Scudder transmits to the reader (student or otherwise) are curiously political, although the extent to which he appears on the surface to be a committed or aligned (as opposed to objective or disinterested) reader is debatable. The expulsion, as Scudder offers it, is seen as understandable and justifiable. Moreover, he implies that the Roman Catholic Acadians brought it down on themselves; had they been good Protestants, the expulsion likely would never have happened. The tragedy (or at least the melodrama) of Evangeline's separation from Gabriel is offered as an accident resulting from "haste and confusion," from "a haste which was increased by the anxiety of the officers to be rid of the distasteful business, and a confusion which was greater from the difference of tongues" (3–4).

In the two pages Scudder allots to the "history" of the poem's composition, he comments on an entry in Nathaniel Hawthorne's notebooks in which he recounts having heard the outlines of the story of "H.L.C." (The Reverend H.L. Conolly, a mutual friend of Hawthorne and Longfellow.) The poem, Scudder observes, "made its way at once into the hearts of people" (7). He also notes the painting and engraving of Evangeline by the Scottish artist, Thomas Faed (engraved by his brother James), "taken from the face of a Manchester working-girl," but he does not otherwise comment on the already extensive illustration of the poem. Scudder likely was unaware that Longfellow particularly admired Faed's painting, which he described in a journal entry of December 18, 1855, as bearing "a certain resemblance" to his wife (Samuel Longfellow, *Life* II, 299).

Finally, in what was to become a feature of nearly every commentary on the poem, Scudder adds a couple of paragraphs on "The Measure," the dactylic hexameter, which he dutifully traces back to Homer and Virgil, while at the same time pointing out that they have little in common, given the quantitative nature of Greek and Latin meters. Scudder also directs the reader to commentaries on the meter and to its use by Arthur Hugh Clough in "Bothie of Tober-na-Vuolich." These connections, though, are of less interest than are Scudder's efforts to discover an appropriate rationale for the unusual and (from the first) controversial meter: "The meter lends itself easily to the lingering melancholy which marks the greater part of the poem" (8). As early as January of 1848, in a review of the second edition of *Evangeline,* George Washington Peck wrote: "We cannot see why this tale should have been written in this measure; there is no consonance between the form and the substance of the narrative" (7).

After observing the value of the medial caesura in the line as a "rest" for the reader, Scudder spins out an analogy whereby the "habit of reading the hexameter" is likened "to the climbing of a hill, resting a moment on the summit, and then descending the other side." He recommends reading the poem aloud, "after a clear understanding of the sense" (8). The metrical commentary is not limited, however, to the introduction. After just three lines of the Prelude, Scudder attaches a lengthy footnote, in which he quotes Oliver Wendell Holmes on the impact of the opening ("we read as we would float down a broad and placid river") and on the hexameter ("the tranquil current of these brimming, slow-moving, soul-satisfying lines"). "Imagine for one moment," Holmes adds, "a story like this minced into octosyllabics" (9). Quoting what he calls a "self-parody," in which Longfellow tried the mockingbird passage from Part Two in pentameter couplets (see Chapter 2), Newton Arvin concludes, "it is hard to resist the feeling that hexameters were 'intrinsically' better suited to the effects Longfellow wished to achieve" (113).

The text of the Riverside Edition of the poem is numbered throughout in five-line increments, and Scudder's footnotes are extensive and mostly informative but occasionally interpretive. Sometimes, as in his note on the Druids, which runs over sixty words, they seem overzealous. Scudder provides 56 notes to the 1,399-line text, but oddly, he offers more than twice as many for Part One (38 notes) as he does for Part Two (18 notes), even though the second part of the poem runs nearly 70 lines longer than the first. It could be argued that because the first part of the poem deals with Nova Scotia (Acadia) and with a French Catholic environment, it is unfamiliar to American readers and so requires more extensive annotation. On the other hand, the second part also concerns a French Catholic context, and it covers much more area geographically, extending as it does from the Louisiana bayous, to the Rockies, to the north woods of Michigan, and on to the streets of Philadelphia. It also covers more time, deals with more numerous species of flora and fauna, and includes an episode that involves Native American lore. One suspects that Scudder simply ran out of gas.

Scudder's choices, what he elects to comment on and what he rejects or avoids, are often idiosyncratic, if not downright eccentric. For example, the reference to "harpers hoar" in the fourth line of the poem elicits a note advising the reader to inquire into the "ancient harper" of Sir Walter Scott's "Lay of the Last Minstrel," and for some reason he provides a rather lengthy note on the word "odorous" (ℓ. 99) with reflections on Milton's accenting of the word. Presumably Scudder's intentions here are those of most teachers, to direct students toward other literary texts. He offers a note of more than a hundred words to define the word "curfew" in line 354, but instead of providing a useful gloss on the legend of Lilinau in the third canto of Part Two, Scudder notes simply, "The story of Lilinau and other Indian legends will be found in H.R. Schoolcraft's *Algic Researches*" (84). He defines the relatively familiar and accessible term "voyageur" (ℓ. 707), but leaves the reader who has no French in a fog with the phrase "ci-devant blacksmith" (ℓ. 970).

The edition concludes with a two-page "Pronouncing Vocabulary of Proper Names and Foreign Words in *Evangeline*," but he supplies no additional apparatus for teaching the poem. The main intent of Scudder's annotations, other than to provide historical, geographical, or lexical glosses, is presumably to establish a literary context, and thereby to imply literary quality or value. This intention is implicit in the first footnote, in which Holmes is quoted as pointing out that the opening clause of the poem, "This is the forest primeval," is "already as familiar" as the openings of *The Iliad* and *The Aeneid* (9). Scudder's literary references range from Homer, Goldsmith, and Tennyson to Charles Brockden Brown.

Claude Towne Benjamin

Of considerably greater value for the classroom is the apparatus provided in Claude Towne Benjamin's edition for the Maynard's English Classic Series in 1893. An English teacher at DeWitt Clinton High School in New York, Benjamin compresses the biographical information into four pages, and although he celebrates Longfellow for his "undeniable genius" (3) and recognizes him as, after Tennyson, "the most popular poet of his day," he rehearses what had already become a litany of the poet's limitations: "His range is domestic. He lacks the power of depicting deep passion, or of robing purely imaginative subjects with ideal grace and color" (6). In these judgments Benjamin echoes E.C. Stedman, among others, who as early as 1885, just three years after Longfellow's death, considers the nearly universal popular appeal of Longfellow's poetic voice to be both his strengths and his weaknesses: "verse whose easy lessons are adjusted to common need [...]; "He often taught, by choice, the primary class, and the upper form is slow to forget it" (190). "Of the higher tests of poetic genius," Stedman asks rhetorically, with reference to "spontaneity, sweep, intellect, imaginative power,—what examples has he left us?" (191). By 1900, Brown University Professor of English Walter C. Bronson can write with casual confidence, "Longfellow is not a great poet": "There are heights and depths, splendors and glooms, in life and the soul, which his muse of the fireside and the library could not touch" (190).

Following his biographical note, Benjamin appends six pages of "Critical Opinions," the sum of which is consistent with the condescending comments cited above: "the moral purity of his verse," "domestic affections," "the poet of the household, of the fireside, of the universal home feeling" (George William Curtis); "it would not be true to say that his art is of the intensest kind or most magical potency [...] he is a good type of the 'bettermost,' not the exceptionally very best, minds of the central or later-central period of the nineteenth century" (William Michael Rossetti); "the essence of his style was simplicity" (*London Saturday Review*); "the sentiment is heartfelt, but a little ordinary [...] he had not that imaginative strength, that spacious vision, that depth of personal individuality which impress somewhat painfully at first, but which alone supply in the long-run the great startling and rousing forces that possess a permanent influence" (*London Athenaeum*); "We know, in reading him, that he will never miss his mark [... but] he will risk nothing. [...] He rarely loses sight of common interests and sympathies" (E.P. Whipple) (7–12).

So why, the students might have asked upon reading such prologue, so reserved, understated, and unenthusiastic in its praise of the poet, why must we read this lengthy poem? It could be argued that unlike the reader of Scudder's prefatory material, the reader of Benjamin's is likely to approach the poem critically because of the qualified praise which he cites, but such speculation would place high expectations on readers of twelve to fourteen years of age. As if anticipating such a tacit question, Benjamin follows with an eight-page commentary on *Evangeline,* including information on the historical context and the meter; implying, that is, that one should read the poem for reasons not directly, or at least not solely, related to the worth of the poem itself. These commentaries begin with a passage from George McCrie's *The Religion of Our Literature* (1875) that typifies the author-centered critical premises of the age before the New Critics: "It holds a place entirely by itself in our literature, in so far as immortal praise is due to its author not only, and not so much for his manner of treating the subject, as for his discovery and conception of the subject itself." McCrie commends not only "this mysterious love-journey," but also the fact that the poem embraces the "vastnesses of the American continent": "for it is the very magnificence of nature in its forests and prairies and rolling rivers that is against her—it is the wideness of space that overwhelms her" (13).

The three-page "Historical Basis of the Poem" is taken from E.S. Robertson's *The Life of Henry Wadsworth Longfellow* (1887) and includes most of the text of Massachusetts Governor Lawrence's proclamation of September 5, 1755, as read to the 1,920 assembled Acadians by Colonel Winslow. In his comment on "The Meter of Evangeline," Benjamin declares, "His success was as wonderful as the attempt was bold" (17), but he does not elaborate. He also offers an analytical breakdown of the poem and a set of eleven composition assignments. The balance of materials in Benjamin's introduction to the poem shifts away from both biographical and historical approaches, as the student is more likely to be swayed by the six pages of critical opinion than by the four pages of biography or the three pages of history. Moreover, as indicated above, the critical opinion is by no means one of unstinting praise.

In 1920 Benjamin provided a revision of his volume for the Merrill series, in which his comments on meter are replaced by "Suggestions for Study." It is instructive, at least in passing, to reflect on the changes Benjamin made in his apparatus after nearly thirty years had passed. For one thing, he cuts the "Critical Opinions" from six pages to only two, and for another, he begins not with the somewhat dismissive praise of George William Curtis ("domestic affections"), but with noted Harvard professor and scholar Charles Eliot Norton's more generous (if perhaps to the contemporary ear somewhat cloying) praise: "The sweetness, the gentleness, the grace, the purity, the humanity of his verse were the image of his own soul" (8). While Benjamin retains some of the damned-with-faint-praise paragraphs, he ends not with Whipple's negative comparison with "the imagination of such poets as Shelley," but celebrates Longfellow as "the people's poet" who voices "universal sentiments" and who, despite the "obvious" limitations of his poetry, treats "the commonplace" in such a way as "to make it eternally interesting and beautiful" (10). Compare the latter observation to Whipple's cited above, to the effect that Longfellow "rarely loses sight of common interests and sympathies." The revision, in short, produces a more balanced critical perspective and at the same time alters the bias somewhat in Longfellow's favor.

Among his "Suggestions for Study" Benjamin advises, predictably, that "the pupils should read it aloud" and "in a good conversational tone" (12) and that they should write frequently "during a period of from fifteen to twenty minutes," observing the rules for punctuation and capitalization, "should not use the same word continuously in the same paragraph," and "should be original." Moreover, students should maintain copies of their "themes" from which they should be called upon "frequently" to read aloud, "and while doing so should be required to take a position in front of the class.

Finally, in their "oral composition," "Pupils should be taught to use complete sentences, and to express their thoughts in a logical manner" (13). Public school teachers of the twenty-first century, desperate to prepare their students to pass standardized tests, might note that not much has changed over the past century or so when it comes to what is expected of their students.

In his assignments at the back of the text for "Written Composition," Benjamin shows some range, from the predictable to the more thoughtful and challenging. The three proposed writing tasks for Assignment 9, for example, begin with a simple hundred-word paragraph "describing the social life of the Acadians," then move to the more imaginative topic in which the students are to think of themselves as witnesses at the reading of Colonel Winslow's mandate and to write up what happens, "in the form of a news story for the daily paper." The third topic, obviously necessitating some research, requires students to "Write a composition of two paragraphs contrasting the deportation of the Acadians with that of the Belgians in the world war" (120). The concept of relevance-based reading and writing has been with us for many years.

Edward Everett Hale

The first edition of *Evangeline* in the United States to provide specific teaching and study guides was that of Edward Everett Hale, in the Standard Literature Series published by Newson and Company in New York in 1897. A Unitarian minister and journalist, Hale had been a student in Longfellow's first class at Harvard in 1856 and was renowned as the writer of the popular patriotic story, "The Man without a Country" (1863). His 23-page introduction includes a brief biographical note, a somewhat lengthier comment on Longfellow's "poetic character," nine pages on *Evangeline* itself, and eight pages of "Suggestions for Study." Hale's extensive footnotes total 167, fairly evenly balanced between the two parts of the poem.

In his comments on "poetic character" Hale formulates the question, "what is a poet," to which he answers, conventionally enough from a post–Romantic perspective, echoing Shelley: an artist "who discovers the hidden beauty of the world." In answer to the implied question, what should a poet be to us, Hale responds, "he should be a friend to us, an older and wiser friend, of nobler and finer nature than our own." He regards Longfellas as an "Apostle" of American poetry: "we had no great poets before Longfellow" (7). Hale adds, "We all read Longfellow early in life, often in school, before we have read much else. [...] It is an impressionable age. Longfellow moulds our taste." He observes also that Longfellow's work is "simple and direct" and that his verse may be read "without difficulty": "Later in life, if we desire, we may pass from his exquisite and gracious mood to poets of a more profound or a more passionate nature" (8). While the foregoing does suggest some qualification when it comes to Longfellow's powers as a poet, the impact on the reader is by no means as negative as that caused by Benjamin's pages of Critical Opinion, particularly in his Maynard's English Classic text. But in any event, a critical inquiry into Hale's unstated but implicit premises might prompt us to ponder this premise: if difficult, therefore profound (one may be reminded of T.S. Eliot's mantra for metaphysical and modernist poetry—it "must be *difficult*"*); and implicitly, if easy and clear, therefore superficial, perhaps the stuff of childhood.

Hale's commentary on *Evangeline* itself is divided into three sections: "Character and Subject," "The Historic Facts," and "The Metre." Under the first of these headings he is most concerned with defining the generic attributes of the poem ("narrative" and "idyll"). Hale's definition of the term "idyll" is worth some reflection, if only because it appears rarely in contemporary literary criticism: "an Idyll is now generally understood to be a narrative poem of no very great length, of a simple, pastoral, homely character, relying for its effect upon the gentle emotions it calls up and on its descriptions of natural scenes" (11). Because Longfellow himself employed the term with reference to the poem—as opposed to "tragedy" or "minor epic," terms which I would like to consider, at any rate—editors of school text editions often refer to the poem as an idyll, probably without the intent of diminishing its status. The phrase "no very great length" is rather equivocal. What other poems run around fourteen hundred lines? The five cantos of Alexander Pope's mock epic "The Rape of the Lock" total 618 lines, less than half the length of *Evangeline.* Book IX of Milton's *Paradise Lost,* the longest in the epic, runs 1189 lines. For the record, as it happens, one of the familiar poems in English closest to the length of *Evangeline* is Walt Whitman's "Song of Myself" at 1,343 sprawling lines collected into 52 sections (one for each week of the year, as some have observed—that division came with the 1867 version of the poem). With its delightfully (or annoyingly, depending on one's tastes) self-indulgent first-person point of view and anti-narrative mode, Whitman's most notable achievement within *Leaves of Grass* might be the ideal antitype of Longfellow's idyll, right down to its disinclination toward "gentle emotions" and "descriptions of natural scenes."

Hale approaches the themes of patient endurance of sorrow and strength of devotion rather casually (note his use of first person): "When I think of

* *See T.S. Eliot, "The Metaphysical Poets,"* Selected Prose, *ed. Frank Kermode (New York: Harcourt Brace and Farrar, Straus & Giroux, 1975), 65.28*

her I am apt also to think of another well-known figure famous for love, devotion, patience [...] the figure of Jeanie Deans in [Sir Walter Scott's] *The Heart of Midlothian*" (12). "But each one will think of Longfellow's heroine in his own way," Hale concludes.

In his comments on the historic context, Hale provides maps of "Evangeline's Home in 'Acadie'" and of "Evangeline's Wanderings in Lower Louisiana," so the student acquires a brief geography lesson into the bargain. In his historical commentary Hale joins those who act as apologists for the English, insisting that it was the New Englanders more than the English who perceived the Acadians as a threat: "It was a harsh act, but it seemed to be an act necessary to self-preservation. [...] The act seems to have been one of the horrible necessities of war. [...] When we read 'Evangeline,' we need not feel fiercely toward the English" (14). In fact, Hale goes so far as to compare the expulsion of the Acadians with the casualties at Waterloo and Gettysburg, an analogy that must have struck some readers as absurd, or at least a far fetch.

The lengthiest of Hale's comments in this section of the introduction is on meter (four pages). Most of his observations have to do with reading the poem aloud, but he concludes with three "inconveniences" of the dactylic hexameter in English, all having to do with the problem of beginning sentences with an accented syllable. Longfellow "gets around the difficulty in three ways, none good in their effect," Hale believes: placing an "unnatural accent on the first word," inverting "the usual word-order," and beginning "a sentence or a clause in the middle of the line" and letting it "run over into the next" (19). On the one hand Hale concedes these are "but slight drawbacks" to the reader's enjoyment of the poem; on the other hand, he devotes considerably more effort and text to illustrating the problems occasioned by the meter than he does to elaborating its felicities. Of three of the earliest school text editions (Scudder's 1883, Benjamin's 1893, and Hale's 1897) Hale's is by far the most concerned with matters of form.

Hale's "Suggestions for Study" (pages 20–27) are of particular interest here, governed as they are by the phrase "if there is time." The first of the three sections is entitled "For a Cursory Reading," in which the reader is advised simply to "read it aloud well and pleasantly" and "to get a good understanding and appreciation of the story." He advises students to write brief abstracts of each of the ten sections or cantos of the poem, and he offers a one-paragraph example of Part II, Canto 3, instructing students to be "simple and direct" and "lively and interesting" in their work. Curiously, Hale composes the summary half in past and half in present tense, and he informs students, "It is well not to use the present tense throughout" (21).

In the second section of his study guide, "For a More Careful Reading," Hale suggests closer analysis of the text, for example, comparing the description of Louisiana in II.3 with that of Acadia early in the poem. "We may also study in a little more detail the characters," Hale observes, and he adds that "it is better to begin with minor characters" (22). He uses the old notary Leblanc to illustrate, extracting ten references to him from the poem and then converting these into a "short sketch" (almost entirely written in past tense). Hale then suggests that a second way to deal with character is to think of the "type" or "kind." For example, Father Felician as "the character of the good pastor," can be compared with such exemplars as Chaucer's parson, although it seems unlikely that an eighth-grader would be familiar with *The Canterbury Tales*. The next step, one might surmise, would be to account for how Longfellow endows his characters with individual as opposed to stereotypical traits. Finally, Hale instructs the student as to the value of contrasting characters, illustrating his point by posing questions concerning Benedict Bellefontaine and Basil Lajeunesse, the blacksmith.

In his brief note on "Memorizing" Hale suggests "sometimes two or three lines will be enough," and he recommends a few passages, none surpassing 21 lines. "It is best for the students," he indicates, "to choose the passages for themselves, and if possible to give good reasons for what they choose" (25). At this stage, after a second reading of the poem, Hale advises "a little study of the poet's life and character." Implicitly, then, Edward Everett Hale's approach to the poem is much less biographically based than Horace E. Scudder's. In his emphasis on close reading, he seems in a way to anticipate the New Critics of a later generation.

In the third section of his study suggestions, "For Textual Study," Hale turns to "a number of minor matters" that can be appreciated "now that we have thought over the story and the characters, now that we know something of the author and of how the poem was written" (25). Over the next two pages he provides examples for five categories of study: allusions (for example, "stand like Druids of eld"), imagery (by which Hale means "figures" like metaphor and simile), words (for example, "What is an amorpha [1. 1091], and whence the name?"), structure of the poem (an odd range of topics, from comparison of passages to "the significance of the stories of Mowis and Lilinau" and a question as to why the poet chose Philadelphia "as the scene of his conclusion rather than New York or Washington"), grammatical study ("Difficult sentences should be analyzed, words of which the syntax gives trouble may be parsed, the derivation and composition of words may be noted").

As to footnotes for the text of the poem, Hale attacks with a vengeance, supplying about three times as many as Scudder, and the nature and quality of the notes vary considerably. Unlike Scudder, Hale, as one might expect of an ordained minister, supplies biblical references, so that When Father Felician refers to Gabriel as a "Prodigal Son" near the end of II.3, Hale advises, "Read Luke xv. 11–32." Often Hale's notes seem to tab the overly obvious, as when he identifies "the blessed image of Mary" (ℓ. 89) as "the mother of Christ." Exactly what to annotate is always a matter of concern for an editor, but it could be fairly said that Hale gets carried away. For example, he supplies a note of more than sixty words to explain lines 41–42, "Flax for the gossiping looms, whose noisy shuttles within doors / Mingled their sound with the whir of the wheels and the songs of the maidens." Scudder offers no annotation of those lines, apparently assuming that if the operation of a loom was not familiar to his readers, the context of the poem was sufficient.

But if Hale is sometimes overzealous in his annotations, that may be preferable to the erratic practices of Scudder, who sometimes takes too much for granted. For example, in the opening twenty lines of II.4 we encounter the "desert land" of the Far West. In this context we meet eight place names, the flower known as the amorpha, and an allusion to "the scattered tribes of Ishmael's children." Scudder offers not one note for all of this, while Hale offers ten, most of which, if not absolutely necessary, are at least worthwhile. In the preface to her edition of the poem in 1896 Mary Harriott Norris, a professor of English at New York City College, argues that it is the editor's duty, "rather than that of the pupil, to supply most of the knowledge obtainable from dictionaries and cyclopaedias. Moreover, it is no help to a student, eager for information, but destitute of library or works of reference, or greatly limited in time, to be told to consult dictionary or cyclopaedia" (iii).

Agnes Lathe

Several text editions of the poem were published between that of Edward Everett Hale in 1897 and the next influential edition, that of Lewis B. Semple, initially published as a Macmillan Pocket Classic in 1900 and last reprinted in 1928. Hale might not have approved of the use of the present tense throughout the thirty-page introduction to the poem by Agnes Lathe, listed as "Late Associate Professor of English Woman's College, Baltimore." Published by Benjamin H. Sanborn & Co. in Boston in 1899 as #5 in the Cambridge Literature Series, this edition follows the pattern of opening with the life and career of Longfellow, but Lathe does not set up a separate rubric for the historical context, and although she includes references to historical events out of Haliburton in her endnotes, she does not foreground those events, as did at least eighteen earlier commentators. Students might be impressed from other commentaries, including H.E. Scudder's, that a primary reason for the poem's importance has to do with its "historicity," but that is clearly not the case here.

Lathe offers the apparently obligatory comment on the meter and then proceeds to her own largely derivative "critical comments" on the poem, having reserved at least a third of the introduction for that purpose. Of the source for the poem, Lathe notes that it "lacks dramatic episodes and movement," but she observes that "though the incident is poor in action, it is rich in feeling" (xix). As to the narrative development, Lathe asserts that "a plain tale should be told plainly" and that "nothing contributes more to the ease and pleasure of a reader than the orderly presentation of events" (xxi). She also finds the language "not only beautiful," but "studiously simple," dominated by "the direct simile and personification" rather than the "less obvious metaphor" (xxii).

While she does take note of the role of the minor characters, Lathe focuses her comments on Evangeline, "for it goes without saying that *Evangeline* is a poem of but one character" (xxiv). Perhaps the problem for some readers is that, unlike her nearest counterpart in American literary history, Hester Prynne, who was to appear on the scene just three years after the publication of Longfellow's poem, Evangeline is flawless. If it can be said that *The Scarlet Letter* concerns the problems of evil and its ambiguities, it can be as readily said that *Evangeline* concerns convictions of virtue and its lucidities. Evangeline is purely sympathetic, and "The sympathy felt for Evangeline is deepened by her youth, her beauty, the death of her father, and most of all by her own attitude toward misfortune. [...] Such unselfishness, such ideal charity, adds beauty and strength to a character which would otherwise be merely pathetic" (xxv).

Whether either protagonist, both of whom might challenge as the first woman to play such a role in American letters, rises to tragic stature might be debated, at least along classical lines, but if the concept of the "tragic flaw" (*hamartia*) has any weight, certainly Hester Prynne has the better claim to the status of the first "tragic heroine" *(pace* Charlotte Temple) of any significance in American literature. The embodiment of patience and self-abnegation, Evangeline "does not doubt, she does not repine; and when she finally yields her own will, she transforms the love concentrated upon one into devotion for many" by becoming a Sister of Mercy (xxvi). Virginal and innocent, faithful to her true love and to her quest, Evangeline could be for many generations the ideal American woman, even a symbol of America in its youth and idealism. Of course in her simplicity and in the seamless transition from her adolescence to old age, she could represent only womanhood of a certain, narrow definition: the good little girl, the virtuous and devoted daughter. To polarize the matter, Evangeline is clearly Sandra Gilbert and Susan Gubar's "angel" rather than their "monster" (17).

Curiously, perhaps, commentators have rarely if ever been inclined to go quite so far in their estimation of Evangeline's character as to consider her as a type of "tragic heroine." Lathe indicates that as the first part ends, the poem "moves on to a tragedy" (xxi), but when she comments on Evangeline as a character she detects "unselfishness" and "ideal charity" that add "beauty and strength" (but not tragic dimension) "to a character which otherwise would be merely pathetic" (xxv). Perhaps it is that she seems too slender a frame to burden with such conceptual freight.

Agnes Lathe backs away from the poem, for the most part, when she turns to her "Suggestions for Study," pointing out that "this one poem should not absorb the entire time and interest of the student," and that one "should add some general acquaintance with Longfellow" (xvii). She proceeds to propose other Longfellow poems for study, wrapping up with a rather bland list of issues for "the special study of *Evangeline*": use of history, use and sources of figures, parallel construction of Parts One and Two, character of Evangeline ("the realistic touches" and "the ideal element"), the lesson of the poem, the artistic beauty of the poem. Lathe appends more than 140 notes to the text, many of which are vocabulary items, and a good number of which seem unnecessary, as in her definition of "Yule-tide" as "Christmas time" and of "sombrero" as "a large soft felt hat." The twenty or so lines at the opening of II.4 that elicited such extensive comment from Edward Everett Hale draw only brief notice from Lathe. Of the numerous place names Longfellow mentions, she writes simply, "The description in the first stanza is exceedingly vague. The land could be anywhere east of Utah and New Mexico, and south of Colorado and Nebraska" (138).

F.M. Muhlig

Perhaps the most singular text edition of *Evangeline* appeared in 1898 in a format similar to what today might be called a casebook. Entitled *The "Evangeline" Book*, the text is intended for "Readers and Students" of the poem. In his single page introduction Muhlig draws attention to the fact that he provides no biographical material on Longfellow because that information is widely available elsewhere. Instead, he begins seventy pages of prefatory material with observations on poets and poetry, proceeding from premises that most readers will find (perhaps sadly) outdated: "Why do we prefer the poem rather than the brief account given in our histories? Because the writer was a poet, and poets write poetry" (7). And the poet, Muhlig confidently asserts, "deals with the ideal more than the real," even though the "true poet finds sweet music and pathos in common things, as the ticking of a clock or the flight of a waterfowl."

The bulk of Muhlig's prefatory pages, however, deal with the history, geography, folk traditions, and social and economic conditions of Acadia. The text is accompanied with maps and ten half-tones picturing Nova Scotia as it appeared in 1898. He then produces, *before* the text of the poem, a dozen pages of explanatory notes and two pages (not numbered) of "Pronouncing Vocabulary." He provides no discussion questions or writing assignments for the poem that follows. Despite his apparent enthusiasm for poetry, Muhlig apparently regards *Evangeline* as a significant text mostly because of its historical connection with Acadia. He offers no information in his preface on Louisiana or indeed on any events dealt with in the second half of the poem, although he does provide some useful glosses in his notes, observing, for example, that Longfellow's geography in II.4 is "rather vague": "The region of the Columbia is so far from the Ozarks that it can hardly be called the same 'land'" (66).

One of Muhlig's variations from the text of the poem as it is usually printed identifies his version as one intended specifically for classroom study. After identifying "Part the First" and numbering the initial canto with a Roman numeral, he identifies all subsequent cantos as "readings": Second Reading, Third Reading, and so on, through the Tenth Reading (II.5). It may be that Muhlig hoped his volume would serve some multiple purposes as both classroom text and guidebook for those making a pilgrimage to the Evangeline Country in Canada.

W.F. Conover

More ambitious as a study guide is the edition published in Chicago in 1899, also by A. Flanagan and prepared by W. F. Conover, a public school teacher in San Diego, who in his introductory note claims considerable success "teaching this delightful poem." Elsewhere, he indicates that the poem "is usually studied in the seventh school year" (117). Conover keeps his preliminary materials to a minimum, so that the student would read no more than a dozen pages before encountering the poem. He sums up the poet's life in just two pages; offers about a page and a half of commentary on the genre and meter, his comments on the former being uncannily close in phrasing to those of Agnes Lathe; and he adds about eight pages, including two maps, on the historical background. As to the historical context and the debate over the expulsion of the Acadians, Conover presents an apologia for the English views very briefly and in terms quite similar to those of Edward Everett Hale. He also cites an article by Francis Parkman in *Harper's Magazine* for November 1884 justifying the deportation. But Conover does not quote from the Parkman article, while he does quote at some length (more than two pages) from Edouard Richards and others sympathetic to the Acadians. The sentiments in these passages are of a piece with those of Eliza Robins mentioned above: "The Acadians were the most innocent and virtuous people I have ever known or read of in any history. They lived in a state of perfect equality, without distinction of rank in society. [...] They were very remarkable for their inviolable purity of morals" (17).

More than any other commentator, Conover stresses the undercurrent of a mythic expulsion narrative that amounts to the destruction of primitive, Edenic innocence by an aggressive, culturally dominant, military and political, colonizing force, though that phrasing would not likely have occurred to him. Other commentators, like Scudder, marginalize this possible reading of the event by citing such authorities as the Abbé Reynal in footnotes or endnotes In fact, after quoting Reynal on the idyllic benevolence of Acadian society at Grand-Pré, Scudder undercuts it when he observes that "His picture of life among the Acadians, somewhat highly colored, is the source from which after writers have drawn their knowledge of Acadian manners" (37).

Conover's 97 endnotes owe much to those of other editors, for example H.E. Scudder, whose definition of "forest primeval" as "one which has not been disturbed by the axe" he pilfers verbatim. But in general his notes strike a balance between those of Scudder and Edward Everett Hale. For instance, Scudder disregards the place names in the opening lines of II.4 and Agnes Lathe shrugs them off as "vague" geographical references, while Hale devotes ten footnotes to the lines. Conover offers a simplified version of Hale's footnotes, and his phrasing is so similar to Hale's that one is led to suspect it is more than coincidental.

His 32-page plan of study at the back of the text, however, particularly interests us here. Conover's approach is implicit in the following passage from the "Argument": "We believe that the common lack of interest and effort in school work is often due to an absence of definite and visible ends, and of proper directions for the reaching of those ends. Pupils do not object to work, and hard work, with something tangible. What they do object to is groping in the dark for something that may turn up—which is too frequently the case in their study of literature" (117). The poem, Conover notes, "is to be studied twice:—First, a general survey to get the story and the characters clearly in mind. Second, a careful study of the text that the beauty and richness, the artistic and ethical values of the poem may be realized" (118).

Conover indicates that the lessons are supposed to "occupy" about half an hour, presumably of an English class that would have run fifty minutes, more or less. In what he labels "A General Survey," Conover lists thirteen lessons, the first three to concern the author and the poem, Acadia and the Acadians, and the structure of the poem, the last ten to entail reading one section (or "canto," to use Longfellow's term) per class session. Over the next four pages Conover breaks the sections into "topics" ranging from five to ten per canto, and he instructs the students to assign line numbers to the beginning and ending of each topic. For instance, the first four topics of I.1, "Acadia," which is largely given over to exposition, are Grand-Pré, Benedict Bellefontaine, Evangeline, and The Home. For I.2, "The Home," however, Conover enumerates six topics, but does not list the captions. These, as well as appropriate line numbers, must be provided by the student. He does the same for I.4 and for three of the five cantos in Part Two.

Presumably, if one were to follow Conover's study plan as outlined, the teacher would have spent some two and a half weeks simply getting through the poem, at which point students would have little more than a plot outline to show for their efforts. It is in the second part of his plan, "Study of the Text," that Conover approaches the "artistic and spiritual values of the poem" (124). To this end he offers no fewer than 27 lessons with accompanying composition subjects.

Followed rigorously, this schedule would amount to another five and a half weeks for a total of eight weeks spent on *Evangeline*, nearly half of the semester. One can only wonder at the "patient endurance" of both students and teachers in 1899.

Conover's analysis and interrogation of the poem in this second stage becomes rigorous from one perspective, and yet from another one might argue that his questions are nearly always so objective as to be answerable at a rather low cognitive level. How perceptive need the student be to answer such questions as the following about the opening 57 lines of the poem: "This is a story of what? What two pictures does the author contrast, lines 6–15? Why murmuring pines? [...] What quality of the people is referred to in line 24? The Acadians are engaged in what industry? Would their lives be more peaceful in this than in other lines of labor?" (125). One suspects that relatively little critical thinking would be needed in order to answer the last question "correctly." The way the question is phrased, almost anyone would answer in the affirmative, whether he or she had read the poem or not.

Occasionally, Conover's questions are rhetorical—not so much questions as they are answers, as in Lesson IX, "Father Felician's Rebuke," which Conover describes as "one of the finest" moments in the poem. "What scene of wild passion Father Felician met when he opened the church door!" Conover exclaims, and then he asks, "Could force have quieted this mob? Could they have been made quiet?" (129). One suspects the answers are "no" and "no." "Who is the 'Prince of Peace'?" Conover asks later, and "What great character in history had a like power over a multitude?" One can imagine the class chorusing as in a responsive reading. "Was it a great thing that the people could say from their hearts 'O Father, Forgive Them'?" (130). One suspects that it was indeed.

Questions that do potentially lead to significant and complex issues of ethical or spiritual value are often buried among those that pertain to routine matters. For example, in his questions on lines 1187–1232, the fourth canto of Part Two, Conover asks, "What do you know of husking bees?" (137). That question may be an indicator of the movement in the United States away from the farm and into urban areas, but it is of slight substantive value. The next question is also one that simply asks the students whether they have actually read the poem: "Who urged patience?" Presumably, the class choruses, "the priest." But the next question does pertain to values that may be derived from the close study of *Evangeline*: "The compass flower illustrates what truth?"

The truth illustrated by the compass flower "that the finger of God has suspended" is that the "blossoms of passion" are bright and fragrant, but they "lead us astray, and their odor is deadly," while "this humble plant" operates like faith, to show us the way "Over the sea-like, pathless, limitless waste of the desert." In short, the values and truths are predictably conventional. After all, the priest is speaking here, and it is he who defines for Evangeline the symbolic meaning of the compass flower. Conover does not, however, pose any questions concerning the conclusion of the priest's analogical discourse: "Only this humble plant can guide us here, and hereafter / Crown us with asphodel flowers, that are wet with the dews of nepenthe." As H.E. Scudder's note indicates, the asphodel are connected with the heroic dead (89), as admirers of William Carlos Williams' *Asphodel, That Greeny Flower* (1955) are likely aware, and nepenthe is a drug that brings forgetfulness, or sweet oblivion (see page). In short, the passage foreshadows the end of Evangeline's search for Gabriel: her love will not be consummated, and she will need some sort of balm for her sorrows. *Evangeline,* it might be argued, tells the only possible story of true love: unfulfilled desire, the love of Keats' "Ode on a Grecian Urn." But Conover and other commentators rarely stray so far from the explicitly stated messages of the poem. Presumably an inquiry into the nature of desire would be too sophisticated an undertaking for a class of twelve to fourteen year-olds. Editors of the school text editions adhere, for the most part, only to the most obvious matters.

In his questions on the last section of the poem, for example, Conover leads the student to the "lessons her life had taught her" (138) which are specifically and unambiguously detailed in the poem: "Patience and abnegation of self, and devotion to others." Conover also asks, "What became of her love?" Here, again, Longfellow's message is clear and straightforward: "So was her love diffused [...] / Other hope had she none, nor wish in life, but to follow / Meekly, with reverent steps, the sacred feet of her Saviour." In her nursing work as a Sister of Mercy, Evangeline is able to act practically on her love, to live a life of what Calvinists would call "practical piety," as delineated in such popular seventeenth-century texts as Arthur Dent's *Plain Man's Pathway to Heaven* (1601) and Lewis Bayly's *Practice of Piety* (1611). Howard Mumford Jones, in fact, suggests that *Evangeline* is part of Longfellow's "campaign" for religious tolerance, an effort to "soften the prejudices of some of his more narrow-minded readers against the Catholic church" (xii).

The "Composition Subjects" Conover lists at the end of his "Plan of Study" are rather perfunctory: 1. Acadian Life. (Contrast with present.) 2. The Notary. 3. Character of Gabriel. And so on, for a total of ten scenes or characters, with no particular end to be achieved. Presumably the students are to describe "The Notary" and to account for his role in the poem, but to whom, or for what purpose, Conover is silent. He adds three sentences, presumably advice for the students in writing about any of the topics: "Select the lines that appeal to you most. Select the lines that show the most beautiful sentiment. Select the lines that contain the best Pictures" (141). Apparently of greater concern to Conover are the lists of nearly five hundred words for spelling and definition (142–149), divided into 33 lessons, though he does warn against allowing the reading to "degenerate into a word-study" (142).

E.O. Vaile

While the annotated texts of such editors as Scudder, Benjamin, and Hale, and perhaps even of such less frequently reprinted editions as those of Lathe and Conover, may represent the mainstream when it comes to turn-of-the-century pedagogy, it is worth at least a glance at the edition of E.O. (Edwin Orlando) Vaile of Oak Park (Chicago), whose 1899 text of *Evangeline* is Volume I, Number 1 in Vaile's Literature Series. Apparently somewhat of a maverick, Vaile prints his biographical notes and "Introduction" *after* the text of the poem, an arrangement which, he notes, "indicates the editor's firm conviction as to the plan which should be pursued in starting young people in the reading of literature. The poem stands first" (87). Ezra Pound would applaud, and he would not be alone. "All notes and commments [sic] should be kept in the background," Vaile continues: "Even notes at the foot of the page are too obtrusive. [...] Nothing should tend to give them the impression, which they too often get, that the work in hand is beyond their power to enjoy without help." Vaile follows up with six captions and brief comments which seem progressive for the period, if not revolutionary:

> The Danger of Formal Study: [...] the editor has grave doubt as to the wisdom of requiring young readers to put much effort on the formal analysis of it, or of any other poem, in fact.
>
> Enjoyment of Literature the Chief Object: [...] When they leave school, as many of them do at the end of the 8th grade, or in the first year of High School, if they do not look back upon their reading in the English classics as a source of genuine pleasure and delight, the literature course has been largely a failure for them.
>
> Don't Abuse Good Literature: The best teachers are careful not to use a choice piece of literature as the basis of an [...] exercise in grammar. [...] Nor should the literature lesson or reading be made a go cart for hauling all sorts of historical and geographical facts into consideration.
>
> How Many Times Should a Work Be Read?: [...] If a class shows no desire to read Evangeline a second time, it would be unwise to press it. [...] The writer has very little sympathy with the advice so often given that a literary work should be read by a class two or three times, each time with a specifically different purpose, to master the plot, to study the characters [...] etc. [88–89].

Vaile adds a couple of more conventional items in support of Reading Aloud and Memorizing, but the comments above set his pedagogical views apart from those of other editors of his era. They are reminiscent, in some ways, of Ezra Pound's pithy observations throughout *ABC of Reading*, guided by this early manifesto: "Gloom and solemnity are entirely out of place in even the most rigorous study of an art originally intended to make glad the heart of man" (13). Among the starry-eyed idealists of the age, Vaile comes off looking like a hard-eyed but compassionate realist.

Maud Elma Kingsley and Frank Herbert Palmer

Vaile's aversion to repeated readings of the poem must have been anathema to Maud Elma Kingsley and Frank Herbert Palmer, whose 1909 text calls for three readings of the poem. A graduate of Colby College (B.A. 1887, M.A. 1890), Kingsley devoted her career to preparing outline studies for public school literary texts. Because of its brevity, the Kingsley-Palmer outline for the first prescribed reading may be provided in complete form. It is listed under the rubric, "The Narrative of the Poem":

Outline of the Narrative.

a. *Introduction.*—Description of the forest; hint as to the character of the story; two aspects of Grand Pré; class of readers to whom the poem will appeal; characterization of Acadie.

b. *Part I.* Acadie, Home of the Happy.
   (1) *Canto 1.*—Grand Pré and its Inhabitants.
   (2) *Canto 2.*—By Benedict's Fire.
   (3) *Canto 3.*—The Ceremony of Betrothal.
   (4) *Canto 4.*—The Tragic Ending of the Betrothal Feast.
   (5) *Canto 5.*—At the Gaspereau's Mouth.

c. *Part II.* Evangeline's Quest.
   (1) *Canto 1.*—Prolonged Separation of the Lovers.
   (2) *Canto 2.*—Down the Mississippi.
   (3) *Canto 3.*—The Home of Basil the Herdsman.
   (4) *Canto 4.*—The Hopeless Quest.
   (5) *Canto 5.*—The Quest Ended.

d. *Conclusion.*—Description of Evangeline's grave; characterization of those who pass by it; description of the Acadia of today; popularity of the story. (6–7)

This outline may appear schematic to the bare-bones point, but for Kingsley and Palmer it is only the beginning. Subsequent outlines to accompany the first reading of the poem deal with historical events and "Place of Action in the Story." Kingsley and Palmer list no fewer than ten specific sites for Part Two of the poem, from the Ohio River and the Mississippi, through the Bayou of Plaquemine, down the Atchafalaya, onto the shores of Lake Wachita, stopping at St. Martins and Adayes, continuing to the Indian Territory and the north woods of Michigan, and ending in Philadelphia.

For the second reading of *Evangeline* Kingsley and Palmer provide a considerably more thorough outline based upon characters and on "details" from the poem. For Part One, for example, we are given eight "Pen pictures of Evangeline" ranging from "Evangeline carrying ale to the reapers" and "Evangeline at her father's door at sunset" to "Evangeline cheering the women" and "Evangeline by the side of her dying father" (12–13). For Part Two we have five such "pen pictures." The section entitled "Details of the Poem" directs the reader to characters like "The stout herdsman of the prairie" and events like "The game of checkers." The section, or verse paragraph, also draws our attention to "Manners and customs of the Acadian peasants," including "proverbial sayings and superstitions," "Allusions to explain," like René Leblanc's story of the Statue of Justice and "Fata Morgana," as well as directions to paraphrase certain passages (15–17). The third reading of the poem concerns "Literary Analysis," with reference to such items as atmosphere and tone; the poem's "wealth of imagery" (19); such figures of speech as personification, simile, and metaphor; and, of course, the meter (18–21). The biblical allusions, the editors note, have been "severely censured," but they assert that these are "appropriate" to the pious nature of the Acadians, as Longfellow defines them, and of course to the saintly Evangeline herself (20).

Arthur L. Hamilton, Lewis B. Semple

Vaile's aversion to repeated readings of the poem also disagrees with A. J. Demarest, Superintendent of Schools for Hoboken, New Jersey, whose 1911 edition of *Evangeline* is founded on the premise that "this poem should be read by the class at least three times" (5). It is only with the third time that the teacher is instructed to allow reading "free from all criticism" and "for the purpose of permitting the student to enjoy the revealed beauty of the poem" (9). Arthur L. Hamilton of Garfield Grammar School in Pasadena, California, does not specify how often the poem is to be read in his 1904 edition (#2 in the Practical Aids to Literature Series), but he suggests that "Combined with a good text book in English Grammar, this may profitably be carried through an entire year" (3). Most of Hamilton's study aids concern "word-building" and "the art of outlining."

Like Hamilton, Lewis B. Semple, who taught at Commercial High School in Brooklyn, begins his preface with the observation that "much attention must be given to definition" (v). His edition of *Evangeline* for the Macmillan Pocket Classics series, first published in 1900, was to be one of the most popular school texts, going into reprint for the sixth time in 1928. In certain respects Semple's format returns to that of Horace E. Scudder: a lengthy introductory essay on Longfellow's life and work (27 pages), a ten-page entry on "The Acadians," in which he exculpates the British even more generously than did Edward Everett Hale, followed by a four-page commentary on the meter. E.O. Vaile would not have been happy with the fifty-odd pages of prefatory material to be leafed through before reaching the opening lines of the poem. Unlike Scudder, Semple employs endnotes rather than footnotes, but he compiles more than 180 of them, even surpassing Hale in that regard, and he frequently produces lengthy, discursive entries.

Semple, who held a doctoral degree, frequently delves into Anglo-Saxon etymology in making his definitions, and such a word as "inkhorn," with respect to René LeBlanc, the notary (ℓ. 244), is sufficient to elicit nearly a hundred words, including a quotation from Thomas Wilson's *Art of Rhetorique* (1553). Longfellow's reference to the asphodel (ℓ. 1226) becomes the occasion for Semple to quote stanzas from Alexander Pope's "Ode on St. Cecilia's Day" and from Elizabeth Barrett Browning's *Sonnets from the Portuguese*. Occasionally Semple poses questions, but they are rarely of much substance. For example, when Evangeline's father is described (ℓ. 62) as "the man of seventy winters," Semple asks, "What common figure in this word? Compare summers, line 65. Are the words suggestive as they are used here?" (115). In other words, Semple focuses so narrowly on lexical matters that the poem becomes little more than an elaborate exercise in vocabulary for the student.

Various commentators have observed (Scudder 6) or complained (Seelye, Chapter 2) that Longfellow never visited the locales in Nova Scotia and elsewhere that he described so memorably, but Semple notes that "Ideal surroundings were demanded" (notably for Acadia), and "ideal they are" (xxix). Perhaps no commentator accounts for the general appeal (one tends to shy away from the more common term of Longfellow's day, "universal") of *Evangeline* as reductively as Professor Semple: "The reason is clear: it is a story of love, ideal love, so simply told that the least imaginative can understand" (xxix).

Eva March Tappan and Margaret Ashmun

The revision of H.E. Scudder's Riverside edition of *Evangeline* prepared by Eva March Tappan and Margaret Ashmun was published in 1916 and reprinted as recently as 1944. Audiences that went to the movies in 1919 to see Miriam Cooper starring as Evangeline, and ten years later to watch Dolores Del Rio, may well have encountered the poem in the Tappan and Ashmun edition. What is most interesting about the new Riverside text, in some ways, is how it differs from Scudder's, which had been frequently reprinted since its appearance in 1883. Some of the phrasing in Tappan's "Sketch of Longfellow's Life" is obviously cribbed from Scudder, but the most significant point is that she devotes half as much space to such matters. Scudder's two-page commentary, "The History of Longfellow's *Evangeline*," is reprinted verbatim, but his comment on the meter is cut by half, to a single page, one new paragraph and one taken directly from his text. The "Historical Introduction" to the poem is cut in half, from four pages to two, and is also adapted (to use the genteel word for it) from Scudder. In effect, then, the bulky preliminary material is streamlined, so that the reader gets to the poem more quickly.

The reader is also saved the sometimes daunting burden of Scudder's footnotes, as the new edition locates them at the end, and while the number is increased from 56 to 134, the length of the entries is trimmed considerably. Scudder's 67-word entry on "Druids," for example, runs to just seventeen words in the Tappan and Ashmun text. The added notes, probably occasioned by those of other editions following Scudder's, typically mingle worthwhile or essential information with glosses of the obvious, but generally they constitute an improvement. For example, the opening twenty lines of II.4 are amply glossed, as in Edward Everett Hale's edition, except at least somewhat more accurately. The rivers "Walleway and Owyhee," probably inserted in the poem for their exotic sound and assonantal euphony, seem to have caused the editors some difficulty. Hale describes "Walleway" (probably the Wallowa) as "a river having its source in north Nevada, and flowing into the Snake River, an affluent of the Niobrara" (87). He says nothing about the Owyhee, though his note appears to confuse it with the Wallowa, as the Owyhee does have its source in northern Nevada. Tappan and Ashmun locate the "Walleway" in northwestern Oregon (116), while in fact it is located in the northeastern comer of the state. The Snake River has its headwaters in Yellowstone and flows through the state of Idaho; it is not a tributary ("affluent") of the Niobrara, which flows through the sandhills of Nebraska and empties into the Missouri.

Margaret Ashmun's "Study Helps," "Brief Outline," and "Composition Assignments" occupy fourteen pages at the back of the text (including two pages of maps). For "Study Helps" she provides questions, from a dozen to twenty or so per section, most of which appear intended to assure the student has read and understood the text (for example, from II.1): "How does the author show the lapse of time? Was it the intention of the English to scatter the Acadians? How do you think the exiles lived?" Some of the questions open up interesting avenues of investigation that might lead to critical thinking, although they may at times suggest interrogation. On I.5: "Why did the English burn the houses of the Acadians? Was such action necessary? Was it excusable? How would it make the people feel? What was the cause of Benedict's death?" On II.1: "Do you think that Gabriel made any attempt to search out Evangeline? Do you think it good advice that was given in the passage beginning, *Dear child* ["why dream and wait for him longer? / Are there not other youths as fair as Gabriel?"]? What does the priest mean when he says, *Affection never was wasted?* Is it true?" (102–103). In most respects these aids to study represent a significant improvement over comparable materials in other early school text editions.

The "Brief Outline" (in topic form) that follows "Study Helps" runs just a page and a half and stands in stark contrast to the elaborate scheme proposed by W.F. Conover (above). Obviously, Conover considers it important that students learn how to construct their own plot outlines and that they do so in some detail, whereas Ashmun considers the outline to be simply a useful device for students on their way to a more thorough engagement with the poem via her "Composition Assignments." Conover's assignments (see above) are quite perfunctory, but his "Suggestive Questions" (set up canto-by-canto, like Ashmun's) are similar in nature to hers, though less numerous and less rigorous. For instance, Ashmun doubles the number of questions posed about the third section of Part Two, but the questions themselves are almost interchangeable:

> Conover—
> "Was Basil's way of breaking the news about Gabriel a good one? Why should she be deeply disappointed? Did Gabriel bear his disappointment as did Evangeline?" [135].
> Ashmun—
> "Why does Evangeline not ask about Gabriel? Why has Gabriel been tried and troubled (ℓ. 946)? What is Gabriel's errand away from home?" [104].

Perhaps the most unusual feature of the apparatus in Tappan and Ashmun's text of *Evangeline* concerns the "Composition Assignments." All eleven call upon the students to "imagine" characters, actions, scenery, or dialogue using the text of the poem or background information as a point of departure. For example, "Imagine yourself a member of one of Longfellow's classes in English. [...] Describe the recitation and your own feelings toward Longfellow." In fact, four of the eleven assignments pertain to Longfellow's life more than they do to the poem. The other assignments are considerably more creative in nature than they are analytical or argumentative: "Write a character sketch of Father Felician as he was in the peaceful days before the exile. Picture him going about his daily duties among his people, and show how they regard him." "Write an imaginary adventure of Gabriel's with the Indians in the Western forests and prairies. Make it exciting and true to life. [...]" (110). One does wonder, perhaps, just how a thirteen year-old might go about making such a narrative true-to-life. "Describe Evangeline at her work among the poor in Philadelphia before she found Gabriel. [...] Follow her all of one morning, and tell what you see" (111).

Jay Earle Thomson

Similar in certain ways to F.M. Muhlig's casebook approach to the poem published about a quarter of a century earlier, Jay Earle Thomson's elaborate text, *The Land of Evangeline: Silent Reading* (1924), aims to "present authentically and truthfully the historical and geographical background of Longfellow's 'Evangeline'" (v). A principal in Jersey City, New Jersey, Thomson proceeds from the premise that a "certain amount of oral reading should be emphasized," but "Inasmuch as the major part of our work in school and life depends upon our ability to read silently we should give increased stress to this modern method of teaching" (vi). He offers no fewer than eighteen chapters (144 pages) of prefatory material focusing, as did Muhlig, on Nova Scotia and essentially disregarding the importance of place and history in the second part of the poem. The 53 accompanying photographs vary from a "View of the Halifax Harbor from the Citadel" and "A Typical Group of Micmac Indians" to "Cape Blomidon," "Evangeline's Well," and eight stills from the 1919 silent film of *Evangeline* featuring Miriam Cooper. He provides ten discussion questions and writing or project topics for each of his preliminary chapters, and he quotes from *Evangeline* frequently by way of arousing the students' interest before they begin reading the poem.

Thomson devotes the two short chapters just before the text of the poem to information on its writing, including two pages of appropriate citations from Longfellow's "personal diary," and a biographical sketch. By printing his two-page commentary on the meter as an appendix, Thomson, unlike most previous editors of school text editions, effectively subordinates formalist issues. He provides minimal footnotes for the poem, just 23 for Part One, and they tend to be very brief, usually just a single short sentence. By way of comparison, H.E. Scudder offers 37 footnotes for the first part of the poem, some of them running a sizable paragraph in length; the 1916 Riverside edition of Eva March Tappan and Margaret Ashmun lists no fewer than 67 entries for Part One set up as endnotes and therefore less user-friendly.

Perhaps Thomson's most important achievement lies in his decision to append discussion questions and topics for writing or projects to the prelude and to each of the ten cantos of the poem along with a topical outline. This process integrates the close reading and analysis of the poem with the lines of the poem itself. More commonly these elements were introduced prior to the text of the poem or appended to it. Predictably, the first of the "Questions and Projects" directs the students to "Commit to memory the first eleven lines" (147). The outline for the first canto of the poem he breaks down into eight topics, from "The beautiful village of Grand-Pré" to "The children grow up together" (157).

Thomson's first writing project asks students to turn out a paragraph "of at least one hundred words" describing the village of Grand-Pré. Like Edward Everett Hale, Thomson prefers the use of the past tense. Others among his "Questions and Projects" for the first canto are somewhat more intriguing, like #13: "Select three passages to show that Longfellow appreciates humor" (158). Although in one instance he offers only eight items for writing or discussion, Thomson usually provides at least ten, and for the second canto of Part One he provides fifteen, ranging in nature from such perfunctory matters as "What were the signs of the advent of autumn?" (166)

and "Pronounce these sounds: Gaspereau, Bellefontaine, glebe, bleating" (167) to #4:

> Assume that you accompanied Basil and Gabriel to the home of Benedict and Evangeline. Using a good heading, a proper salutation, and an appropriate conclusion, write a letter to a friend describing your experiences [166].

Although he subtitles his text "Silent Reading," Thomson fairly often includes oral assignments among his "Questions and Projects," like the following at the end of II.4: "Impersonate Evangeline and give an account of the interview with the Shawnee woman" (233); "Memorize the eleven lines beginning with the word 'Patience'" (234).

Subsequent School Text Editions

Between the initial publication of Tappan and Ashmun's Riverside Edition in 1916 and its republication in 1944, the torrent of text editions of *Evangeline* dwindled to a trickle. At least ten teacher-scholars tried their hands at such editions of the poem in England and the United States in the five years from 1896 through 1900, and school text editions of the poem were also available with notes and other apparatus in French (1884) and German (1885). After 1900 the number of new annotated text editions declined, but new editors surfaced even as previous editions (notably that of Semple) were reissued. Arthur L. Hamilton's 1903 text (mentioned above) was reprinted in 1904, the same year P.H. Pearson, a professor of English at Bethany College, contributed an edition for the Crane Classics series in Topeka, Kansas. In 1905 Mary O'Reilly, who taught seventh grade at the Darwin School in Chicago, arranged a five-act *Evangeline Entertainment* for "School Exhibitions and Private Theatricals," and that same year an elaborate annotated German edition was published in Heidelberg, edited by Ernst Sieper. In 1906 the Educational Publishing Company reprinted its 1899 annotated text as a Ten Cent Classic, and in 1909 Maud Elma Kingsley and Frank Herbert Palmer collaborated on a text that included an introduction, prefatory notes to each canto, footnotes, and an extensive outline of study predicated on the assumption of three readings of the poem. The study outline includes twenty "Theme Subjects" and 25 "Examination Questions" (see above).

Prior to the Tappan and Ashmun text of 1916, several smaller publishers released school text editions, including that of A.J. Demarest (see above) in Philadelphia and that of Jane M. Cutts for D.H. Knowlton and Company in Farmington, Maine, both of which appeared in 1911. The Beckley-Cardy Company of Chicago released an edition in what it called the "Progressive School Classics" series in 1914, but without apparatus other than a one-page biography. While the text itself is not significant, perhaps the publisher's selection of a title for its series is. Also in 1914 appeared a text with extensive apparatus by Lucy Adella Sloan, head of the English department at Central State Normal School in Mount Pleasant, Michigan, for the Interpretation Series of English Classics. Sloan's apparatus is perhaps noteworthy for two features, her "Suggestions for Notebook Work," which almost invariably advise the students to "make a list" of some sort, and her almost obsessive interrogations. Her three pages of questions on the first canto of the poem include the following: "What expression in 1.11 personifies sea-fogs? What expressions in 1.12 personify the mists? How do both mists and fogs favor the valley? What are next described (11. 13–17)? From these four lines give at least six statements describing the houses" (79). It is difficult to read through Sloan's "Suggestive Questions" without feeling harassed, or at least exhausted.

But the 1916 Riverside Edition appears to have exhausted the market for such texts. A revised edition of Claude Towne Benjamin's text was printed in the Merrill's English Texts series in 1920. Jay Earle Thomson's *The Land of Evangeline: Silent Reading* (1924), described above, may prompt us to wonder whether teachers weren't growing weary of listening to their pupils butcher Longfellow's hexameters. Increasing years were separating new text editions of the poem. The 1922 prose version of the 1919 film starring Miriam Cooper (a novelization accompanied by the poem and by scenes from the movie) may have given rise to Olive Price's dramatic adaptation in 1925. Price, who taught in the Pittsburgh Public schools, offered her dramatic adaptations partly in response to the demands of the new "Platoon System," which required "regular work on the part of all classes in grammar schools in some branch of Drama" ("Foreword" by William D. Davidson, Superintendent of Pittsburgh Public Schools). At the end of her introduction to her *Short Plays from American History and Literature,* Price asserts that the plays are intended to "bring to the hearts of school-children throughout the land the high idealism and love of the beautiful in thought and action that we find revealed in the pages of American history and literature" (x).

The appropriateness of *Evangeline* as a school text for early adolescents (before that term was in general use) appears to have been self-evident. The virginal heroine, a dutiful daughter who is beautiful and is the belle of her village, remains devoted to her love (Platonic, in effect, and hence never consummated) until death. Her heroic search for Gabriel, who remains a safely distant male throughout, is rewarded so late and so slightly (that is, so devoid of eros) that only a saint could murmur her quiet words of submission. Evangeline's odyssey, unlike that of Odysseus or Huckleberry Finn, never places her in jeopardy. If one asks no difficult questions of the poem—and clearly no such questions were posed by the many commentators—then the reader is led to concede the inevitability of Longfellow's messages: patient endurance *is* godlike, affection *never* was wasted, sorrow and silence *are* strong. Those who promoted use of the poem in the classroom appear also to have been reasonably consistent in their perception of collateral lessons: historical, geographical, literary, and lexical.

That *Evangeline's* fall from the curriculum, if not from the canon altogether, was not simply a matter of changing tastes is implicit in the efforts of the commentators who edited the new Riverside Edition of 1962. The commentary and discussion questions provided by Harriett Tippett, a junior high school teacher from Needham, Massachusetts, direct students outward from the poem instead of back (historically) inward on details from the text: "Review the poem for idealization of setting, character, or narrative. Compare your findings with a farm with which you are familiar, or a slum area; people you have known or seen in films; news accounts of violence and disaster you have witnessed on radio and television. [...] Do you find Longfellow's optimism a pleasant change from the realities you know at firsthand? Do you like a story to provide ideals and dreams for you to shape your life by? or do you prefer a story to give an unflinching record of *all* facts—including the unpleasant?" (85). Tippett's questions apparently encourage the students to read the poem as an escapist text. Clearly, though, the trend in education had shifted from teacher-dominated to student-centered. Tippett insists that the message of the poem is "still timely": "In an age of moral bewilderment, of broken homes, juvenile and adult delinquency, race riots, and religious intolerance, his message is a call for charity and personal loyalties" (86). Mixed in with the creative "Suggestions for Writing" ("Imagine you are Evangeline." "Assume that Gabriel returned briefly to his father's plantation from his Michigan hunting trip.") we find some more contemporary angles ("Prepare 'lost person' notices" for various characters. "Select an organization in or near your community dedicated to the cause of racial or religious tolerance" and explain and evaluate its work). The demand for relevance in the activist Sixties affected even the teaching of *Evangeline.*

Evangeline as it existed in school curricula even into the early 1960s appears to have been what one might call a vestige of the literature of edification. The time for romantic idylls had passed, and so too, perhaps, the time for lessons in love and patience. Harvard University professor Howard Mumford Jones appears to be almost painfully aware of this at the end of his introductory essay, "*Evangeline*: An American Idyll," for the 1962 Riverside Edition of the poem: "[This] poem, if it is to be understood and valued, must be read from a certain point of view and in a certain way. *Evangeline* is not a story by Hemingway. It is a legend, poignant and beautiful, out of American History" (xiv). Jones was to win the Pulitzer Prize in General Non-Fiction three years later for *O Strange New World: American Culture—The Formative Years*. The love idyll of that period, after all, was the winner of ten Academy Awards, *West Side Story*, which appeared in 1961.

In his chapter on the "aftermath" of Longfellow's life and work, Charles C. Calhoun draws our attention to the strange power of the Evangeline myth as it exerted its historical influence: "[I]t was Longfellow's world-famous, much translated, hugely selling poem that put the Acadians, and the plight of the Acadians, on the map" (259). Calhoun might well have added "much taught" to his explanation of how this particular poem has played a socio-political role in both Canada and the United States. He also connects the poem to Cajun culture in Louisiana, noting that in his survey of the Lafayette, Louisiana, yellow pages he found "some two dozen entities named for Evangeline, from a Boy Scout troop to a Laundromat" (260).

Subtract *Evangeline* from its hundred or so years in the school curriculum as reflected in its many textbook editions, and we would be unlikely to detect much influence, either historical or commercial. Based on statistics from the U.S. Department of Education, Lawrence A. Cremin concludes that "By 1940, the average American twenty-five years of age or older had completed 8.6 years of schooling" (544). In effect, this means that the last substantial poem most Americans would have read on the eve of the Second World War would almost certainly have been *Evangeline*. Ironically, it may be that the ancillary lessons connected with the poem in the text editions would have occluded the primary rationale for introducing the poem into the curriculum at what would be for most Americans their last year of formal schooling. Presumably, that is, the intention was not to impress students with the character and personality of Henry Wadsworth Longfellow, the intricacies of dactylic hexameter, or even the historical events on the North American continent during the two decades preceding the Revolutionary War. The close reading and study of *Evangeline* calls upon us to be compassionate. The poem constitutes a drama and meditation on loss, on loss of innocence in the broadest sense, and more narrowly on lost love. It calls readers to reflect on the nature of justice and on individual courage, particularly that of Evangeline herself, extended to encompass her gender, "the beauty and strength of woman's devotion," as Longfellow phrases it in his prologue. The poem also celebrates a virtue that one does not necessarily associate with the American temperament, but which William Faulkner implicitly commends in the character of Dilsey from *The Sound and the Fury*: patient endurance.

4

Evangeline Illustrated

Given Longfellow's flair for the pictorial and the picturesque, it is not surprising that *Evangeline,* his most scenic work to date, appeared in an illustrated edition within just two years of its publication in November of 1847. His Boston publisher, William D. Ticknor (later, Ticknor and Fields) ran nineteen editions of the poem, not illustrated and with minimal changes to the text, by 1865. Meanwhile, his London publisher, David Bogue, produced an edition with no fewer than 45 wood engravings (dated 1850, but apparently printed in 1849), which Ticknor (then Ticknor, Reed, and Fields) imported and issued under their imprint. Bogue's was the first of nine different illustrated editions in the century. More than a dozen illustrators and designers were to make their contributions to the text of the poem by the time of the Peter Pauper Press edition, which marked its hundredth anniversary. In effect, a considerable iconography has developed around the character of Evangeline and her story.

Illustrators, some of whom have legitimate claims as artists, concentrated their efforts on four visual aspects of the poem: Evangeline herself; other important characters, like Father Felician and Basil Lajeunesse the blacksmith; group scenes depicting such specific events as the betrothal feast and the expulsion from Acadia; and natural scenery or landscape. The preferences of individual artists and illustrators varied, of course, and we find some merging among the four aspects; that is, Evangeline may be depicted alone: or she may appear as the principal character in a group scene, for example, when she serves "Flagons of home-brewed ale" to the reapers, and a group action scene may be depicted in, and subordinated to, details of a landscape, as in Birket Foster's representation of Evangeline and other Acadians boating on Têche Bayou amid the lotus blossoms.

Portraits of Evangeline

The various illustrators, most of them American, record images of womanly beauty during an era that witnessed a dramatic change in the way that beauty, and womanhood itself, was conceived. William Wasserstrom describes it as a transition from the genteel "Steel Engraved Ladies" of the antebellum decades to the vital, if not vivacious, All-American Gibson Girls of the turn of the century (14–16). In *American Beauty* Lois W. Banner elaborates on those terms and their implications, arguing in addition for the existence of a transitional image of feminine beauty during the 1860s, which she calls "The Voluptuous Woman," fleshy and buxom (106). Although Longfellow's depiction of Evangeline in poetry obviously did not change, the readers' perception of her, at least of how she looked, altered radically in the sixty or so years following the poem's publication. These alterations in Evangeline's physical appearance affected even the portrayal of her ethnic attire, though most illustrators did make some effort to follow descriptive passages in the poem, and the variations also indicated changing attitudes toward women and their roles.

A sensible consideration of the illustrated editions of the poem requires various kinds of limit and focus. Certain of the editions, for example that of Charles Howard Johnson in 1894, are rather rare, while others, like those of F.O.C. Darley, which first appeared in 1866, were frequently reproduced even though they are inferior to his 1882 designs. The first color illustration of the poem *appears* to be that of British illustrator Arthur Dixon, about whom fairly little is known. His illustrations were published in London by Ernest Nister and in New York by E.P. Dutton, and the title page bears what looks like the date 1856. Inasmuch as printed, as opposed to hand-tinted, color illustrations did not appear until the 1860s, however, such an early date is unlikely, and the compilers of the bibliography for *Illustrators of Children's Books,* 1744–1945 indicate that Dixon's appeared mostly in the early years of the twentieth century and that he was active as of 1920 (Mahony 404). According to the *British Library Catalogue,* the rather strikingly illustrated book was published in 1907 and printed in Bavaria. Dixon's color illustrated edition and his illustrated and undated edition of *The Courtship of Miles Standish* (*BLC* date, 1902), is a collector's item, along with such curiosities as the 1887 edition of *Evangeline* "Decorated with Leave from the Acadian Forests." I will limit my observations primarily, although not exclusively, to the following: The first illustrated edition, the work of Birket Foster and Jane E. Benham, for the most part; the 1856 edition, which featured the illustrations of John Gilbert; the first illustrated edition featuring the work of an American artist, F.O.C. Darley, published by Ticknor and Fields in 1866 and a subsequent edition with much improved designs published in 1882 by

Houghton Mifflin; the 1882 London edition of Cassell, Petter, Galpin & Co., which included 23 illustrations by Frank Dicksee and was much later issued in an edition with illustrations by Gilbert; the 1905 Bobbs-Merrill edition with sketches by Howard Chandler Christy; and the 1909 edition by Reilly and Britton with drawings by John R. Neill.

The feature artist for the first illustrated edition was [Myles] Birket Foster (1825–1899), whose 31 wood engravings for *Evangeline*, engraved by the Dalziel brothers, were to help make him "much in demand for illustrations of country scenes in the 1850s and 1860s" (Ray 122), but his contributions are limited to landscape images, and those will be considered hereafter. The best known of the illustrators for the 1850 edition was John Gilbert (1817–1897), who produced just three designs, all portraying characters other than Evangeline. Little is known of Jane E. Benham, all of whose eight designs for the poem feature Evangeline herself. In his *Dictionary of British Book Illustrators and Caricaturists, 1800–1914* Simon Haufe considers her to be not "a particularly strong draughtswoman [...] outdistanced by the suavity of Gilbert and the decorative sense of Foster" (88). Her work, according to Haufe, shows some influence of William Blake, but perhaps it is closer to the feeling of the emerging Pre-Raphaelites. "Where she triumphs," Haufe adds, "is that her illustrations are very personal statements, unconventional in their simplicity of outline and lack of modeling; a great deal is left to the imagination of the reader, evoking a mystical rather than literal response to the work" (89).

Figure 1. "Homeward serenely she walked with God's benediction upon her." Jane Benham (1850).

In every one of Benham's illustrations, as in the first, which appears early in the first canto of Part One, eyes are modestly downcast (Figure 1). Evangeline's hair shows in only three of Benham's illustrations, not including this one, in which she looks already nun-like in her shapeless hood, cape, and gown: "Homeward serenely she walked with God's benediction upon her." The book she is carrying close to her chest is almost certainly a missal, for she is coming home from confession. Longfellow's lines call for "a celestial brightness—a more ethereal beauty" to shine on her face and encircle her form, and indeed, alone and set apart from several background figures, she appears to cast only a faint shadow on the earth. Benham is almost singular among the illustrators for making no attempt to capture Evangeline's ethnic costume, as if the famous blue kirtle and Norman cap were too terrestrial, or as if such clothing might compromise her idealized image. As Wasserstrom observes, the morally upright, "good woman" of the 1840s was to embody "a living victory of the spirit over the flesh. [...] Womanliness came to mean sexlessness and in the 1840s and later, fiction relied on this conviction whenever it presented an ideal woman" (24).

The "Ideal Woman" of the steel engravings as Lois Banner describes her, possesses an oval or heart-shaped face, soft and retreating chin, "eyes cast into the distance or [...] downcast," and a tiny mouth. Her body is "short and slight, rounded and curved": "Her shoulders slope, her arms are rounded; a small waist lies between a rounded bosom and a bell-shaped lower torso, covered by voluminous clothing. Her hands are small, her fingers tapering. Her feet, when they protrude, are tiny and delicate" (46). Minus the "rounded bosom," Benham's Evangeline conforms to most of the details of this description, right down to the toes.

A couple of pages later Benham captures Evangeline kneeling in prayer, and while the boy (possibly Gabriel) kneeling next to her cannot seem to keep his eyes on his missal, her eyes are devoutly closed and her hands folded, a rosary looped around her wrists. In her penultimate portrait Evangeline appears in full nun's habit, her hands loosely folded at her waist and her eyes downcast. Benham's design suggests an emblem, framed in what appear to be palm branches, inscribed with a double motto: "Patient Endurance is Godlike" and "Sorrow and Silence are Strong" (Figure 2). She scarcely seems nun-like, however, when she is saying goodnight to Gabriel Lajeunesse at the end of the third canto of Part One, her head against his shoulder, her eyes fixed on his feet or on the doorstep (but still downcast).

The only scenes in which Benham depicts Evangeline in action are at the opening of the fourth canto, when she brings drink to her father's guests outside; a later scene in that canto, in which she attempts to cheer "the disconsolate hearts of the women" as they are about to be expelled; and at the

Figure 2. "Thus many years she lived as a Sister of Mercy." Jane Benham (1850).

end of the poem, when she supports the dying Gabriel. As she extends a cup to one of the guests in I.4, Evangeline smiles, and we are aware of her eyes, which appear to be closed in the next illustration. In the former scene, too, Benham allows a touch of sensuality, as Evangeline's arms appear to be bare, there is some hint of a bust, and her hair is decked with flowers (Figure 3). Gabriel's hand is poised all too clumsily at her waist. In the picture that illustrates her attempt to cheer the women of Grand-Pré, Evangeline again appears nun-like, if not saint-like, her right hand raised as if in benediction, her rosary conspicuously evident at her waist. Her own placid facial expression is overwhelmed by the twisted agony of the woman at her feet and the confusion of the plump child, who appears to be a refugee from a Rubens painting.

Longfellow's reactions to the London illustrated edition of *Evangeline* are a matter of record. In a journal entry dated 28 January 1850, he writes of having received a copy of that edition, "which is very beautiful,—the landscapes in particular" (Samuel Longfellow, *Life* II, 169). Although he mentions no names, his compliment was directed at Birket Foster's designs. "But alas!" Longfellow adds, indirectly referring to the work of Jane E. Benham, "Evangeline herself fares poorly with her limner." His disappointment with Benham's designs, however, may have had nothing to do with the artist's failure to capture either her ethnic dress or her womanly figure, and in a letter to his daughter Anne dated 7 March 1850, he expresses pleasure with "an English copy" of the poem, presumably the David Bogue edition *(Letters* III, 247), and in another letter to her, dated 12 April 1850, he refers to the

Figure 3. "Bright was her face with smiles, and words of welcome and gladness / Fell from her beautiful lips, and blessed the cup as she gave it." Jane Benham (1850).

"nice English copy of 'Evangeline'" as "the handsomest, that has yet been published, with many illustrations" (253).

Nathaniel Hawthorne apparently was even less impressed with Benham's work, writing in a letter to the publisher James T. Fields dated 12 January 1851, that the illustrations led him to a new interpretation of the poem:

> It is my idea (Evangeline being so infernally awkward and ugly as Miss Benham depicts her) that Gabriel was all the time running away from her, and that, when at last she caught him, it was naturally and inevitably the instant death of the poor fellow [383].

Hawthorne finds Benham's likeness of Gabriel to be no more handsome than that of his beloved.

The portrait of Evangeline that would most impress Longfellow was that of Scottish artist Thomas Faed (1826–1900), engraved by his brother James (1821–1911). In a letter to Thomas dated 30 July 1855, Longfellow thanks him for the "etching" and expresses his "sincere acknowledgements for this beautiful illustration of my poem. It touches me very deeply. The landscape,—the melancholy seashore,—the face and attitude of Evangeline, so full of sorrow and patience, tells the whole story with great power and truth. It is very beautiful and very pathetic" (*Letters* III, 490). This is the image that others told him resembled his wife (see frontispiece).

The Bogue edition was reprinted frequently in the 1850s and 1860s, but the familiar designs of Foster, Benham, and Gilbert were replaced by those of American illustrator F.O.C. Darley, to be considered hereafter. Benham's depiction of Evangeline reappeared, however, along with the work of Foster and Gilbert, in the early 1890s, starting with printings by John B. Alden and William L. Allison, both New York publishers, in 1892. Several of Foster's designs and a few of Gilbert's are also resurrected in the "Minnehaha Editions" of Smith-Andrews Publishing Co. (1895) and Thompson and Thomas (1903), both of Chicago, but none of Jane Benham's appear in them. Generally, the Minnehaha editions are attractively bound and gilt-edged but not costly, what one might call gift or parlor-table books for the middle class. These are generously illustrated texts—perhaps overly so—in which often blurry half-tones mingle promiscuously with Gilbert's sharp-edged wood engravings. The Faed brothers' illustration is often reprinted as the frontispiece; it appears as the cover illustration on an undated paperback edition (probably ca. 1915) by F.A. Owen Publishing Co. of Danville, New York.

Apparently Gilbert, who would be knighted in 1871, felt particularly drawn to *Evangeline,* as he produced nine designs for a printing of the poem by George Routledge (London) in 1853, and a much more elaborate set of 31 illustrations three years later. He was known for his "dependability, speed, and extraordinary productivity" (Hodnett 123). The illustrations were to resurface almost seventy years later in Grosset and Dunlap's edition, an odd combination of Gilbert's designs with those of Frank Dicksee, which first appeared in Cassell & Company's London edition of 1882, and were reprinted by A.L. Burt (New York). I shall comment on Dicksee's illustrations hereafter. My references to Gilbert's designs pertain to the Grosset and Dunlap edition of 192_, which is much more readily accessible than the Routledge editions.*

As in Benham's designs, the seventeen-year-old Evangeline is walking

* *Nineteen of Dicksee's illustrations accompany Noah Porter's* Evangeline: The Place, the Story and the Poem, *a limited edition (500 copies) published with a 30-page essay on the geography and history of Acadia.*

alone, pensively, missal in hand, eyes downcast, but the similarities end there (Figure 4). Gilbert uses no background detail to emphasize, as Benham does, the distance that separates Evangeline from the villagers. After all, Longfellow describes her as "the pride of the village." Moreover, Gilbert is much more attentive to details of her dress, about which Longfellow is fairly precise:

> Down the long street she passed, with her chaplet of beads and her missal,
> Wearing her Norman cap, and her kirtle of blue, and the ear-rings,
> Brought in the olden times from France, and since, as an heirloom,
> Handed down from mother to child, through long generation.

Figure 4. "Down the street she passed, with her chaplet of beads and her missal, / Wearing her Norman cap, and her kirtle of blue, and the ear-rings, / Brought in the olden times from France [...]." John Gilbert (1853).

Gilbert dispenses with the formless gown of Benham's portraits in favor of Evangeline's ethnic costume, at least in the illustrations for the first half of the poem. The other designs for that half show her standing between Gabriel and her father before Father Felician; holding hands with Gabriel, presumably after the announcement of their betrothal; sitting alone by the kitchen table after hearing the bad news of their expulsion, her hands folded in apparent prayer; and trying to cheer up her father, the only design that shows Evangeline taking significant action, and also the only one that shows her without downcast eyes

In his illustrations for the second half of the poem, Gilbert depicts Evangeline in a rather formless gown and cloak, as if to indicate her loss of Norman identity. In none of his designs does

Gilbert show her hair or emphasize her eyes, even though Longfellow directs our attention to both: "Black were her eyes as the berry that grows on the thorn by the wayside, / Black, yet how softly they gleamed beneath the brown shade of her tresses!" In his portrayal of her as a nun, Gilbert, unlike Benham, ages Evangeline and fills out her face. While Benham carefully details the nun's habit, however, Gilbert represents it as a nondescript robe. But, despite the differences in costuming, Gilbert's definition of Evangeline is consistent with Benham's: she is more saint than woman, and he thoroughly conceals any vestige of sensuality.

Several features distinguish the portraits of Evangeline by F[elix] O[ctavius] C[arr] Darley (1822–1888), the Philadelphia artist who was to be the first American illustrator of the poem and whose designs were reprinted more than those of any other artist after their appearance in 1866. Longfellow describes Darley as a "distinguished artist" in a letter dated 12 August 1859, and he mentions having him over for dinner in a journal entry for 10 March 1861 (*Life* II, 391, 413). His ten initial designs, including a frontispiece and a tailpiece, were replaced with sixteen new designs in the 1881 Riverside edition of Houghton Mifflin. For the first time, readers would encounter an animated Evangeline portrayed always in the company of others and always attracting attention not the sort reserved for putative saints, but that which one might expect would be shown to a pretty young woman. She smiles, she converses, she dances, she shows her ankles. From Darley's pen flow portraits of a human being living among other people, "a woman now," as Longfellow notes at the end of the first canto, "with the heart and hopes of a woman." It should be added, however, that Darley does not offer the reader a sensual Evangeline: she does not fit Lois W. Banner's description of the "Voluptuous Woman," vigorous, hearty, and large-bosomed (106–107). Evangeline remains the chaste, wholesome "girl" of every mid–nineteenth-century American "boy's" dreams, but in Darley's engravings she does look decidedly healthier and livelier than in Benham's or Gilbert's.

The first of Darley's portraits in the 1866 edition shows Evangeline serving "flagons of home-brewed ale" to the reapers in the fields at noon (Figure 5). Her dress may be a "kirtle of blue," but here her sleeves are rolled up against the heat, and her hat, which hangs at her back, is not a "Norman cap" but an American style, wide-brimmed hat appropriate for wearing in the fields. Her hair, which is accentuated here, is tied back with a bow, and her long lashes draw our attention to her eyes. While her blouse may not qualify as décolletage, we do see more of her torso than has been revealed by other artists. In short, while not exactly voluptuous, Darley's Evangeline does exhibit some sensual appeal.

Figure 5. "When in the harvest heat she bore to the reapers at noon-tide / Flagons of home-brewed ale, ah! fair in sooth was the maiden." F.O.C. Darley (1866).

The first portrait of Evangeline in the 1882 edition shows her walking in the town of Grand-Pré and associates her with the passage cited above ("Down the long street she passed"), but Darley shows her neither isolated nor set apart significantly from her fellow villagers (Figure 6). Here she is wearing a Norman cap and, presumably, a blue kirtle, but she shows a slen-

Figure 6. "Down the street she passed, with her chaplet of beads and her missal, / Wearing her Norman cap, and her kirtle of blue, and the ear-rings, / Brought in the olden times from France [...]" F.O.C. Darley (1883).

der ankle and close inspection reveals a long braid of hair hanging below her waist, fastened with a bow. She holds a missal and rosary, but although she seems to be rapt in thought, her eyes are not downcast, but fixed straight ahead. She looks serene, pleasant, self-confident. Two teen-aged boys seem to be talking about her admiringly, or maybe the one behind is gossiping to his friend about Evangeline and Gabriel. The old man sitting on the bench and leaning on his cane gazes at her and smiles, perhaps in happy reminiscence of his own youth. Of equal importance, however, is the fact that other figures in the scene are *not* preoccupied with Evangeline. A middle-aged man in a wide-brimmed hat appears to be talking to his daughter, and an old man walking behind Evangeline is halted temporarily as his granddaughter stops to pick up something on the path. In short, some of Darley's most engaging designs imply a narrative secondary to, but connected with, the one Longfellow tells. Whether this constitutes an addition to the poem, as opposed to a distraction from it, may be debatable.

In Darley's illustration depicting Evangeline with Gabriel as their fathers play "draughts" or checkers (a popular subject among the artists who created designs for the poem), Evangeline, hand at her breast, actually looks a little flirtatious. In the design that accompanies the celebration of their

Figure 7. "And as she pressed once more the lifeless head to her bosom, / Meekly she bowed her own, and murmured, 'Father, I thank thee!'" F.O.C. Darley (1883).

engagement, we find Evangeline dancing and smiling, in effect, living up to Longfellow's portrait of her as hostess: "Bright was her face with smiles, and words of welcome and gladness / Fell from her beautiful lips, and blessed the cup as she gave it." She is distinguished, however, at least in one way from the other dancing woman in the picture, who ducks under the arch formed by Evangeline and Gabriel: The décolletage of the other woman reveals an ample bust-line, while Evangeline's bust is clearly subordinated to the cross she wears around her neck.

In his final illustration for the poem Darley offers a deathbed scene predictably popular with the artists. Evangeline appears in full nun's habit, aged and in anguish, her head on the chest of Gabriel, who appears to have just died (Figure 7). The stark simplicity, among other things, recommends this design. An hourglass and an open book (presumably a bible) lie on the table and an empty chair sits stiff in the foreground, where Evangeline has left it to throw herself on her old lover. Benham's design may be more dramatic, for Gabriel is not yet dead as Evangeline supports him, and his left hand seems almost to project from the page as it feebly pushes against death (Figure 8).

Figure 8. "Vainly he strove to rise; and Evangeline, kneeling beside him, / Kissed his dying lips, and laid his head on her bosom." Jane Benham (1850).

At least three other men lie on their pallets nearby dying of yellow fever (notes associate the scene with an outbreak that occurred in 1793). A framing arch surmounted by a halo studded with eight stars makes the design appear an overt effort to beatify Evangeline. Indeed, Benham's use of frames tends to distract the reader both from the text of the poem and from the illustration; that is, the frames dissociate the illustration from the text of the poem. Significantly, neither Foster nor Gilbert employed them in their designs.

The illustrations of Benham and Gilbert are generally located on the same page as the text of the poem, so it was essential that the lines in the drawings be in keeping with the cut of the type. Darley's engravings are usually placed on a facing page, and in the 1882 and subsequent editions they were separated from the text with a blank page intervening. Effectually, this means that the illustrations acquire greater autonomy and integrity as works of art. The illustrator is at least set free from the dictates of the typesetter.

This holds true, to some extent, with the designs of Frank Dicksee (1853–1928), who studied at the Royal Academy in London, where he had his first exhibit in 1876. A renowned Pre-Raphaelite painter, Dicksee was knighted in 1925. A good sense of the nature of Pre-Raphaelite painting generally and of Dicksee's work in particular may be gained from a visit to the internet, where at least two dozen of his pieces are available, including a popular painting for Keats' "La Belle Dame sans Merci" and Longfellow's "The Village Blacksmith."* The Pre Raphaelite commitment to the interrelationship of all of the arts helped elevate book illustration to its height as an art form, as opposed to a type of mere decoration or ornamentation. Ideally, the picture and text would enhance each other. Paintings that alluded to literary texts would necessarily rely for part of their power on the viewers' recall of the poem.

Dicksee's 23 illustrations of *Evangeline,* which first appeared in 1882 in a limited London edition (1,000 copies), represent the work of a new generation. Had they not been reintroduced in a New York printing by A.L. Burt in 1900, Dicksee's designs might have survived only in rare book collections, but their eventual reappearance in the Grosset and Dunlap editions of the early 1920s along with the designs of John Gilbert have made them probably the most familiar illustrations to American readers of the poem. In both the A.L. Burt and the Grosset and Dunlap editions, unfortunately, Dicksee's illustrations appear on glossy paper in somewhat murky half-tones, so that even the texture of the paper sets them apart. Moreover, while the half-tone process, using metal plates, was much less laborious and much cheaper, the results were often disappointing, with some designs blurring into charcoal shadows. Finally, we see frequent evidence that Dicksee was a painter rather than a drawer or draftsman. While his sense of texture is often appealing, his sense of line too frequently falls short. A design showing Evangeline with Father Felician (II.2) appears to have been taken from an oil that would likely have been quite striking in color as opposed to black-and-white.

Dicksee's frontispiece (Figure 9), also used as a cover illustration, depicts Evangeline in perhaps her most sorrowful expression, but despite her melancholy, Dicksee's Evangeline appears to be able to cope, as she proves in the poem. As Wasserstrom notes, "After 1860 Americans of even the straitest gentility preferred girls with spunk" (27). Her eyes are darkly circled as she gazes beyond the left margin of the page (or cover), as if anticipating her long journey westward. Presumably, the picture relates to II.3 as Evangeline, having wandered alone from the reunion celebration in Louisiana, sits beneath the oak on the Têche Bayou. Basil the blacksmith, now "herdsman," has informed her that Gabriel, his "moody and restless" son, has headed north and west into the Ozarks: "And the soul of the maiden, between the stars and the fireflies, / Wandered alone, and she cried, 'O Gabriel! O my beloved! / Art thou so near unto me, and yet I cannot behold thee?" But her lips are full and her chin is anything but "soft and retreating" (as in

* *http://www.artcyclopedia.com/artists/dicksee_sir_frank.html; http://www.illusionsgallery.com/dicksee.html*

Figure 9. "And the soul of the maiden, between the stars and the fireflies, / Wandered alone, and she cried, 'O Gabriel! O my beloved! / Art thou so near unto me, and yet I cannot behold thee?" Frank Dicksee (1882).

Banner's description of the "Ideal Woman," above). Here and elsewhere in Dicksee's portraits she wears the French earrings passed on to her by her mother as an heirloom. Her expression, though sad, seems determined. Evangeline's hands are folded not in prayer but on her lap, and they are not "tiny." Her fingers seem to be tightly clenched. Her feet, which are shown several times in Dicksee's illustrations, are rather sizable.

One problem attendant on mixed illustrations of a text is that one artist's Norman cap and kirtle may not resemble another's (see Gilbert's illustration, Figure 4, which is included in the Grosset and Dunlap edition). Dicksee's striking portrait of Evangeline bringing ale to the reapers (Figure 10) differs considerably from Darley's 1866 design (Figure 5), though the discrepancy is not problematic in this case because the illustrations are not included in the same edition. Significantly, Darley's design shows Evangeline in conversation, whereas Dicksee's portrays her concentrating intently on her pouring. In Dicksee's illustration we are much more aware of the weary, even haggard, workers. The muscled forearm of the long-haired reaper in the foreground is set off powerfully by the sickle gripped in his other hand, and, typical of Dicksee's work, we are made aware of myriad textures: his loose hair, his baggy trousers, his heavy-looking wooden shoes. Evangeline is more obviously the center of our attention in Darley's illustration, which is considerably less detailed and less naturalistic.

One of Dicksee's more evocative illustrations shows Evangeline in I.3 heading up the staircase, "a luminous space in the darkness, / Lighted less by the lamp than the shining face of the maiden." Here she appears serene, anticipating her betrothal celebration the next day (Figure 11). Against that optimistic moment one might place the illustration used as the frontispiece of the Burt edition and as cover art on the undated (apparently early 1900s) M.A. Donohue edition published in Chicago. Evangeline walks home from church, her eyes familiarly downcast, hands folded loosely at her waist, a cross pendant from her necklace (Figure 12). This image of Evangeline differs from the lone portraits of her by Benham and Gilbert that accompany the text from I.1: "Homeward serenely she walked with God's benediction upon her" (Figures 1 and 4). Dicksee's image shows a decidedly melancholy and troubled expression following the proclamation of their eviction by the British commander in I.5: "Meanwhile, amid the gloom, by the church Evangeline lingered." Although she has done her best to cheer the villagers, now, at sunset, "on her spirit within a deeper shadow had fallen," and she can find no consolation among the graves.

Probably because the then exotic scenery of Louisiana and the West were attractive subjects for illustrators, the second half of *Evangeline* features fewer portraits of the heroine and more of the varied landscape. A curious exception however, is an illustrated edition by H. Hirschauer, C.S.

Figure 10. "When in the harvest heat she bore to the reapers at noon-tide / Flagons of home-brewed ale, ah! fair in sooth was the maiden." Frank Dicksee (1882).

White, and Louis Meynelle published in1893, in which four half-tone landscapes, all by White, illustrate the first part, while three portraits of Evangeline, all by Hirschauer, illustrate the second. A Hirschauer picture of Evangeline and Gabriel serves as the frontispiece for the book, and a landscape by White appears at the end of the text. All of the illustrations appear to have been taken from watercolors. Only Meynelle, who apparently contributed just a couple of designs, is an illustrator or artist of record. Sue Rainey's study of the "Picturesque America" Series run in *Appleton's Journal* (1872–1874) and supposedly edited by William Cullen Bryant but actually the work of Oliver Bell Bunce testifies to the popularity of landscape engravings in the decades following the end of the Civil War: "Through inexpensive prints of scenery and cities in popular periodicals and books, many Americans were seeing for the first time what they had only abstractly imagined as their country" (3). In an anonymous review of the illustrated edition of *Longfellow's Complete Poems* in Houghton Mifflin's Riverside Press Household Edition for the *New York Times* (December 5, 1880) the critic opened with the observation that "Longfellow furnishes better material for picturesque illustration than any other American poet" and compared the volume favorably with the designs offered in "Picturesque America."*

Figure 11. "Up the staircase moved a luminous space in the darkness, / Lighted less by the lamp than the shining face of the maiden." Frank Dicksee (1882).

* *http://query.nytimes.com/mem/archivefree/pdf?_r=1&res=950DEEDD123FEE3ABC4D53 DFB467838B699FDE&oref=slogin*

Figure 12. "Meanwhile, amid the gloom by the church Evangeline lingered." Frank Dicksee (1882).

The first Bogue (London) edition of *Evangeline* offers seven fewer illustrations in Part Two (26 to nineteen), and only three of those feature Evangeline. Fifteen of the remaining designs, mostly landscapes, are by Birket Foster. Most readers of the poem will likely agree that Longfellow devotes more lines to landscape description in Part Two than he does in Part One, so some shift in focus from characters to setting is predictable. Evangeline fares somewhat better in Part Two of the Grosset and Dunlap edition, where she figures prominently in eleven of the 25 illustrations, several of which pertain to events from Part One and are therefore incorrectly distributed. Some artists, Dicksee among them, depict her still wearing her ethnic costume until the last canto of the poem, in which she has become a Sister of Mercy. Her appearance at age 55 in a nun's habit, sometimes with a large wimple, constitutes a dramatic contrast with Evangeline as a seventeen-year-old maiden wearing Norman peasant garb.

Readers of the Household Edition of *Longfellow's Complete Poems*, published around the turn of the nineteenth century by Houghton Mifflin, would have encountered illustrations by Philadelphia native E[dwin] A[ustin] Abbey (1852–1911), who was to become a member of the Royal Academy and would paint murals for the Boston Public Library and the Pennsylvania

Figure 13. "Long at her father's door Evangeline stood, with her right hand / Shielding her eyes from the level rays of the sun [...]" E.A. Abbey (1880).

State Capitol. In her "Special Commemorative Edition" of *Evangeline* published in 2004, Françoise Paradis includes eight of Abbey's designs along with others by such engraver-illustrators as C[harles] S. Reinhart (1844–1896) and Granville Perkins (1830–1895), whose work also appears in the Household Editions. Abbey's picture of Evangeline near the end of I.4, standing at her father's door and "Shielding her eyes from the level rays of the sun, that, descending / Lighted the village street with mysterious splendor," is perhaps the most poignant portrait of all (Figure 13). Her right hand is gracefully poised, slightly cupped, over her eye; her nose appears to be small and nicely shaped; her lips are delicately formed and arched; her large eyes gaze emptily into the distance. In what some might regard as a postmodern commodification of art, a different portrait by Abbey is featured on moulds used for the six varieties of Evangeline Soaps, "made of 100 percent biodegradable vegetable oils with no artificial colors and no animal testing."* The illustration of *Evangeline* did not cease by any means with the designs of Frank Dicksee and E.A. Abbey, but it may be argued that the artists' fancy begins to run amok in portraits for some later editions of the poem. Or perhaps artists were simply striving to follow changing trends in the identity of American womanhood. The publisher who wishes to attract the interest of readers in the new century would need to offer them a different image of Evangeline, presumably one in which downcast eyes would not be featured prominently. For example, I have not been able to identify the artist whose work led to the half-tone in Figure 14, but apparently this alluring Evangeline, whose hat certainly is not a "Norman cap," is posing at the well with its "moss-grown" bucket. She holds a tin cup in one hand and a hay rake in the other. Her sultry, come-hither eyes and shapely lips seem quite tempting. The text in this case is from the undated M.A. Donohue edition. The *National Union List of Pre-1956 Imprints* describes a copy at the University of Virginia library with a bracketed date of 191_, but the copy I consulted at the St. Martin Parish Library in St. Martinville, Louisiana, is inscribed "Christmas 1907."

Figure 14. "Farther down, on the slope of the hill, was a well with its moss-grown / Bucket, fastened with iron, and near it a trough for the horses." Unknown artist (M.A. Donohue edition, n.d. [ca. 1900]).

The half-tone used in the Van Cleve-Andrews Minnehaha printing of 1895 shows an openly flirtatious Evangeline who appears more at home in a colonial pub

* *http://www.francoiseparadis.com/soaps.html*

than in her father's house at Grand-Pré, where she is presumably serving guests on the day of her betrothal announcement (Figure 15). Similar halftones, apparently by the same unnamed artist, throughout this heavily illustrated text feature Evangeline in an array of dresses and gowns appropriate to an eighteenth-century aristocrat, while Gabriel comes off looking very little like the humble blacksmith's son and very much like a dandy. The effect on the reader is jarring, but perhaps the casual guest sitting in the parlor in 1900 and leafing through the pages of the poem she or he had read as an unillustrated text in the eighth grade was diverted. No fewer than 55 illustrations clutter this 98-page edition, many of them clearly not prepared with *Evangeline* in mind, but what we would now recognize as "file photos." One could quite plausibly claim not to have read the poem, but to have enjoyed the pictures.

Figure 15. "Bright was her face with smiles, and words of welcome and gladness / Fell from her beautiful lips, and blessed the cup as she gave it." F[red] H[ines] (1895).

The drawings by John Rea Neill for the 1909 edition of *Evangeline* published in Chicago by Reilly and Britton were printed in flesh-toned ink and are highly stylized. In general, Evangeline, as seen in the frontispiece by the artist who had illustrated Frank Baum's *Wizard of Oz* just two years earlier, is very girlish, and while her eyes are indeed downcast (Figure 16), her image on the color front cover is quite another matter. Neill offers us a profile of her head and shoulders with enough of her bust to reveal a rosary around her neck. She wears white and her brown hair peeks out just a little saucily from her white Norman cap, which is firmly fastened under her delicately sculpted chin. Fastened to the cap is an orange rose. Her nose is small, her red lips parted slightly in a near smile, her eyes open, but not widely. The design that follows the prologue in the text, however, sets a different image for the reader as he or she enters the narrative: an almost bacchanal visage (Figure 17). Evangeline smiles at us with what I would describe as a "demure naughtiness," her lips full, eyes wide-set, cheeks aglow, a bucket of grapes in her lap. A few pages later we encounter her walking home from church alone, "serenely [...] with God's benediction upon her," but her face is closer to that of the frontispiece (Figure 16) than to the "ethereal beauty" Benham attempted to capture. In general, Neill's portraits (ten of the total fifteen focus on Evangeline) show her to be girlish and—there really is no better term for it—"cute." Just five of Neill's illustrations appear in Part Two, two of them showing her in nun's habit tending to the stricken Gabriel.

Figure 16. "Homeward serenely she walked with God's benediction upon her." John Rea Neill (1909).

Lois Banner observes that the "voluptuous woman was never as powerful a model of beauty as the steel-engraving lady before her or the natural woman later" (155). She describes the Gibson Girl, as defined by Charles Dana Gibson between 1895 and World War I as "tall and commanding, with thick, dark hair swept upward in the prevailing pompadour style. Her figure was thinner than that of the voluptuous woman, but she remained large of bosom and hips. Her mouth was small and her nose snub" (154). The rather athletic Gibson Girl might be college-bound and headed for a future apart from hearth and home.

Unlike the cheaply produced Minnehaha editions, illustrated indiscriminately, the Bobbs-Merrill edition published in 1905 featured the artwork of Howard Chandler Christy (1873–1952), an imitator of Gibson in some ways, and being almost certainly intended as a gift edition, it was not inex-

Figure 17. "Black were her eyes as the berry that grows on the thorn by the wayside, / Black, yet how softly they gleamed beneath the brown shade of her tresses." John Rae Neill (1909).

pensive. Printed with color tinting throughout, a sort of salmon or flesh-tone background for the text with splashes of that color occasionally introduced into the black-and-white pictures, the illustrations portray a sultry young woman who can appear alternatively flirtatious and sweet or pensive and dreamy. She smiles, for example, while on her knees in prayer at church, well aware of handsome Gabriel staring at her. Six of the 39 illustrations are offered in full color, albeit not very vividly or brightly. Christy's Evangeline never looks either "ethereal" or deeply melancholy, but she does look "interesting," as in the frontispiece (Figure 18). Her eyes, which have been altered to blue, despite Longfellow's insistence on black, are emphasized in several illustrations, as is her long dark hair, which she braids sensually in one design (Figure 19).

Figure 18. Frontispiece of Howard Chandler Christy's illustrated edition of *Evangeline*. Howard Chandler Christy (1905).

Perhaps for the first time, the reader encounters an image of Evangeline that instead of being intent on foreshadowing her eventual role as a nun bodies forth her romantic promise and femininity. In short, Christy gives her "sex appeal"; note, for example, his picture of Evangeline bringing "flagons of home-brewed ale" to the reapers in a rather ornamental ewer (Figure 20). Christy imparts an almost haughty turn of her head, and her right arm cocked against her hip suggests that she will brook no nonsense from the thirsty workers. Her slender waist is accentuated for perhaps the first time, and while the cross and rosary figure prominently in Benham's portraits, they are absent in 25 of her 26 portraits by Christy, appearing only when she is shown at the end in her nun's habit. He sustains her ethnic costume, in fact, until that point, and he depicts Evangeline as a 55 year-old Sister of Mercy scarcely altered by age. Sad-eyed and wasp-waisted, she looks like a Gibson Girl who has taken orders.

Christy's most poignant portrait of Evangeline appears at the end of

II.2 and is rendered in full color. At this point the reader knows that Gabriel's boat has passed hers unnoticed on one of the lakes of the Atchafalaya River, a hundred or so miles west of New Orleans. It is most likely the evening during which she hears "the mocking-bird, wildest of singers" with his "floods of delirious music." They are about to meet Basil, now herding cattle in the "Eden of Louisiana." Still in her ethnic costume, Evangeline wears an open-necked white blouse, a dark blue or black long-sleeved bodice laced with red, and a red-orange skirt. Her dark hair falls lushly from under her white Norman cap over her right shoulder. She looks sadly but unaware over her left shoulder at the ghostly outline of Gabriel who seems to emerge from a garden of waist-high yellow and pink flowers (Figure 21).

Perhaps it is well to recall at this point the advice of Frank Weitenkampf with respect to book illustration: we must "always remember that the relation of the illustration to the book as a physical product should never take precedence over its relation to the author's text" (6–7). As intriguing as the designs by illustrators like Neill and Christy often are, they tend sometimes to project a character rather at odds with the woman portrayed in the lines of Longfellow's poem. "At first shocked" at the feminist movement's aims and ideals, Wasserstrom notes, "society later came to prefer rebellious, vigorous young women to debilitated and self-effacing girls" (82). It could be argued that Evangeline fits right between these extremes: she is vigorous, but not rebellious, self-effacing, but not debilitated. If she is not quite as stiff as a Steel-Engraving Lady, Evangeline remains something short of a voluptuous Gibson Girl.

Figure 19. "She was a woman now, with the heart and hopes of a woman." Howard Chandler Christy (1905).

One result of the changing definition of womanhood in the United States, Wasserstrom suggests, is that "all the brisk young men, reared to idolize Steel-Engraving Ladies, married Gibson Girls." What is remarkable about this version of "ut poesis pictura" (to reshape the Latin proverb) is the effort to convert Evangeline from what she is in Longfellow's poem, a proper young Steel-Engraving Lady though with a more daring and venturesome spirit and a much greater commitment to action, into something palatable to an audience that had changed over the generations. While the artists never go so far as to render her voluptuous, they do recreate her in images vastly different from those generated by artists like Jane Benham and Thomas Faed.

Figure 20. "When in the harvest heat she bore to the reapers at noon-tide / Flagons of home-brewed ale, ah! fair in sooth was the maiden." Howard Chandler Christy (1905).

Portraits of Other Important Characters

Although Evangeline herself remains the dominant character in Longfellow's poem, illustrators dealt with all of the named minor characters or supporting cast, from Gabriel to the Shawnee widow who tells her the haunting story in II.4 of "the fair Lilinau, who was wooed by a phantom." Portraits of certain prominent characters, like Father Felician, "Priest and pedagogue both in the village," would have been required by nearly any publisher. Jane Benham depicts the priest as young and with short hair as he instructs two children,

Figure 21. "Nearer and round about her, the manifold flowers of the garden / Poured out their souls in odors, that were their prayers and confessions." Howard Chandler Christy (1905).

presumably intended to represent Gabriel and Evangeline in their childhood (Figure 22). But no other illustrator appears to have followed her lead. All illustrators, of course, portray him wearing a cassock. F.O.C. Darley shows him with a wide-brimmed hat and shoulder-length hair (Figure 23) and displays a fine sense of

***Right:* Figure 22. "[...] Father Felician, / Priest and pedagogue both in the village, had taught them their letters / Out of the selfsame book with the hymns of the church and the plainsong." Jane Benham (1850). *Below:* Figure 23. "Solemnly down the street came the parish priest, and the children / Paused in their play to kiss the hand he extended to bless them." F.O.C. Darley (1883).**

Figure 24. "Solemnly down the street came the parish priest, and the children / Paused in their play to kiss the hand he extended to bless them." John Gilbert (1853).

detail and of scene—he depicts not simply the priest teaching a pair of children, but the priest as he exists in the context of the entire village. In this, one of the finest illustrations of the poem, Darley represents the "Matrons and maidens" with their "distaffs spinning the golden / Flax for the gossiping looms," and while some of the children reverently kiss his "extended hand," per the poem, Darley shows us the artist's capacity to conceive beyond the limits of the text, as one child gazes off into the distance untouched by the great moment and a dog worries a string in the lower foreground. "Solemnly" and "reverend" the priest walks down the street, and the children pause in their play to kiss his hand, but not all of them do. And not the dog.

A quick comparison of the scene as visualized by John Gilbert, who perhaps shares an equal control of the art, of fine detail and composition, reveals the superiority of Darley's illustration. Gilbert's Father Felician appears to be much more elderly than Darley's, which might cause readers to wonder how he would be up to serving as Evangeline's companion and guardian in the second part of the poem. Father Felician reminds his congregation in I.4 that he has spent forty years of his life in their service, so he would be in his sixties during most of the events that occur in the poem. Darley

Figure 25. "Solemnly down the street came the parish priest, and the children / Paused in their play to kiss the hand he extended to bless them." Violet Oakley (1897).

most likely followed Gilbert's lead (Figure 24) in giving us a priest with shoulder-length hair. Perhaps the most attractive illustration of the priest with the children is that by Violet Oakley (1874–1961) in an 1897 edition of the poem published by Houghton Mifflin. The ten full-color illustrations, five each by Oakley and by Jesse Willcox Smith (1863–1935), both of whom were students of renowned illustrator Howard Pyle (1853–1911) at Drexel Institute of Art in Philadelphia, demonstrate an intentionally exaggerated sense of line (one can follow the sharp outer edges of the figures in every design). What distinguishes this portrait of Father Felician (Figure 25) are the happy faces of the children who have come out to greet him, particularly that of the boy on the right who is biting into an apple. Oakley also produced a design for what might be regarded as the priest's most important moment, when in the midst of I.4 he chastises the citizens of Grand-Pré, led by the angry Basil the blacksmith, for rebelling against the British soldiers.

The old notary and raconteur, René Leblanc, "Father of twenty children," who retells an allegory about a statue of justice that was related to him when he was a prisoner at Port Royal, captured by the British in 1710, is represented in Gilbert's second set of illustrations for the poem surrounded by no fewer than eight of his grandchildren scrambling for a place on his lap (Figure 26). Gilbert also offers memorable images of snow-white-haired Michael the fiddler, whom he imagines as perhaps a midget, as he shows him seated on a keg that has been placed on a table during the betrothal party in I.4 and being triumphantly carried on the shoulders of two young Acadians in II.3 as children strew flowers (Figure 27). The contrast of Gilbert's designs with

Figure 26. "Father of twenty children was he, and more than a hundred / Children's children rode on his knee, and heard his great clock tick." John Gilbert (1853).

Figure 27. "'Long live Michael,' they cried, 'our brave Acadian minstrel!' / As they bore him aloft in triumphal procession [...]." John Gilbert (1853).

Jane Benham's borders on the comical (Figure 28). Her version of Michael shows him not playing his violin but holding it in his right hand as he perches rather nervously on the arms of two young men. Unlike Gilbert's Michael, Jane Benham's does not smile.

Gilbert draws Evangeline's father, Benedict Bellefontaine, a man of "seventy winters" as opposed to his daughter's "seventeen summers," as the wealthiest and most prominent citizen of the town (Figure 29). Even when he is shown in the company of his daughter, as in Christy's color portrait, or playing checkers with his old friend the blacksmith, as in Dicksee's pic-

Figure 28. "'Long live Michael,' they cried, 'our brave Acadian minstrel!' / As they bore him aloft in triumphal procession [...]." Jane Benham (1850).

ture, he appears unable to muster a smile. The impression made, at least retrospectively, is that we are looking at a doomed man, an old man nearing his last days. Gabriel's father, Basil Lajeunesse, fares much better; after all, he represents one of Longfellow's favorite occupations—the village blacksmith. Both Gilbert and Darley offer illustrations of Basil working at the forge, watched with "wondering eyes" by Gabriel and Evangeline as children. Neill appears to be singular in creating a design that depicts a wide-eyed, clench-fisted Basil raging in church against the British (Figure 30).

Figure 29. "Benedict Bellefontaine, the wealthiest farmer of Grand-Pré." John Gilbert (1853).

Surely one reason the illustrators paid so much attention to Basil is that his character, anticipating Evangeline's in some ways, undergoes a significant change in the second part of the poem. Basil's reappearance in Louisiana (II.3) as a prosperous rancher also became one of the most popular moments in the poem for illustration, perhaps because of the way Longfellow engineers that scene. We see him first as an anonymous "herdsman" wearing a sombrero and appearing to be "master" of the "peaceful scene." He blows on his horn and the cattle bellow in response, then rush across the prairie. But when he sees the priest and Evangeline, he jumps from his horse and embraces the weary travelers, revealing himself as their old friend, the "ci-devant blacksmith." Dicksee's portrait shows the cattleman astride his horse, his elbow jutting out (Figure 31). His exotic sash and the rowels of his spurs may grab our attention. Gilbert's portrait shows Basil blowing his horn, his back turned to the viewer. Jessie Willcox Smith's image also focuses on Basil blowing his horn as the sun sets serenely. The crown of the sombrero as she imagines it has a much more pronounced conical shape than we find in other designs. Although Basil's anger at the British is not fully quelled, he is clearly pleased with his new home "that is better perchance than the old one" and presumably with his new occupation as well.

Of all the significant characters in the poem other than Evangeline, it seems to me that Gabriel has fared least well at the hands of the illustrators. While Longfellow makes a great deal of Evangeline's walking "serenely" homeward after confession, of her patience and forgetfulness of self, and of her physical traits and items of her wardrobe, Longfellow offers few details on Gabriel

except that he is "a valiant youth" with a face "like the face of the morning," whatever that is supposed to suggest (I.1.141). As we encounter him in I.5 Gabriel's face is "pale with emotion": "Gone was the glow from his cheek, and the fire from his eye." We hear from his father in II.3 to the effect that Gabriel has grown impatient with "this quiet existence," that he has become "uncertain and sor-

Left: **Figure 30. "Flushed was his face and distorted with passion; and wildly he shouted: / 'Down with the tyrants of England! we never have sworn them allegiance!'" John Rea Neill (1909).** ***Below:*** **Figure 31. "Mounted upon his horse, with Spanish saddle and stirrups, / Sat a herdsman, arrayed in gaiters and doublet of deerskin." Frank Dicksee (1882).**

Figure 32. "As apart by the window she stood, with her hand in her lover's, / Blushing Evangeline heard the words that her father had spoken. John Gilbert (1853).

rowful," "silent," and "tedious" even to his own father. But aside from being told that Gabriel has become a hunter and wanderer, we do not encounter him again until he is on his deathbed. At the hands of his illustrators Gabriel risks becoming a generically handsome and "noble" young man.

Benham offers two images of Gabriel in Part One, both of which depict him with an arm around Evangeline's waist, his right hand drawn clumsily (Figure 3). Although Gilbert's drawing is more skilled, Gabriel does not acquire much character in his scene with Evangeline, where he holds her hand and looks down seriously and quietly into her eyes (Figure 32). He is

Figure 33. "Into this wonderful land at the base of the Ozark Mountains, Gabriel far had entered, with hunters and trappers behind him." F.O.C. Darley (1883).

taller than she is, of average to slender build, and wears his hair at shoulder length. Neill offers an image of the couple on the verge of a kiss under a full moon. Gabriel's dark full hair looks a little tousled; his nose is rather large and hawk-like; he has what most would call a "strong" chin. Christy's Gabriel has long, wavy hair and much finer features than Neill's, and we see more of him. I count ten images of Gabriel in Christy's book, including the "ghost" mentioned above. Christy is all but unique in *not* creating a deathbed design for the poem. E.A. Abbey's image of Gabriel holding Evangeline's hand on the evening of their betrothal shows him clasping his broad-brimmed hat and smiling shyly at her. He is narrow-shouldered and boyish. But in Abbey's design depicting Gabriel with Evangeline on the beach during the deportation, his face is serious and he appears already to have matured. In Darley's illustration of the lovers, Gabriel is seated with his back turned to us, but he imagines Gabriel in II.4 on horseback, carrying his long rifle in the "wonderful land" of the Ozarks (Figure 33). His hair is long and dark, but while the other hunters sport beards, he is clean-shaven. Over his fringed deerskin jacket he wears a striped cape or blanket, and on his head sits a broad-brimmed dark hat. His facial features are handsome. He stares down and ahead seriously and maybe a little sadly. He may be intent on tracking, but given the context we are inclined to assume he is thinking about Evangeline.

Group Scenes

Although most of the illustrations examined in the previous section involve group or action scenes, they tend to be focused on the single character under discussion. Various artists, however, among whom F.O.C. Darley and Frank Dicksee appear to have been foremost, were inclined to stress group or action scenes, and most of the illustrators aimed at least some of their talents in that direction. Predictably, certain dramatic events, like the dance at the betrothal celebration and the uproar in the church over Colonel Winslow's proclamation, proved especially popular topics, whether the preference of the book publisher or that of the artist would be difficult if not impossible to ascertain. From the welter of possibilities I will select just two illustrations each by Darley and Dicksee of two group scenes: the Acadians with their loaded ox-carts heading toward their enforced embarkation at the

Figure 34. "Soon o'er the yellow fields, in silent and mournful procession, / Came from the neighboring hamlets and farms the Acadian women, / Driving in ponderous wains their household goods to the seashore [...]." F.O.C. Darley (1883).

beginning of I.5, and Evangeline with fellow Acadians in their "cumbrous boat" floating through the Louisiana bayous early in II.2.

Darley's design shows a heavily loaded cart drawn by two straining oxen, one black and the other white (Figure 34). The black ox slobbers painfully while the white ox appears to be distracted by the dog at its right. Another dog sits in the loaded wagon amid plowshares, tools, a chair, and covered household goods. Significantly, we cannot see the faces of the three principle female characters in the foreground, two women and a girl probably in her teens. The girl has turned her face away to look back at her home or at friends who are loading or driving their carts in the background (three are visible). The two women, one of them holding a baby, are weeping and have covered their faces. A little girl attempts to comfort the woman holding the placid baby, who must be her little sister or brother. Her big sister, face averted, holds the hand of another sister, who carries a doll over her left shoulder. In what I take to be a typical example of Darley's humor, a goat appears to be nibbling at the doll. To the mother's right her son, the only male in the picture, looks straight out at us, sad and apparently stunned, perhaps in shock at what is happening to him and his family.

Not one of the seven female figures in Dicksee's design looks directly at us; in effect, they are looking back at what they have lost. But details from the illustrations are similar; both, for example, feature one black and one white ox, although only the white one is fully visible here (Figure 35). (The picture, which concerns action in I.5, is placed, or rather misplaced, in II.2 in the Grosset and Dunlap edition.) One other loaded cart follows this one closely, but we can make out no details. Dicksee's cart is loaded with household items, most prominent among them being a wardrobe, a spinning wheel, and a couple of cooking pots. The elderly woman in the foreground driving the oxen appears to be the matriarch of the family. Her shaded, downcast face is lined with worry. Behind her a young woman who may be her daughter holds a baby and turns to converse with a young woman walking behind her. Consequently, we do not see her face, nor do we see that of her baby. In the left foreground of the picture a young girl, perhaps nine or ten years old, holds the hand of what could be her little sister or brother, and she seems to be consoling him as he looks up at her somewhat fretfully. The woman to whom the young mother is talking appears to be tired. Beside her walks a little girl whose face looks blank. In both portraits the characters are dressed in traditional costume, and in Dicksee's we typically see special attention to texture, particularly in the clothing.

Darley's design shows greater attention than Dicksee's to fine details and to perspective, portraying events in the distance, and he captures a broader emotional range. Darley's illustration also capitalizes on the bitter

Figure 35. "Soon o'er the yellow fields, in silent and mournful procession, / Came from the neighboring hamlets and farms the Acadian women, / Driving in ponderous wains their household goods to the seashore [...]." Frank Dicksee (1882).

grief over the expulsion, but it might be argued that Dicksee shows us the next stage in the emotional response to their tragedy, as a kind of resigned numbness appears to pervade the faces of these women.

The placid boat scene from Part Two amounts to a sort of counterpoint to the anguished *déportation.* Although the publisher (Houghton Mifflin) has accompanied Darley's illustration with the passage, "Day after day they glided down the turbulent river" (the Ohio or the Mississippi), the design indicates no turbulence at all and suggests the Bayou of Plaquemine where the Acadians find themselves "lost in a maze of sluggish and devious waters," or the "slight undulations" of the lakes off the Atchafalaya River. A small boat powered by two oarsmen accommodates no fewer than ten passengers, including Father Felician and Evangeline in the stern, five children of varying ages, a baby, and two young women we might assume are the wives of the rowers (Figure 36). Darley has not bothered to account for luggage, and there appears to be no shelter from the weather. In the bow of the boat a

Figure 36. "They, too, swerved form their course; and, entering the Bayou of Plaquemine, / Soon were lost in a maze of sluggish and devious waters [...]." F.O.C. Darley (1883).

woman holding a child over her shoulder shades her eyes and looks hopefully ahead—directly at the viewer, in fact. In nearly all of Darley's designs one character or another makes eye contact with us. Evangeline, her eyes typically downcast, apparently looks at a little boy who leans over the gunwales and plays in the water. One might like to think Evangeline is warning him that a gator might snap off his hand, but she does not appear to be speaking. Instead, she is hearkening to the words of Father Felician, who may be advising her that "Feeling is deep and still," or that she should trust to her heart "and to what the world calls illusions." While the trees near the shore in the background are not festooned with Spanish moss, the man who faces toward the viewer pulls his oar through weeds and lily pads, so we may assume that the boat is moving through a swampy area.

Similarly, Dicksee shows us a boat moving through quiet, almost glassy waters, but while the boat is near shore, signified by a cluster of lily pads in the lower right, we can see to the left that they are situated either on a large river or a lake (Figure 37). Dicksee provides Evangeline, sitting in the prow and gazing dolefully ahead, directly at the viewer, with a considerably larger boat, but he has textured the planking so that it looks scarcely seaworthy. Dicksee's "cumbrous boat" accommodates four oarsmen and features a small

Figure 37. "Dreamlike, and indistinct, and strange were all things around them; / And o'er their spirits there came a feeling of wonder and sadness, / Strange forebodings of ill, unseen and that cannot be compassed." Frank Dicksee (1882).

mast for a sail. I can count at least twenty passengers of varying ages, from a baby in arms to an elderly man to Evangeline's right (the viewer's left) who most likely is Father Felician.* Two young girls lean over the gunwales near the bow and stern, both apparently asleep, or at least bored. The old priest appears to have his mind on other things in Dicksee's picture, for he does not engage Evangeline in conversation as in Darley's illustration. Near the stern an older woman tends to a baby in Dicksee's design, but while she appears preoccupied, we can see at least four other faces, those of three men, including one of the rowers, and a woman, and each appears to be at least mildly apprehensive about something. Despite the publisher's citation pertaining to the cumbersome boat, Dicksee may have had in mind a more somber passage: "Dreamlike, and indistinct, and strange were all things around them; / And o'er their spirits there came a feeling of wonder

* *Granville Perkins' illustration of the "cumbrous boat," reprinted in Paradis'* Special Commemorative Edition *(111), may have set the record for carrying capacity: I count at least thirty on board (presumably four oarsmen and a man at the tiller provide the locomotion).*

and sadness, / Strange forebodings of ill, unseen and that cannot be compassed" (II.2). As the foregoing demonstrates, group pictures, particularly when action is involved, invite speculation that reaches beyond the text being illustrated. Whether intentionally or not, such illustrations invite viewers to interpret both what they see and what they have been reading. These illustrations expand the dimensions of the printed text. Whether that expansion constitutes an enrichment of the literary experience or a possibly irrelevant digression will doubtless vary with the reader.

Pictures of Natural Scenery or Landscape

Aside from initial designs intended to illustrate the "forest primeval" or the idyllic and "thatch-roofed" farms that resemble English cottages transported to Acadia, the first part of *Evangeline* offers relatively little opportunity for the landscapist, but the second provides ample possibilities, from the "towering and tenebrous boughs of the cypress" in the Louisiana bayous to the West where "jagged, deep ravines" and gorges form something like a "gateway" to the "wheels of the emigrant's wagon." Birket Foster and F.O.C. Darley contributed designs for the prologue of which Foster's comes closer to the text of the poem. The design itself frames the opening six lines, and two snags frame the picture in the left and right foreground with some windfall at the bottom. Beyond them loom large healthy trees that might be pines or more likely hemlocks, and occupying the mid-ground are ocean waves breaking on rocks (Figure 38). How much of Longfellow's metaphoric reference the picture manifests ("Druids of eld" or "harpers hoar") must be left to the viewer. Darley's design shows a triangle formed by snags and a fallen tree on the left balanced by healthy conifers to the right and in the background (Figure 39). A mountain stream rushes over boulders at the center of the picture, but the stream does not connote the loud roar of the "deep-voiced neighboring ocean" called for in the prologue.

Foster provided illustrations of idyllic village and farm life for Part One, but they are not particularly distinctive. For the second part of *Evangeline,* however, he created images that would likely have had a particularly exotic appeal in his day. Certainly they make some contribution to the premise of a "picturesque America" mentioned above. The five designs he created for II.2, which recounts Evangeline's river voyage down the Ohio and Mississippi and into the bayous of Louisiana, are especially fine. Rather than make sport of his portrayal of the Ozarks as barren, snow-capped peaks reminiscent of the Rockies, I will focus my comments on three images, the first two of which appear in the second canto of Part Two. In the first design Foster captures the "plumelike / Cotton Trees" (that is, cottonwoods) nodding

Figure 38. "This is the forest primeval." Birket Foster (1850).

Figure 39. "This is the forest primeval." F.O.C. Darley (1883).

"their shadowy crests" amid "large flocks of pelicans" (Figure 40). In a fashion similar to that of painters like Asher Durand (1796–1886) and Thomas Cole (1801–1848) of the Hudson River School, he minimizes the human place in the great scheme of nature, the small boatful of Acadians being scarcely visible in the distant mid-ground. A dozen pelicans stand, wade, or fly off near what appears to be some sort of palm in the foreground of the peaceful scene. A towering cottonwood soars overhead, and in the background Foster has added an improbable mountain.

In his design for the boaters on "the lakes of the Atchafalaya" with its "Water-lilies in myriads" and the "resplendent" lotus, which "Lifted her golden crown above the heads of the boatmen," Foster produces his most imaginative artwork for the poem (Figure 41). Several water lilies in the lower foreground are dwarfed, as are the figures in the boat, mid-ground, by a shock of giant lotus flowers, four in full bloom and four huge buds, with several large leaves. Although the American lotus can reach a height exceeding three feet, the effect of Foster's picture approaches the surreal. If Longfellow was aware of the special place of the lotus in Buddhist and Hindu mythology, we find no evidence of it here. Emerson and other of the so-called "Boston Brahmans" were well read in the Vedas, as was Walt Whitman, but apparently Longfellow was not. Nevertheless, the evocative image combines with Longfellow's personification of the lotus as feminine to make the passage suggestive of sensual or creative energy.

As opposed to his somewhat daring illustration of the lotus, Birket Foster's picture of Basil the herdsman's house at the start of II.3 looks bland and domestic, studiously picturesque and perhaps more at home in Kent or Wessex than in Cajun country (Figure 42). The house as he draws it bears only a faint resemblance to the one described by Longfellow as "Hewn from the cypress-tree, and carefully fitted together" and as sporting a "low" roof. Close inspection, however, reveals that Foster took pains to depict the "slender columns" encircled with roses and vines and the "broad and spacious veranda." As Evangeline and the other Acadians disembark, they might notice the carefully placed, triangular dove-cot perched on a pole, "love's perpetual symbol" (not so much the dovecote, of course, as the doves, birds sacred to Aphrodite). The house is shaded by large trees that might well be oak, but in the distance

Figure 40. "Then emerged into broad lagoons, where silvery sand bars / Lay in the stream, and along the wimpling waves of their margin, / Shining with snow-white plumes, large flocks of pelicans waded." Birket Foster (1850).

Figure 41. "Water lilies in myriads rocked on the slight undulations / Made by the passing oars, and, resplendent in beauty, the lotus / Lifted her golden crown above the heads of the boatmen." Birket Foster (1850).

Foster does not sketch "great groves of oak" skirting "the limitless prairie," but a pair of tall and unlikely palm trees.

Landscape illustration is almost inevitably static, and in this respect it reflects in picture what happens in the descriptive "purple patch" so popular in the writing, both prose and poetry, of Longfellow's day. At their worst it might be argued that such designs provide mere ornamentation for the poem, but at their best they enhance the vividness of some passages and underscore the symbolic suggestiveness of certain images.

* * *

It may be fairly said that every decade after its publication in 1847 was

Figure 42. "At each end of the house, amid the flowers of the garden, / Stationed the dovecots were, as love's perpetual symbol [...]." Birket Foster (1850).

to find at least one new illustrator for *Evangeline* until about 1910. The quality of illustration varied wildly, from the fine wood engravings of the presentation or parlor-table book (today's coffee-table book) featuring the work of a single artist, like John Gilbert or F.O.C. Darley or Howard Chandler Christy, to the hodge-podge of the Minnehaha editions of the late 1890s and early 1900s, which combined work of at least half a dozen "various" illustrators along with what we would now call "file photos." As Frank Weitenkampf has observed, the camera was to aid the wood engraver in the "refinement of his art," but ultimately the photomechanical process "drove him to the wall" through the use of halftones, which was to mean "the surrender of line to tone" in his art (184).

Although other illustrated editions have appeared over the years, including a 1929 edition in German blank verse with a dozen silhouettes and a dual language Italian version in 1930 with a dozen brown-tones by Carlo

Above: **Figure 43. Miriam Cooper as Evangeline (1919).** *Below:* **Figure 44. Dolores Del Rio as Evangeline (1929).**

Nicco, along with a fascistic and poorly translated introductory essay, the hey-day of the illustrated book was past and the popular demand for such books was to be satisfied largely by the novel medium of the *moving* picture. The Peter Pauper Press edition commemorating the hundredth anniversary of the poem's publication features pen-and-ink drawings by William Moyers, who specialized in the illustration of children's books. His designs are shaded in gray-green ink that gives the impression of watercolors: The most recent illustrated version of *Evangeline* worthy of note appeared in 1966 and features the line drawings of Howard Simon (1902–1979), a professor of Art at New York University. Along with Moyers' designs Simon's reflects the tendencies toward abstraction in modern art and simplification of the fine detail so prized by early illustrators and engravers.

The Milton-Bradley Company of Springfield, Massachusetts, published a prose version of the poem in 1922 by Carolyn Sherwin Bailey illustrated with stills from the Miriam Cooper film produced by William Fox (Figure 43; compare Abbey's design for the same scene, Figure 13), and in 1929 A.L. Burt, which had revived Frank Dicksee's illustrations in 1900, published a prose rendition by Oklahoma film producer, director, and screenwriter Finis Fox (1881–1949) and stills from the Edwin Carewe production starring Dolores Del Rio (Figure 44). Both volumes reprint the poem in its entirety. Subsequent images of womanly beauty and of women's roles in society would owe as much to celluloid as to the artist's brush or pen.

5

Evangeline on Stage, in Song, and on the Silver Screen

As a playwright Henry Wadsworth Longfellow is known mostly for the closet drama, *The Spanish Student* (1842), which was never staged professionally, but which famously drew the ire of Edgar Allan Poe, who accused him of plagiarism (see page). As Walter I. Meserve notes, however, drama "held a certain fascination for Longfellow, who could write dialogue consistent with that produced by poetic dramatists during his lifetime and superior to the work of many of them" (180). Meserve aptly describes *The Spanish Student* as a "romantic melodrama" with a clearly defined hero, villain, and damsel in distress. Newton Arvin describes the piece as "essentially lyrical; a dramatic poem, at the best, not a play" (85). Longfellow's continuing infatuation with poetic drama is demonstrated in the *New England Tragedies,* "John Endicott" and "Giles Corey of the Salem Farms" (1868), which Arvin describes as "purely literary performances" and closet dramas "in the most thoroughgoing sense" (259). The lengthy fragment *MichaelAngelo,* started in 1872, testifies to Longfellow's engagement with drama into his last years. His journals and letters indicate that he attended plays and opera frequently, but was not an avid theatergoer.

It would be appropriate to say that Longfellow was more interested in "the dramatic" than he was in theater, and it may be fitting that his greatest stage success was not one of his dramatic poems, or even *The Courtship of Miles Standish,* which William Dean Howells dramatized in 1882 as *Priscilla: A Comedy* (it was never staged professionally). *Evangeline* (1847) was adapted for the stage as early as 1860, but the immensely popular poem experienced greater contemporary success, ironically, in a parody or musical burlesque version than as "legitimate" theater.

Brenda Murphy describes "legitimate drama" in the United States in the mid–nineteenth century as a "minor enterprise" among such other stage productions as minstrel shows, burlesque, and vaudeville, which reflect the "peculiarly American genre of the 'extravaganza'" (3). Murphy's list of six categories of drama dominant prior to the emergence of realist theater in the 1880s suggests why *Evangeline* might have been a compelling text for adaptation: the one-character vehicle (the now lost 1860 adaptation was prepared by Sidney Frances Bateman for her daughter, and *Evangeline* is sometimes regarded as a one-character poem); plays based on American history, legend, or literature (the single category the poem fits best); the melodrama (although, *not* technically a melodrama for several reasons, including the lack of a proper villain, the poem is sentimental and in many ways "melodramatic"); the local-color play (the poem focuses on shifting scenery and locale, arguably at the expense of plot action); the Western play (a significant portion of the poem involves Evangeline's search for her lost love on the western frontier); the drama of contemporary life (that is, the "domestic" drama that comes closest to realist tenets—the only one of the six categories from which *Evangeline* would be excluded, inasmuch as the opening domestic scenes are clearly depicted as those of another place and time (the mythic Golden Age in Acadia).

In effect, as a stage piece *Evangeline* had five lives: as "legitimate theater," as a musical comedy or burlesque, as opera, as a popular school play, and as a motion picture. With the first silent film versions, which came as early as 1914 and which included a 1919 production starring Miriam Cooper, and a 1929 version with Dolores Del Rio, the stage life of *Evangeline* came to an apparent end, except for school classrooms and auditoriums. The Del Rio film, produced and directed by Edwin Carewe, is currently available in a refurbished format by Milestone Films.

Stage Adaptations

The earliest recorded dramatic rendition of the poem is that of Sidney Frances Bateman (1823–1881) mentioned above, which she wrote for her daughter, Kate, then aged seventeen. While Sidney Bateman was not considered a great actress, she is described in the *Dictionary of American Biography* as a "guiding force" in the careers of her three daughters, all of whom were actresses. The play appears to be lost, and little is known about it except that it was staged on March 19, 1860, at the Winter Garden in New York. We have no record of how Longfellow responded to Bateman's adaptation, nor to the premiere, on July 27, 1874, of the next dramatized version of *Evangeline,* and perhaps that is just as well. Longfellow was 67 years old when

John Cheever Goodwin and Edward Everett Rice collaborated in the production of an *opéra bouffe* based on the poem, which in its original form is something between a tragedy and a melodrama. The Goodwin and Rice production has the distinction of being the first American play to be specifically labeled a "musical comedy." I will deal with it hereafter.

Of greater interest from a literary point of view, and in some ways from the perspective of the stage as well, are two dramatic adaptations by practically unknown playwrights, that of Robert Traver, published in 1878 but perhaps never staged, and that of Thomas W. Broadhurst (1857–1936), first performed at the Park Theater in New York on October 4, 1913. The lost adaptation of the poem by Sidney Frances Bateman in 1860 would likely be of considerable interest here as it precedes the burlesque version.*

Traver subtitled his adaptation "A Legitimate Spectacular Drama in Five Acts," and in his brief introduction, he exculpates the printer, pointing out that the copy was set "out of a fount of Burgoise that has seen over thirty years hard service west of the Missouri." In this context the term "legitimate" likely signifies "literary" as opposed simply to "not burlesque," inasmuch as most of Traver's additions to the poem involve comic roles and music. The term "spectacular" suggests not only the use of elaborate stage scenery, but also that a certain element of spectacle is involved, as the cast of characters calls for "Villagers, Soldiers, Priests, Indians, Plantation hands, Boatmen, &c. &c. &c." (n.p.).

In one of his less sensible decisions, Traver conflates the characters of René Leblanc, the old notary ("bent, but not broken, by age [...] father of twenty children was he"), with that of Father Felician, the parish priest ("priest and pedagogue both in the village"), under the name of LaBlanche. As a result, in the midst of Act I, when Gabrial [sic] refers to the priest as "the father of twenty children, and a score of grand children," Traver runs afoul of probability, or at least of propriety. Thereafter, however, "Father LeBlance" (the orthography varies, or perhaps it's the typesetting) is consistent with Longfellow's portrayal of Father Felician, and no further reference is made to the presumably celibate priest's twenty children (n.p.).

Although Traver does create a mildly comic subplot, it was certainly not his intention to deride "Longfellow's Beautiful Poem," as the title page has it. Traver indicates that he began work on the play "some three years ago," for Joplin, Missouri, stage manager Selden Irwin who desired its completion "for representation at that place." Irwin and his actress wife Maria

**Jean Appleton's adaptation in classic French hexameters,* Évangéline: pièce en trois actes *(Paris: Alphonse Lemerre, 1891), like that of Robert Traver, is available in only half a dozen libraries worldwide.*

Rainforth were active throughout the northern Plains during the 1860s and 1870s. Harold and Ernestine Briggs, in their extensive essay on early theater in that region, indicate that Irwin and his wife were engaged for some 56 nights in Salt Lake City in 1863 (234n). The most popular play of that era was, predictably, *Uncle Tom's Cabin* (256). "It was the age of the actor," the Briggses observe, and "also an age of oratory: democratic audiences liked exaggerated roles with emphasis upon gestures. The frontier public demanded novelty, variety, and excitement" (257). Traver claims to have outlined the last four acts in a single afternoon, but "the Joplin engagement was not remunerative to the Irwin's [sic] and the work progressed no further." Traver adds, "Throughout this drama the argument of the Poet is closely followed and care has been taken not to put into the mouths of the characters a word that conflicts with the original conception" (n.p.). The text is set in prose, but direct passages from the poem cause it to slip at times into dactylic hexameter. Only a single word separates Traver's prose early in Act I from two lines of Longfellow's hexameters in 1.2: "Welcome Basil, my friend; come, take thy place on the settle, close by the chimney side which is ever empty without thee." Traver alters the adverb, replacing "always" with "ever."

In his dramatic adaptation of "Longfellow's world-famous poem," staged in 1913, Thomas W. Broadhurst (1857–1936) stays even closer to Longfellow's text, though he, too, creates a largely comic subplot. It has been his aim, Broadhurst points out in his foreword, "to do it reverently and to preserve [the poem's] beauty and its spiritual significance" (3). Meserve notes a revival of interest in poetic drama during the decade before World War I; although his adaptation is mostly in prose, Broadhurst's play is related to that revival (197). Broadhurst presents the play in twelve tableaux with a prologue and an epilogue ("This is the forest primeval") recited by the Spirit of Acadie. Obviously a more experienced playwright than Traver, Broadhurst provides elaborate stage directions, as in the following for the Prologue:

> The overture (which should breathe the whole poem with Evangeline for its main theme), dies down as the curtain rises on a dark stage which gradually lightens, revealing "Indistinct in the twilight," the Forest Primeval as described by Longfellow [7].

The Spirit of Acadie speaks "to the orchestral accompaniment of the murmuring pines." At first she is not visible; then she "steps forward and makes the direct appeal to the audience." She is "revealed as an ethereal creature clad in trailing robes of brown and green that blend into the background of the forest" (7).

The first tableau depicts a village street scene featuring a group of women singing as they spin flax, and the play proper begins with dialogue between two characters Broadhurst creates for his subplot, Toinette, "a buxom woman of twenty-four, with light hair and blue eyes," and Marie, "a black-haired, black-eyed girl of eighteen" (10). Also on stage are Louise, "a woman of twenty-six" and several children, including five year-old Felice, whose character is eventually developed in some detail.

Both Traver and Broadhurst do all they can to include Longfellow's original phrasing in their adaptations, although Broadhurst, who also cast the play in prose except for two appearances by the Spirit of Acadie and the Indian Woman's story, echoes the poem less often. His play runs about twice the length of Traver's, so he is able to accommodate more of the poem, even though his subplot is more involved and more sophisticated. In general, Traver adheres closer to Longfellow's rhythm than does Broadhurst.

Of greater importance for the audience are certain decisions Traver and Broadhurst make when it comes to inclusion or exclusion of details. Gabriel's first lengthy piece of dialogue in Broadhurst occurs near the end of the first tableau, when he rails against the British: "For nearly a hundred years we have been between the upper and nether millstones. On one side, France, to whom we are bound by the ties of blood and a common religion; on the other, England, who rules us, but sees in us only a foe" (20). Gabriel's outburst runs nearly another twenty lines, none of it taken from Longfellow. In this passage Gabriel informs the audience of an important context which is not fully elaborated in anything Traver offers; moreover, he establishes Gabriel as his father's son, as we learn in the next tableau. Both men are outspoken, and in Broadhurst's version, Father Felician counsels patience, a prevailing thematic motif in the poem, against which Gabriel argues, "We cannot longer be patient. We are men, and it is time to proclaim ourselves men; to strike for our freedom; to die, if we must to secure it" (20–21). After all, it might be argued, Gabriel is the son of "the hasty and somewhat irascible blacksmith," as Longfellow describes him in the third canto of Part One, the same man who in the fourth canto shouts wildly, "Down with the tyrants of England! We never have sworn them allegiance!" The fact that Gabriel acquires a voice in the dramatic renditions constitutes a significant departure from his muteness in the poem.

While Longfellow does describe Basil as an embodiment, before the fact, of American revolutionary zeal, he does not ascribe such bellicose sentiments to Gabriel, and Traver's mild portrait of Gabriel is altogether at odds with Broadhurst's. For American theater audiences, Broadhurst's Gabriel comes across as a patriotic figure who argues for freedom in general and for independence from England and from tyranny in particular, whereas Traver's Gabriel comes across as poetic and lyrical, a man in love, aptly matched with Evangeline, whose response echoes the sentiments of her lover.

Perhaps the most striking aspect of the dramatic versions is that Evangeline necessarily acquires considerably more of a voice than she has in the poem. For instance, the third-person narrator speaks in the poem (1.2): "Now recommenced the reign of rest and affection and stillness. / Day with its burden of heat had departed, and twilight descending / Brought back the evening star to the sky, and the herds to the homestead." In Traver's play Evangeline responds to Gabriel, who has just spoken Longfellow's words, slightly modified, notably in verb tense, "Filled is the air with a dreamy and a magical light": "Yes, Gabrial [sic], this is the hour of rest, of affection and of stillness. Day with its burdens of heat has departed and twilight descending brings back the evening star to the sky and herds to the homestead" (6).

The difference in the impact of the two plays derives most of all from how the playwrights conceived them with respect to plot structure. Here the adaptations differ considerably, as Traver's emphasis is much at odds with that of Broadhurst. In general it might be argued that the difference is implicit in their organization: Traver's five-act structure suggests the conventional mode of Freytag's Pyramid, with its exposition, rising action, climax, falling action, and dénouement, while Broadhurst's twelve tableaux suggest the popular practice of the nineteenth-century French stage, with emphasis on the "framed picture" effect (appropriately, given the highly pictorial and scenic qualities of Longfellow's poem).

Traver's first act, set up in three scenes, runs about ten pages and covers fully half of the events (all of Part One) of Longfellow's poem: betrothal scene, celebration feast, incursion of the British soldiers, and expulsion of the Acadians, which includes the burning of the village of Grand-Pré and the death of Evangeline's father. The second scene and part of the third, almost wholly of Traver's contrivance, involve some punning on the part of old Michael the fiddler. The scene features the coquettish Christy (a more American than French moniker), who delights in referring to her suitor Herman (more Germanic than French) as a "stupid fellow." The lovers have quarreled, but Michael suggests to her that "men are like fiddles: not always in tune, and an overstrain may break them. But handle them right, and they will respond to your touch and play any note you may desire" (10). They do make up, of course.

Traver's second act, also three scenes, runs only six pages and signals the haste with which he composed the later acts of the play. It opens at the cabin of Herman and Christy on a lake, as they await Evangeline's return "home" and tell their two children, Benedict, whose name echoes that of Evangeline's father, and Annette of their expulsion from Grand-Pré "many a weary year" ago. Traver describes them in the cast of characters as "hopeful scions of posterity." In this scene Baptistie (an odd version of French) proposes to Evangeline, a prospect suggested in Longfellow's poem, but not carried through (in II.1 a villager urges her to marry Baptiste LeBlanc, the Notary's son, who has loved her "many a tedious year"). In Broadhurst's play Toinette, a character somewhat similar to Traver's Christy, rather awkwardly pushes for the marriage, but Evangeline "cannot" accept (72). In both plays, as in the poem (II.2), she promptly sets out in search of Gabriel, who is said to be living with his father in Louisiana.

One curious aspect of Traver's characterization concerns what might be called the Americanization of Herman, who has acquired distinctive dialect features in his ten years of exile, as in his response to Christy's teasing about marrying a rich man: "You wouldn't have done nothing of the kind, and besides rich men ain't picked up any thicker than gold dollars" (19). Later, the practical Herman, who cannot see why Evangeline doesn't simply settle down and marry Baptistie, exclaims, "Pshaw! It's all bosh" (20). In Herman, Traver creates a conventional American voice of common sense, against which Christy effectively argues for the unfathomable mysteries of the human heart. So effective is her argument, in fact, that Herman ends up asserting, with comic vehemence, that "Evangeline shant marry Baptistie, no, not even if she wants to; the hard hearted rascal to pester the girl against her will" (20).

With the third act, Traver's patience appears to have waned, or perhaps Selden Irwin and his troupe had already left town, as he provides only a single scene, a practice he continues in the remaining two acts; and for the final three acts, he writes only three pages each. The third act is set on a Louisiana plantation ("Scene, as before the [Civil] War") at the home of Basil the blacksmith, where Evangeline finds that her lover has just departed. While the shifts in setting offer an opportunity for local color, Traver appears to be in too much haste to exploit it, and the act set in the West also falls short on dialogue, though it runs long on stage effects which center around the entrance of Michael the fiddler, dance and song, and a conclusion featuring a tableau vivant in which Evangeline kneels in prayer as Gabriel kneels similarly at the back of the stage.

Traver's fourth act is located at an Indian mission, with a mountain landscape in the background. In a touch that would have seemed quite realistic for an audience west of the Mississippi in the 1870s, he shows "Government officers issuing supplies to Indians." The initial stage action involves soldiers on guard, a priest, and Indians, in short, more spectacle. In the latter acts, in fact, Traver appears to have moved away from dialogue toward scenery, as the Indian maiden, Tame Fawn (she is an unnamed Shawnee woman in the poem), tells the story of Lillineau [sic] and the Mowas [sic], shortly after which the scene changes, disclosing a "beautiful Landscape" of an Indian village at the foot of a mountain, cascades, a stream, and "a 'dreamy and a mystical splendor' over all" (29).

The final act brings Evangeline to the streets of Philadelphia where, coincidentally, young Benedict (now "Benny") and Annette (similarly Americanized as "Netty"), now college age, attend a boarding school and are awaiting a visit from their parents, Herman and Christy. As Herman and Benedict support the dying Gabriel, Father LeBlance [sic] appears with Evangeline, who is a Sister of Charity (founded a century before the anachronistic Sisters of Mercy in the poem). The appearance of the priest is especially significant in this stage adaptation, for instead of the play closing with Evangeline's famous line, "Father I thank Thee," Father LeBlance has the last words: "Man is unjust, but God is just; and finally justice triumphs" (32). Whether this assertion of divine justice reflects Longfellow's intent may be argued, but certainly the emphasis in the poem falls rather on Evangeline's stoic acceptance and self-abnegation than on the tension between human and divine justice. Diminishing the Roman Catholic impact at this crucial moment, Broadhurst omits the priest altogether, introduces a Quaker doctor and nurse in his final tableau, and ends the play with Evangeline's line, as in the poem.

Throughout, Broadhurst's adaptation is closer than Traver's to the plot structure of the poem. Prior to each of the twelve tableaux he quotes a dozen or so lines from the poem, though these apparently were not intended to be read in production. In his foreword Broadhurst suggests "The play may be used to advantage in the study of the poem, especially by such as are interested in the drama. It will afford them an opportunity to note what use the adapter has made of his material; what he has omitted; what condensed; what he has rearranged; what characters he has added and what dialogue, and to ascertain why he thought best to do so" (4). Clearly, then, the play as published by Samuel French in 1926 is intended as a reading text as well as a script. In addition to villagers, soldiers, Indians, and guides, Broadhurst creates no fewer than twenty-four speaking parts (there are fifteen in Traver's adaptation). Longfellow creates nine speaking parts in his poem, not including Gabriel, who never utters a word.

The limitations of space prevent a close analysis of each tableau, but some additional observations are in order. First, Broadhurst keeps the balance of his tableaux closer to what one might expect, given the two-part structure of the poem. He devotes five tableaux to the first part, which is divided into five cantos in Longfellow's poem. The first tableau has been adequately described above. In the second, which has been mentioned in passing, the betrothal is contracted at Benedict's house after he and Basil argue over the British presence, as in the poem. In the third tableau, which deals with the betrothal feast, Basil teases René the notary about his many children, and Benedict adds that if all were as productive as the notary, "there would soon be no room in Acadie to swing a scythe" (42). When Gabriel tells her to kiss René Leblanc, Evangeline demurely replies, "It's a wife's duty to obey, and I will do as you command, monsieur" (43). In short, Broadhurst endows her with a more lively personality than does either Traver or Longfellow. When Baptiste kisses her hand and claims that "To be by Evangeline's side is as near heaven as I ever hope to be," Evangeline wittily responds, "Hear that, Father Felician? Is not that sacrilege?" (45). When the priest sides with Baptiste, saying, "He has just kissed the hand of an angel," she "throws up her hands in mock despair," and replies, "Oh, you men! You are all alike!" (45).

This humanization or demythologization, perhaps even "desacralization," of Evangeline in the early scenes of the play is significant. More than in Traver's adaptation, and even more than in the original poem, Evangeline acquires here a dimension of personality and character that makes her more appealing initially and that causes her eventual saint-like heroism to stand out more sharply. In Longfellow's poem we see her at first in "a celestial brightness" (I.1) and are told that an "ethereal beauty [...] Shone on her face, and encircled her form, when, after confession, / Homeward serenely she walked with God's benediction upon her" (I.1). We are informed that when at church, "Happy was he who might touch her hand or the hem of her garment!" (I.1). But in Broadhurst's adaptation, when Gabriel says, "I'll swear she's a saint," Evangeline curtseys and says pertly, "Oh, thank you kindly, monsieur!" She insists upon being a young woman.

Broadhurst, even more than Traver, adds considerably to Evangeline's speaking part; she acquires more voice than in the poem, where she is practically mute throughout Part One, uttering only the word "Gabriel" in the fourth canto and whispering two lines of encouragement to him in the fifth. In Part Two, she speaks three lines near the end of the first canto, four or five toward the end of the second, and her longest speaking part in the poem, just eight lines, in the third. In the final two cantos of the poem she breaks silence to the tune of no more than two lines (II.4, lines 1171 and 1203) and two phrases (II.5 lines 1363 and 1380). What happens in II.3 lines 941–58 is indicative of her place in the poem. Here, tearfully and rhetorically, she asks Basil of his son, "Gone? is Gabriel gone?" The "good Basil" responds in no fewer than fifteen lines. Obviously, both Traver and Broadhurst would have to augment her voice for stage production, the alternative being to have her part played by a mime. Traver generates about a dozen such passages for her, and Broadhurst offers nearly twice that amount of dialogue.

Broadhurst's fourth tableau, a relatively short one, involves the reading of the edict of British Colonel Winslow, Basil's protest, and Father Felician's intervention. After an intermission follows the highly dramatic fifth tableau, which is set on the cold, bleak beach, and in which Broadhurst gives full rein to his sense of stage action. The British sergeant struggles comically with the French names. Broadhurst introduces characters like Louise and Henriette, who are separated from their husband and father, respectively. The cheeky Toinette provides comic relief when she takes on the sergeant: "You may steal my home, and you may steal my goods, but you cannot rob me of my tongue." She "snaps her fingers under the Sergeant's nose and turns away" (55). In an unusual twist of Longfellow's plot, perhaps his gesture to Anglo-American comity, Broadhurst has the sergeant offer Evangeline a place on the boat with Gabriel, but she will not leave her father and instead offers her place to Louise and Henriette so they can rejoin their husband and father. The tableau concludes with the death of old Benedict on the beach, which completes the tragedy of Acadia, as Grand-Pré burns in the background.

Between the two major sections of the play Broadhurst inserts a brief interlude, in which the Spirit of Acadie appears on a stage before "an allegorical picture of THE DESERT OF LIFE, vast; mysterious; arid" (64). As at various places in Traver's adaptation, we are made well aware of spectacle, as we see "a procession of shadowy figures representative of The Journey of Life, from youth to old age," some of whom follow "the mirage of Love," while others "gather the flowers of Pleasure," and still others "follow the phantom of Success," and so forth. All, we are told in the stage directions, "are blind to the nameless graves and the bleaching bones of those who have gone before." The Spirit of Acadie recites lines from the opening of Part Two of the poem, "Many a weary year has passed since the burning of Grand-Pré," including a passage on Evangeline: "Dreary and vast and silent, the desert of life, with its pathway / Marked by the graves of those who had sorrowed and suffered before her" (65).

The lengthy sixth tableau depicts the Acadian camp on the shores of the Atchafalaya, complete with the vegetation described at some length in the poem: roses, cedar, trumpet flowers, grape vines, Wachita willows, water lilies, lotus, magnolias—local color with a vengeance. Now married to Pierre, Toinette continues to tease him, thus sustaining the generally comic subplot, and we find she has raised Felice as her own daughter. Toinette exerts considerable impact as a secondary character. For example, after Father Felician speaks at length to Evangeline of affection and patience, and of love that is "greater than faith, stronger than death," Toinette responds, "Well, saving thy presence, Father, we can't all be saints and angels. I think a girl is foolish to wait all her life for any man. There's none of them worth it" (72). This startling practicality is incongruent with Longfellow's Romantic vision, but it is reminiscent of the role played by Herman in Traver's adaptation of the poem. Moreover, it provides an almost essential leavening for the audience of 1913, for whom the drama of sentiment was passé.

When Evangeline appears, she recounts her search for Gabriel, which has led her even back to Grand-Pré, and Baptiste reports that he has not seen him in Philadelphia. Following Evangeline's dream of Gabriel passing nearby, Basil appears and promises to pursue him with her. Broadhurst covers the wandering of Evangeline, recorded in the fourth canto of Part Two of the poem in Tableaux VII–XI of the play. These vary considerably in length and substance. The seventh constitutes a protracted account of Evangeline's arrival at the Jesuit Indian mission, where she meets an Indian woman (unnamed, as in the poem—Traver's Tame Fawn), who tells her the story of Lilinau. While Traver covers the story with a brief prose summary and a sort of dumb show "seen in mid heaven," Broadhurst sets out the story in considerable detail. Longfellow summarizes it in five lines, while Broadhurst devotes nearly a hundred lines to it, cast in the familiar trochaic tetrameter of *The Song of Hiawatha* (first published in 1855).

Tableaux VIII through X are silent *tableaux vivantes* of the same scene in autumn, winter, and spring, intended to give the audience the impression of passing time. Once more, Father Felician (Broadhurst leaves Basil out of the picture) counsels patience, reciting with very slight alteration the passage on the compass plant near the end of II.4, where a Jesuit priest spoke the lines. Evangeline again sets off with Father Felician, and Tableau XI shows a scene from "the depths of the Michigan forest: a gloomy pine wood, with trunks, riven by lightning and blackened by fire in the foreground" (95). Here they find the deserted hunter's lodge, presumably Gabriel's, and here "her courage leaves her" (95).

The last tableau parallels events of the last canto of the poem, except for the addition of the Quaker doctor and nurse, which provides an oddly clinical note that jars with the spiritual tone of the scene. Broadhurst imparts to Gabriel none of the overwrought lines that Traver puts in his mouth, perhaps signifying the decline of melodrama by this period, at least on the sophisticated stages of New York City. In her imagination, Evangeline informs the nurse just before discovering the dying Gabriel, "Over him years have no power. He is not changed but transfigured" (99). When he dies in her arms, Evangeline recites the last words of the poem almost verbatim, concluding, "Father, I thank Thee." After the curtain, the Spirit of Acadie reappears to recite the epilogue: "Still stands the forest primeval [...]" (102).

In his comments on the 1913 performance of Thomas W. Broadhurst's "tableaux," which he describes as "a polychromatic picture play," an anonymous reviewer describes the music of William Furst as "atmospheric," but concludes that the effect is that of "a dirge" (n.p.). Of the two playwrights, only Broadhurst adds dimension to major characters, specifically to Gabriel and Evangeline, as indicated above, and only he expands episodes, as with the Indian Maiden's rendition of the Lilinau story. Both writers cut René Leblanc's allegorical story on "the brazen statue of justice" (1.3), among other episodes. Both adapters reflect the possibly insurmountable difficulties of transporting a narrative poem, much of the appeal of which derives from its lyrical and imagistic qualities, to the stage.

The anonymous reviewer for the *New York Times* commended the "exceedingly pretty Scenery" of the "pictorial presentation," but complained that Broadhurst's play "is lacking in any real dramatic quality, and, save for the pictures, provides mighty little reason for enthusiasm." The review indicates that the play was offered "in Four Acts," rather than in "Twelve Tableaux," as set up in the printed version, perhaps an indication that Broadhurst decided to capitalize on the visual qualities mentioned by the reviewer in a later version of his adaptation. Thanks, "For what?" the reviewer asks, as readers of the poem must have asked over the years, when Evangeline thanks God at the end of the play: "Certainly no heroine of melodrama pursued by an unrelenting black-mustached and silk-hatted villain ever had so little cause for thanks." Overall, in fact, he argues that the play comes off as "a stretch of unrelieved and unnecessary gloom."

The most significant additions to Longfellow's poem by both Robert Traver and Thomas W. Broadhurst indicate their efforts to alleviate that "unrelieved and unnecessary gloom" by way of fairly extensive comic subplots. Perhaps coincidentally, they provide Evangeline with girlfriends, young women of her own age with whom she might converse, but who are absent in the poem. Longfellow does provide a few passages of mild humor, as when the "lordly turkey" is pictured with his "feathered seraglio" in I.1 or when in I.2 Basil tells old Benedict, "Happy art thou, as if every day though hadst picked up a horseshoe." But both playwrights perceived a need for more extensive comic relief and from the reviewer's responses cited above, it would appear that even Broadhurst's rather considerable efforts in that direction were not sufficient, at least for the theater audience of 1913. The fact, according to the reviewer, that some of the British soldiers were chewing gum would not qualify as effective comic relief.

* * *

At the present moment the most interesting addition to the Evangeline story when it comes to serious dramatic production does not qualify as an adaptation so much as a revisionist version, a "demythification" that at the same time amounts to a sort of deconstruction of Longfellow's poem:

New Brunswick–born French Canadian playwright Antonine Maillet's *Évangéline Deusse* (1975), translated in 1987 as *Evangeline the Second.* The play, featuring what Renate Usmiani calls a sort of "anti–Evangeline" (11), premiered in March of 1976 in Montreal. The eighty year-old heroine of this two-act play holds court on a park bench in Montreal, where she has been exiled, in effect, from Acadia and where she is visited by other elderly exiles, including an eighty year-old Breton man and a man who calls himself a "Wandering Jew." Something of this Evangeline's irreverent, highly colloquial dialect (as translated into English) can be had from reading just the opening lines, where she offers her own special version of Longfellow's familiar "forest primeval": "A spruce. Yep! Nothin' but a sapling just now, but some day he'll be a spruce tree. You don't get 'em around here cause this ain't a city tree. [...] Nope, they belong to the woods ... 'n to the coast. Yeah, to the sea. Look, even the salt can't kill this little bugger here" (21). The play, Usmiani observes, is "about exile and old age" and it is also "a hymn to life" (15). Evangeline comes across as a salty character in her own right, compassionate and endearing, a "new archetype," Usmiani suggests (16). As the play ends, Evangeline greets the seagulls and recognizes that "The sounds of home are here"; then she remarks, in the last words of the play, essentially a parody of Longfellow's quiet, reverent, and submissive heroine, "Who's the son of a bitch that said a person can't make a fresh start when she's eighty!" (78).

Musical Comedy

One reason the reviewer for the *New York Times* might have reacted so negatively to the "gloom" of Broadhurst's play—after all, why wouldn't a playgoer assume some gloom would be in store, given the poem—has to do with the most incongruous aspect of *Evangeline* as fare for the public stage: Its appearance in 1874 as an *opéra-bouffe* or musical comedy. According to the *Oxford Companion to American Theatre* the successful staging apparently launched the careers of John Cheever Goodwin (lyrics) and Edward Everett Rice (music): "this most popular and enduring of American musical burlesques was played incessantly for the remainder of the century, although it produced no songs of note" (211). Presumably their timing was right; as Margaret G. Mayorga has noted, following Charles M. Barras' highly successful production of *The Black Crook* in 1867, *opéra-bouffe* "spread like an epidemic" (173).

Subtitled "The Belle of Acadia," the musical burlesque in three acts features such improbable characters as "a dancing heifer, an amorous whale, and the Lone Fisherman, who is forever looking for the sea with his telescope

Figure 45. Scene from Edward Everett Rice and John Cheever Goodwin's *opéra bouffe* stage version of *Evangeline* (1874).

but never utters a word." Two actors were featured as the dancing heifer, doubtless suggested by Evangeline's "beautiful heifer" in 1.2, "(Proud of her snow-white hide, and the ribbon that waved from her collar"), which was "Quietly paced and slow, as if conscious of human affection." According to Robert C. Toll, the production featured "a woman in tights playing the male lead" and "the three-hundred-pound George Fortesque" in drag, *not* in Evangeline's role, but as a heavy elderly woman (171). The play opened at Niblo's Garden in New York, where *The Black Crook* had experienced great success, and although it initially ran for just sixteen performances, it was to hold the stage for thousands of performances by the end of the century. Some sense of the elaborate staging may be had from reference to Figure 45.

The play opens with two tenors and two basses singing as follows:

> We must be off without delay,
> The wind is fresh, the sky is clear,
> Come, boys, arouse, and work away,
> Too long we linger here [...].

They then address the audience:

> There's a man you all have heard about,
> Who poetry has written,
> That all of you have often read,
> And on it have been smitten.

Chorus:
Longfellow, Longfellow, Longfellow,
Fellow, Fellow, Fellow, Fellow [n.p.].

Any connection between what ensues and the poem as written by Longfellow is, in the parlance of movie disclaimers, "strictly coincidental." The action sprawls from Nova Scotia, to Africa, to the wilds of Arizona. Clearly, Goodwin and Rice had no interest in doing justice either to the poem, or to Longfellow, but one might argue that the parodic treatment proves how thoroughly familiar *Evangeline* was to the American audience by 1874. Clearly, however, a theater audience aware of this stage production would not likely have warmed to that of Broadhurst.

Although he offers little substantial commentary in his *Annals of the New York Stage,* George Odell traces the progress of "one of the longest-lived successes on the lighter side of our country" (193) from 1877 through 1892, mostly being content simply to list the casts of the musical comedy's many revivals. The play at Daly's Fifth Avenue Theatre, which featured a cast of sixteen (the "shapely and attractive" Lizzie Harold playing the part of Evangeline), emerged as "a mad, merry thing 'fever there was such.'" Odell notes that the part of Captain Dietrich, created by Goodwin and Rice, was played by George S. Knight, who "made a great hit in his burlesque make-up as General Benjamin F. Butler." This refers to the pompous political officer from Boston, known during the Civil War in the South, notably in New Orleans, as "Beast Butler." Although he describes the play as "a hit, of a sort," Odell adds that the "account book shows at times shockingly low returns in money" (193).

Barnard Hewitt, in his textbook, *Theatre U.S.A., 1665 to 1957*, cites a review of the "bright and sparkling extravaganza" published in 1877. Describing the play as "purely American," the critic notes that it "never once ventures upon dangerous ground" of subtle wordplay and that "The action is now and then tinged with coarseness, but never too much to be disagreeable to the most refined" (232). The reviewer describes the costuming as "bouffish, with a vengeance" (232) and observes, "The auditorium was filled, and, judging from the applause and continued laughter from the beginning to the end, Evangeline may be set down as a drawing card" (233). The actress who played the part of Gabriel, we are told, "carried off the honors," and the mute Lone Fisherman "made a great hit. [...] He gives a briny flavor to the atmosphere, and in his perpetual silence becomes ghostly, yet indescribably droll" (233).

On August 28, 1880, Odell refers to Rice's "never-dying Evangeline" playing at Haverly's Fourteenth Street Theatre, and in October of 1885 he describes an "elaborately staged" version that ran 250 performances, concluding that "Evangeline never had so glorious a career as in this season" (XII, 31). By 1888, however, Odell was referring, to "the *inescapable,* but lively Evangeline" staged at the Windsor Theatre (XIII, 467—italics mine). On March 18, 1889, he notes the 5,000th performance of the play at the Star Theatre (XIV, 27). The burlesque version of Longfellow's sentimental narrative poem was to hold the New York stage until at least 1892, a full decade after the poet's death.

The text of Goodwin and Rice's play, as the excerpts above suggest, is not very readable. Indeed, one would hardly expect a "good read" from the text of a musical burlesque. What is remarkable about the history of *Evangeline* as a burlesque theater piece is what one may infer from its considerable success. Obviously, the poem had already acquired not just popularity, but a sort of universality in its twenty-seven years of existence. Numerous illustrated editions had been published, beginning with a London edition in 1850, effectually establishing its scenic status; that is, many readers would have images in mind of how characters like Evangeline and Gabriel might look and of how certain settings might be framed. Annotated texts appeared as early as 1848, although the renowned Riverside Literature Series, which brought the poem into the public schools, generally at the eighth grade, the last year of formal schooling for most Americans at the time, did not appear until 1883 (*Evangeline* was #1 in the series). Longfellow was the best known American poet in both the United States and Europe, and by 1874 *Evangeline* had been translated into several languages, including German, Polish, Norwegian, and Portuguese (at least four different translations into French had been published).

Whether the poem had become a standard or privileged text in the ever-evolving canon, however, might be debated. From the outset Longfellow had had his detractors, like Edgar Allan Poe and Margaret Fuller, and the lead essay in The *American Review* of February 1848 by George Washington Peck (see Chapter 2) laid bare nearly every shortcoming of the poem, from meter to metaphor, with special emphasis on the heroine, whom he finds "so childish as to be silly" (12). A new "gunner" seems to have taken Poe's place, Longfellow claimed in a letter dated April 4, 1848, but "The shots do not hit" (169).

At the very least, Goodwin and Rice's comic opera version of *Evangeline* implies a critique of sentimentalism. It also illustrates what some might regard as a healthy predisposition toward iconoclasm in the American character, or at least in American theater after the Civil War. Perhaps it is in the nature of a democracy to refuse to deify, or even to lionize, its authors; or perhaps the literary parody, like the celebrity roast, constitutes an expression of genuine admiration. The burlesque version of the popular poem also indicates the broad and irreverent sort of humor often connected with the elusive American character. It is difficult to conceive of a text that would have been more dear to the heart at the time than Evangeline (although *Uncle Tom's Cabin* does come to mind), yet the parodic assault on the poem and its author was obviously quite successful. It is equally obvious, however, that the musical comedy version of the poem did not compromise its acceptance as a serious literary text, nor did it provide the poem's only dramatic identity, as its subsequent life as a theatrical vehicle would attest. Moreover, *Evangeline* was to serve as the subject for more serious musical treatment of various sorts for years to come.

Musical Performance and Opera

Among the hundreds of relevant items in the World Catalog pertaining to *Evangeline*, dozens concern widely scattered musical scores of considerable variety and rare accessibility. The poem directly and indirectly deals with music throughout, sometimes instrumental, as with Longfellow's references to Michael the fiddler and to specific tunes like "Le Carillon de Dunquerque" I.4 and other times "natural," for lack of a better term, as in his often quoted passage concerning the song of the mockingbird, "wildest of singers," at the end of II.2, which "Shook from his little throat such floods of delirious music, / That the whole air and the woods and the waves seemed silent to listen." In fact, Longfellow appears to be coaching would-be composers at this point in the poem:

> Plaintive at first were the tones and sad; then soaring to madness
> Seemed they to follow or guide the revel of frenzied Bacchantes.
> Single notes were then heard, in sorrowful, low lamentation;
> Till, having gathered them all, he flung them abroad in derision [...].

The whippoorwill in II. 3 sounds like "a flute in the woods," and in the concluding canto we are made aware of the "chimes from the belfry of Christ Church" in Philadelphia and of the distant sound of psalms "sung by the Swedes in their church at Wicaco."

The earliest music of which I can find a reliable record is "Evangeline: Song with quartette adlibitum" by J.R. Thomas and William Percival, printed in New York by William A. Pond & Company in 1855. Perhaps more momentous, but equally difficult of access, is the *Overture to "Evangeline"* by William Henry Fry (1813–1864), one of nineteenth-century America's most prominent composers of operas and symphonic music (he produced seven symphonies). Fry composed the overture for H.L. Bateman's production of the play in 1860 (now lost), written by his wife Sidney Frances and starring their daughter Kate. Other musical compositions during the century include songs by the prolific John J. Blockley (1800–1882), who specialized in setting Longfellow's verse to music. These include "Evangeline," words by Charlotte Young, in 1855; a song entitled "Gabriel and Evangeline," a vocal duet written in 1860: "Whisper, love, thy words are music"; and "Gabriel's Lament for Evangeline": "Thy last look haunts me like a spell." Other period listings include cantatas by George Carter (1873) and Virginia Gabriel (1876), and individual songs from the 1874 musical comedy by Goodwin and Rice, like the "Evangeline March," also appeared as sheet music.*

Without much doubt, however, the most renowned sheet music concerning *Evangeline* to appear in the nineteenth century was "Evangeline: Song and Chorus" (1862) by the prominent Kentucky composer William Shakespeare Hays (1837–1907), whose 350 songs are said to have sold in excess of twenty million copies.† Hays' most admired song during the Civil War was "The Drummer Boy of Shiloh" (1863). An instrumental version of the melodious tune of "Evangeline" is available online,‡ and the sheet music, illustrated with the Faed portrait of Evangeline, is also available.§ In fact, a barbershop version of the song is also obtainable making use of synthesized voices.** Having survived in defiance of Longfellow's poem, Gabriel laments that "Sweet Evangeline, My lost Evangeline" is "gone" and white-robed angels are now watching over her "green and mossy grave." Those who find this song overly lugubrious would do well *not* to introduce themselves to "The Drummer Boy of Shiloh," which is said to have been popular with both the Blue and the Gray.

French composer Xavier Leroux (1863–1919) may deserve credit for having produced the first serious operatic version of the poem, *Évangéline, Légende Acadienne en Quatre Actes*, in 1895. The first two acts take place in Acadia, the third in Louisiana, and the last in Pennsylvania. Although the chorus concludes with lines from Longfellow's prelude, it ends not with the "deep-voiced, neighboring ocean" answering "in accents disconsolate" the "wail of the forest," but more hopefully with a couplet celebrating the lovers: "Uniront dans les coeurs, uniront sous les ciel / Le nom d'Évangéline au nom de Gabriel!" (258–9). I have found reference, but no text, for *Evangeline: An American Grand Opera from Longfellow's Poem* (1906) by Charles Raymond Weills and William Edgar Weills. In the early decades of the twentieth cen-

* *In the era before radio and phonograph records, the best measure of the popularity of a song was sheet music sales.*

† *http://www.nfo.net/cal/th6.html and http://www.pdmusic.org/hays.html*

‡ *http://www.pdmusic.org/hays/wsh62evangeline.mid*

§ *http://louisdl.louislibraries.org/cdm4/document.php?CISOROOT-/AAW&CISOPTR989&RC-2; http://www.traditionalmusic.co.uklsongs-collection-fs/fs-songs%20-%200264.html*

** *http://emersonguys.com/hughlmp3slbbmp3.html*

tury *Evangeline* remained attractive to musicians, as indeed the legend does today (whether Longfellow's poem remains attractive may be another matter). Noble Cain (1896–1977) composed *Evangeline: A Cantata for Soprano and Alto* in 1929, and Irving Berlin produced the score for the song sung by Dolores Del Rio in the not-absolutely-silent film that same year, with music by Al Jolson and words by Billy Rose. Will Earhart's review of Cain's cantata published in the *Music Supervisors' Journal* for 1930 praises its "sterling worth" and recommends its use to "all teachers of public school music" (91).* Also in 1929, on the brink of the Depression, Otto Luening was asked to compose an opera for the American Opera Company for the 1931 season, and, as he puts it in his autobiography, in search of a "foolproof story" that would "make it possible for me to use folk music, that could be done effectively with a medium-sized orchestra" he decided on *Evangeline.* Seeing that the hexameters would not suit his purpose, Luening wrote his own libretto. Earhart notes in his review of Cain's cantata, above, that the composer "has not entirely freed himself" from the "restraints" of Longfellow's meter (91). Perhaps following the Dolores Del Rio film (although he makes no mention of it), Luening decided on ten scenes, "to contrast strongly musically and visually" (307). Assisted by a Guggenheim Foundation grant, he was able to visit the pertinent sites in both Nova Scotia and Louisiana.

Luening's comments on his plans for both the stage and the music are instructive: "I planned more and more dreamlike stage pictures, right up to the very last scene in a Quaker almshouse in Philadelphia" (308). "Formally, the work was like a suite and avoided symphonic developments. [...] I conceived the work as a singers' opera, with the orchestra supporting and underlying but never overwhelming the voices" (308). He decided not to emphasize the stringed instruments, but to rely on "winds, percussion, or harp to provide the main color" (309). As to the singers' movements on the stage, he promoted "nonoperatic and nontheatrical, but expressive and dignified projections of their emotional tensions"; he wished to "loosen up stilted operatic acting" (309). But no sooner had Luening completed the first two acts than he learned that the American Opera Company was folding, a victim of the Depression. "Only a long rest and much self-discipline," Luening writes, enabled him to pursue work on the third act in St. Martinville, Louisiana, along Bayou Têche. The opera was finally performed at Columbia University in May of 1948 to what Luening describes as "mixed" reviews.

**A considerably more sophisticated two-part cantata, the first part of which premiered in 1994 in Winnipeg, Manitoba, was composed by Malcolm Forsyth (the full piece premiered in 1997). It features a soprano, trumpet obbligato, women's chorus, and chamber orchestra. www.camargofoundation.org/fellowdetails.asp?recno=373-9k*

Although on opening night "the principals and the chorus were applauded after each scene" and he was "called out repeatedly at the end" (466), performance of this operatic version of *Evangeline*, with its forty-voice chorus and 25-piece orchestra, was over. Luening did perform scenes from the opera, however, on a few occasions. The same year Luening's opera debuted in New York, Canadian composer Graham George (1912–1993) saw his *Evangeline* premiere in Kingston, Nova Scotia.

In the published vocal score, Luening approximates the duration of the three acts at three hours: "For a medium-sized stage, the string section of the orchestra would balance best with 4-4-3-3-2, and double winds, trumpets, and horns, one trombone, two percussion, and harp, making a total orchestra of thirty-two" (n.p.). His cast lists eighteen characters and a narrator, with Michael the fiddler playing a non-singing role. The action begins with Benedict singing and then asking Evangeline to "Sing me the song of the Nightingale, the one your mother loved so well" (5). The sad piece, a "haunting melody" of parting and a "Song of death that awoke in my heart" (7), foreshadows the sorrowful events to follow. When Basil enters, he and his old friend Benedict debate the danger of the British ships approaching, as in the poem, and when René LeBlanc the notary appears, he sings his tragic story of the Statue of Justice, intending by it to celebrate the triumph of justice, but Benedict responds poignantly, "The poor little orphan girl!"(17). As the two men play draughts (checkers), Evangeline and Gabriel sing a duet with Gabriel praising her as "the saint whom I have chosen" and associating her with "'The sunshine of St. Eulalie," as in the poem (23).

The second scene of Act I features the wedding celebration and a choral "song of the sea" that Benedict requests, which might be regarded as foreshadowing events soon to come (42–47). In fact, as that song ends a British captain appears with the proclamation requiring all the men to meet that afternoon at the church. The act ends with more dancing, but Act II opens in the church where Colonel Winslow sings of his "present duty," which he finds "distasteful" to his "natural inclinations" (61–62). Protesting against the treachery, the chorus rush at the soldiers, but Father Felician quiets them, and they sing the "Ave Maria Stella" (usually translated as "Hail Star of the Sea"), which was adopted as the Acadian national anthem in 1884 (French lyrics were written in 1994).* The brief second scene depicts the women, packing up, fearful of their exile to Louisiana, where "thousands die of the fever each year" (81). The chaotic embarkation dominates the third

* *Words and commentary on the Acadian connection may be found online at http://en.wikipedia.org/wiki/Ave Maris Stella*

scene: Gabriel is dragged away from Evangeline as Grand-Pré burns. The chorus sings "let us bear the cross" as Benedict dies (94).

Act III is set at night on the banks of Bayou Têche and shows Father Felician helping the Acadians set up camp as Evangeline sings, "Ah, lovely moon, your silent rays shining so softly bring me new hope" (110). At the end of the scene Father Felician tells her he believes Gabriel is living one day's journey away in St. Martin. Gabriel sings a lament offstage "as in a dream" as the second scene of Act III begins, set at an Indian mission in the Ozarks. An Indian Maiden then sings the song of Lilinau for Evangeline, which causes her to wonder if she, too, is "pursuing a phantom lover" (130). Luening's phrasing is the same as Longfellow's near the end of II.4. In the brief closing scene of the opera, set five years later at an almshouse in Philadelphia, Evangeline sings "memory, memory, why do you torture me?" (133). We hear the familiar sixteenth-century German hymn, "A Rosebush Gently Blooming," often regarded as a Christmas carol, being sung offstage as the opera ends. In his stage directions Luening indicates that

Evangeline and Gabriel recognize each other and "seem through lighting to be transfigured into their former youthful selves" (132). Like Leroux and others who adapted the poem for the stage or for opera, Luening eschews Longfellow's "Father, I thank thee" for Evangeline's last words. Here, each of the lovers sings out the other's name, in the process offering a more congenial dénouement. Indeed, one might prepare a fairly substantial paper based on alternative endings for the one Longfellow offers, not so much alternatives to Gabriel's death, but alternatives, rather, to Evangeline's submissive and saint-like expression of gratitude.

At least two additional elaborate versions of the poem composed for the musical stage deserve some comment: Canadian composer and literature professor Marc Gagné's *Évangéline et Gabriel*, which premiered at Laval University (Quebec City) in 1987 and Jamie Wax and Paul Taranto's *Evangeline: The Musical*, which saw its first full-scale production at Louisiana State University in June of 1999 and was subsequently aired (October 2000) on PBS stations throughout the United States and Canada. Gagné's libretto, which he regards as "á la fois poème dramatique et livret d'opéra" (9), was published (in French) in 1994; the "concept album" of Taranto and Wax's musical, featuring eighteen songs, some of them (like "To Our Memories" and "Matt from Ville Platte") quite comical, is available on CD or MP3. The attractive songs of *Evangeline: The Musical* may be sampled online.*

Gagné's verse play, to use an apt designation, is constructed in two parts (in effect, a two-act opera), as is Longfellow's poem. The first act, set up as

* *http://cdbaby.com/ed/pauljamie*

five scenes separated by four interludes, he entitles "La tendresse et la détresse," which I would prefer to translate perhaps too loosely for the sake of alliteration as "Affection and Anguish." The second act constitutes four scenes and three interludes and is entitled "La patience et la passion" (the English cognates provide an acceptable translation here). Gagné departs from Longfellow's poem in various significant ways. For one thing, he ages Evangeline and Gabriel so that both are 25 years old; their fathers, Benoit and Basile respectively, he makes sixty, which at least seems more probable than the huge age gap that separates Longfellow's Evangeline from her father Benedict (seventeen and seventy). Gagné creates a substantial role for an Indian servant to Evangeline's family, Katery, who speaks in broken French and apparently has prophetic powers.

The scene opens with the announcement of the betrothal accompanied by dancing, and it ends with the following duet sung by Evangeline and Gabriel celebrating their love and urging each other to press the wine from that beautiful day and not let it turn into vinegar on the morrow. A similar proverb is probably implied in their promise not to toss stones into their basket of bread:

Je t'aime, ô fils/ô fille de la Grand-Prée.
Puisse du bel aujord'hui le vin
Ne pas tourner vinaigre demain,
Et dans la corbeille les pains
Ne pas virer pierres des chemins [31].

Directly after the musical interlude, we hear the voice of Colonel Winslow, and British troops appear. When the Acadians assemble at the church we become aware that while Gagné has kept the character of LeBlanc the Notary, he has eliminated a very prominent figure in Longfellow's poem, that of Father Felican. Consequently, while his version of the story clearly has spiritual dimension (the last scene is entitled "L'Extase" and both lovers speak of rapture, "ivresse" and "ravissement"), it loses most of its specifically religious—Christian—Roman Catholic identity despite the occasional appearance of lines from hymns in Latin. Gagné treats the British soldiers and Colonel Winslow harshly, featuring them in a name-calling confrontation with the Acadian women in Act 1, Scene 4. Driving them into the boats and separating old men, women, and children from the heads of families and young men, Winslow refers to the Acadians as "une race de chiens" (74). A soldier kicks Katery. Act 2 of Gagné's opera opens with another of his surprising alterations: Basil the blacksmith is carried to his grave in Louisiana as the chorus of Acadians sings the "Miserere Mei, Deus." Gabriel laments that he has now lost everything, and far from embracing their alter Eden on the American frontier, Gabriel leads the Acadians in building a boat to take them back to "le merveilleux jardin de la Grand-Prée." Leblanc and Benoît, who hopes that his wife Anne and his daughter Evangeline are still alive, present Gabriel with a sculpted image of his "fière et belle fiancée." Gabriel affixes the bust to the prow of his boat, which he names (of course) "L'Évangéline." But at that moment Katery suddenly enters with news that Evangeline is ill and her mother Anne has died up north. We then hear Evangeline's voice in a vision declaring that she is dying and that it is now "trop tard"; Gabriel replies that he is coming; she insists she is heading back to Acadia.

In the final scene, the "ecstasy," the battered Gabriel, now blind, and Evangeline, now ill, discover each other on the shore of Acadia. Their touch cures them, and they strip away their tatters, at least metaphorically discarding the limits of their physical identities, until as Gabriel proclaims, "Nous voilà femme et homme nouveaux." And not only new woman and new man, Evangeline adds, but new for a new country, "Pour un nouveau pays" (127). An ecstasy, after all, as in John Donne's poem "The Extasie," is an out-of-body experience by definition. Evangeline sees herself as a symbol of fruitfulness: "Mon corps est une amphore neuve: / Imprime en lui les stigmates de l'amour" (128). Gabriel responds enthusiastically, "ô mon avenir!"—my future, that is, my posterity. They fall into an embrace as a mist rises into which they disappear. The chorus then sings in praise of Evangeline as "Our Lady of Acadie":

> Salut, gente Dame,
> Ancêtre féconde,
> Tu créas notre âme
> D'air, de sel, et d'onde [129].

Evangeline, then, is transformed from Longfellow's Sister of Mercy into a sort of earth-mother. In effect, Gagné's opera, or verse drama, amounts to a radically revisionist version of Longfellow's poem, in some ways a repudiation of it. The influential role of Father Felician, and all of the religious convention clinging to it, is expunged. Basil the blacksmith does not discover a new identity as an American "herdsman," or proto-cowboy, and Gagné's Acadians do not embrace a new home "that is better perchance than the old one." Perhaps most significantly, even if one regards the final scene of the opera as more symbolic than literal, Evangeline and Gabriel reunite physically, and in effect, they transcend both the limits of death and of the "disconsolate" wailing that conclude Longfellow's poem.

* * *

A brief coda is in order here. Because of their narrative link to the poem, my focus in this section has favored dramatic or stage productions by various composers. But the interest in Longfellow's poem as a source for individual song lyrics has also been sustained over the past century and a half. Since the early 1990s a New Orleans–based women's band calling itself "Evangeline" has been publishing successful albums with a Cajun-folk sound. Their *Evangeline,* featuring such ballads as "Bayou Boy," "Hey, René," and "Gulf Coast Highway," dates from 1992. Probably the best known of several songs entitled "Evangeline," some of which, like Mary Gauthier's, have no apparent connection to Longfellow's heroine, is that of Emmylou Harris, in which Gabriel is metamorphosed into a riverboat gambler, "Bayou Sam from South Louisian'."*

An early version of the lyrics appears in Robbie Robertson's "The Last Waltz."† Essentially, only the theme of lost love and the fact that Evangeline is "from the maritime" (that is, the provinces of Canada, including Nova Scotia) connect the song to the poem. In her website Harris comments, "It started out being about me. But then I got this idea about Evangeline, whom we all think died for love and died young after her long travails. But the real Evangeline actually ended up being an old woman."‡ Presumably Harris has in mind such supposed historical counterparts as Emmeline Labiche, proposed by Felix Voorhies in his 1907 account, *Acadian Reminiscences,* as an historical counterpart, or one Leona "Tootie" Guirard, as recorded in Barry Jean Ancelet's essay on folkloric elements in the story (124–126). Harris also connects her "chiseled" song with the singer Mimi Farina, concluding her entry with remarks that pertain both to Farina and to Evangeline: "I also wanted to leave the song open to interpretation. I think it can be seen as a lot of things. This woman is both heroic and tragic, because everyone's life is ambiguous, really." One suspects that Longfellow would have been surprised to think that the life of *his* Evangeline might be thought "ambiguous."

Somewhat closer to the mark when it comes to Longfellow's Evangeline may be the Jerry Garcia Band's 1987 recording (music and lyrics by David Hidalgo and Louis Perez), which features a seventeen-year-old Evangeline, "the queen of make-believe," who leaves home uncertain of her destination. Hidalgo and Perez have the age right, and they impart Longfellow's black eyes "just staring / At this mean old world," but aside from that, the lines of connection run thin, as their Evangeline, "all alone" and dressed in her "new blue jeans," pursues "some American dream."§ So recent popular music does suggest the lingering attraction of the name and the legend, but it may not say much about any lingering fascination with Longfellow's poem.

* *http://www.myvideo.de/watch/1496808/Emmylou_Harris_Evangeline_1976*
† *http://theband.hiof.nolyrics/evangeline.html*
‡ *http://www.emmylou.net/ehsongs.html*
§ *http://www3.clearlight.com/~aesa/songfile/EVANGELINE.html*

Dramatic Renditions for School Performance

Exactly when *Evangeline* entered the classroom or when it became established as a text in the public schools is hard to say, but it was Number One in Houghton Mifflin's Riverside Literature Series, which began in 1883, school texts of the poem were printed in England as early as 1878, and an annotated French edition with text in English, "Enseignement secondaire des jeunes filles," appeared in 1884. The dramatic "Church Scene," which includes the reading of the king's proclamation, is excerpted in *McGuffey's Sixth Eclectic Reader*, revised edition of 1879. A German edition of 1885 is listed as "English authors for the use of schools," and an 1886 Houghton Mifflin edition is labeled "Riverside School Library." In short, within forty years of its initial publication, *Evangeline* had been firmly established as a classroom text not only in the United States, but also fairly widely in Europe. Various teachers may have produced dramatic adaptations of the poem independently over the years, but the first such effort to see print was apparently that of Mary O'Reilly, a seventh-grade teacher at the Darwin School in Chicago, which was published in 1905. In her brief preface she points out that most of the "incidents suitable for acting are at the beginning of the story" and that she felt obliged to create dialogue for Gabriel, who "said not a word the whole book through," a point that has drawn relatively little comment over the years. Although she attempted to "preserve the delicate spirit of the poem," O'Reilly found it necessary to "write more and more blank verse as the play progressed" (n.p.). She provides fairly elaborate advice for costuming, stage setting, music, and dance, and in her preface she credits F.M. Muhlig, author of *The "Evangeline" Book*, which had been published in 1894 by A. Flanagan, the same Chicago press that printed her play.

The classroom adaptation by Pittsburgh grade school teacher Olive M. Price, which was published with her other "short plays from American history" by Samuel French some twenty years later, differs considerably from O'Reilly's version. O'Reilly offers little in the way of pedagogical context, observing simply that "Dramatic expression is inherent in child nature and needs but to be guided" (n.p.). Price proceeds from fully asserted premises: that this sort of play can "stimulate the imagination of young people" (vii); that there is particular "educational value" in "teaching history and literature through Drama"; that such materials will "bring to the hearts of schoolchildren throughout the land the high idealism and love of the beautiful in thought and action that we find revealed in the pages of American history and literature" (x). To her introduction the school superintendent, William M. Davidson, added a foreword in which he offered that in addition to the "recreational" and "educational advantages to be derived from the production of plays in schools, is the humanitarian aspect of the whole matter. [...] There is no doubt that the proper enjoyment of plays by young people is one of the most effective means of developing character" (xii).

It is not essential to go much into detail with these adaptations, mostly because they involve very little of the adapter's art. Neither of the teachers, who, after all, do not claim to be professional playwrights, add characters of consequence or generate a subplot. Both adhere to the text of the poem so far as it is possible, and they present their plays in line form, and not as prose (as is the case with the adaptations by Traver and Broadhurst). O'Reilly's adaptation runs five acts, the titles of which fairly well indicate both the plot elements included and the structural balance: The Betrothal, The Mandate, The Embarking, The Search, The Search Ended. The most distinctive feature of O'Reilly's adaptation, perhaps, is her inclusion of musical scores for every act except the third: "The Chimes of Dunkirk," "Ave Maria" (Schubert, in English, not the "Ave Maria Stella," the Acadian anthem mentioned earlier), "In the Land of France" ("A la Monaco," in French), "Evangeline's Lament" (by Mary S. Conrad—music only).

Olive M. Price apportions her four acts evenly among the two parts of the poem and allocates two scenes per act, but the last act is rather slight. Despite her prefatory disclaimers regarding the staging of the play, Price does provide fairly detailed directions for each of the eight scenes. As with O'Reilly's, the structural outline of Price's adaptation is implicit in the titles of the scenes: Living-room (I.1); An orchard (I.2—site of the betrothal celebration); Interior of a church (II.1—where the proclamation is read); A beach (II.2); A garden (III.1—Basil's plantation in Louisiana); The same (III.2); Open space in the forest (IV.1—the deserted hut of Gabriel in Michigan); Room in an almshouse (IV.2). She introduces music more sparingly and does not provide scores or suggest titles of songs.

Price is somewhat more daring in her adaptation than is O'Reilly. In the first scene of the third act Price expands Gabriel's role considerably, as he tells his father of his intention to leave their plantation on Bayou Têche, as in the third canto of the second part of the poem. In Longfellow's poem it is Basil who describes his son as "Moody and restless grown, and tired and troubled." In Price's adaptation Gabriel demonstrates some self-awareness: "My heart is restless and sad, and bitter, with pain and with longing, / To wander o'er the vast earth would harmonize more with my spirit." As in the poem, his father decides to send him to "trade for mules with the Spaniards," and hence "to the Ozark Mountains" to hunt and trap. But in Price's version we also encounter Gabriel's feelings when he informs his father, "Peace I expect to find not—but relief from my troubled spirit" (75).

Like O'Reilly, Price does not attempt to follow Evangeline in her search for Gabriel, so both adapters eliminate the scene at the Indian mission, along with the story of Lilinau. O'Reilly simply ends her fourth act with Evangeline and Basil setting out on the search and begins the fifth act at the hospital in Philadelphia. Price shows us Evangeline at Gabriel's deserted cabin in Michigan in the first scene of Act IV. There, she summarizes her odyssey, and in the second scene we find Evangeline at the almshouse, as indicated above. In fact, Evangeline speaks the entire twenty-five lines of IV.1 as well as the six lines of IV.2, thus dominating the end of the play as in no other dramatic adaptation. While she is given four or five significant passages of dialogue in O'Reilly's version, Evangeline is overshadowed as a speaking character by both Basil and Father Felician, just as she is in Longfellow's poem.

Perhaps protected by their lack of sophistication as playwrights, and certainly relieved from the burden of appealing to an adult audience, with its particular demands for entertainment, the adapters of Longfellow's poem for school presentation stay much closer to the original in spirit, and often in substance as well, than do those who worked it over for the legitimate stage or for operatic or other musical performance. Mary O'Reilly and Olive M. Price also had the advantage of creating adaptations that would have a considerably shorter performance time than the plays fabricated by Robert Traver and Thomas W. Broadhurst, or than the musical comedy by Goodwin and Rice, or than the operatic productions by Leroux, Luening, Taranto and Wax, and Gagné. Of course no serious adaptation will produce a play that surpasses the sentimentality of the poem itself. The most successful adaptation of the poem to the stage would be that which would somehow capture both the pathos and the pictorial qualities of the poem while at the same time avoiding bathos and the perils of inertia.

Evangeline on the Silver Screen

In his essay, "Imagining Paradise: The Visual Depiction of Pre-Deportation Acadia, 1850–2000," Canadian historian A.J.B. Johnston notes that between 1908 and 1911 "short, one-reel adaptations of Longfellow's story" appeared, and he includes a still from the 1913 feature-length film released by a company in Halifax, Nova Scotia, now apparently lost. He indicates that the five-reel movie played "to a packed house in Halifax in 1914" (115). Miriam Cooper, who had played a role in the D.W. Griffith classic *The Birth of a Nation* in 1915, is said to have suggested the poem to her husband, director Raoul Walsh. It debuted successfully in 1919, and the Milton Bradley Company published Carolyn Sherwin Bailey's prose version along with a complete text of the poem in 1922. It includes sixteen stills from the movie

Figure 46. Miriam Cooper and Albert Roscoe as Evangeline and Gabriel (1919).

(see Figure 46, Miriam Cooper and Albert Roscoe as Evangeline and Gabriel).

In 1929, however, United Artists released its version starring Mexican-born actress Dolores Del Rio, whose girlish beauty (she was about 24 at the time; Evangeline is 17 in the first part of the poem), dark eyes and hair ("Black were eyes as the berry that grows on the thorn by the wayside, / Black, yet how softly they gleamed beneath the brown shade of her tresses!"), and spirited stage presence injected vitality into the role. Del Rio plays anything but the part of a silent, passive object of wooing or victim of circumstance. In her brief biography, *The Invention of Dolores del Rio* (2000), Joanne Hershfield says little about Del Rio's part in *Evangeline,* which qualifies as an early "talkie" because she and her co-star Roland Drew sing a couple of love songs. Hershfield's particular angle on Del Rio concerns her use, or possible exploitation, in "a variety of roles as an exotic, foreign woman" (18). For the American audience of the 1920s, she suited well: she looked French, or Canadian, or Acadian, or at least "foreign" enough. This film has been restored by the UCLA Movie and Television Archive and is available on DVD in superb condition.

Produced and directed by Edwin Carewe, who had directed more than fifty silent features since 1914, the movie was released simultaneously as a novelization by Finis Fox, the screenwriter, along with a full text of the poem. The book offers four stills from the movie, including one that shows Del Rio as Evangeline in her native costume, with prominently displayed wooden shoes, on the eve of her betrothal festival (see Chapter 4, page). The subtitle heralds the film as Longfellow's "immortal love epic." The production follows the poem closely, as a brief survey of the ten scenes selected for the DVD version (87 minutes running time) will attest. The exposition occurs mostly in "Simple Life," which begins with Father Felician and the children; then moves quickly to scenes featuring Basil at his forge; a clearly inebriated Michael the fiddler, who plays the low comic role throughout; the old notary René, who regales us with a silly jig; and on to Benedict and Evangeline, shown at her spinning wheel apparently singing. The only significant action in this scene involves the fruitless efforts of Baptiste, the notary's son, to win over Evangeline, who politely turns him away.

The second scene, "True Love," opens with Gabriel guiding his sailboat into the harbor and singing (the sound quality is marginal). Father Felician blesses Evangeline as she rushes off to greet Gabriel, who improbably scales the rocky cliffs to embrace her. She plays the coquette and comes off as a credible seventeen year-old, but when the church bells toll, both lovers drop to their knees in prayer. That Del Rio plays a more playfully flirtatious role than did Cooper may be suggested by a still from the Finis Fox text (Figure 46). Perhaps the most startling aspect of the third scene, "Wedding Plans," is the huge dowry to be attached to Evangeline in marriage: a thousand acres, some fifteen hundred sheep, and five hundred head of cattle, to touch upon the major features. This dowry contrasts comically with that of Luening's opera: fourteen cows and one bull, twenty sheep, and a keg of wine over which Basil quibbles for a second (19). The black-and-white film is tinted with a blue filter for outside scenes that occur at night; inside scenes in the evening generally are shot with a sepia filter.

In the fourth scene, "Conflicted Loyalties," the Acadians (notably Basil) react angrily to a British proclamation demanding that they join against their French countrymen in the hostilities known in the American colonies as the French and Indian War (the Seven Years War in Europe), and in the next scene, "The Crown Responds," Carewe indulges in the most spectacular moments of the story as armed British troops load into ships. Using familiar cross-cutting techniques, Carewe shifts back and forth between the festivities of the betrothal feast (Michael, for example, coaxed into action with ludicrously foamy beer) and the ominous preparations for the confrontation (Colonel Winslow questioning whether the colonial governor should act without the approval of the crown): Michael's fiddle, British drums, Acadians dancing, soldiers marching. When the deportation orders are read, both Basil and Gabriel rage "Vive la liberté!" until Father Felician calms them with his "Father forgive them" prayer. The cinematography of "Shattered Lives" is rather striking, moving us from Evangeline's fireside, in sepia tones, where she insists to the anguished Gabriel that nothing will separate them, to the very murky gray tones at the seashore, where the British are enforcing the embarkation. Hollywood must have its moments, so we are treated to a soldier stomping on Michael's fiddle and to Gabriel being restrained bloodily and hauled to the boat unconscious as Evangeline attends to her stricken father. Evangeline wades into the surf as far as she can in pursuit of her lover, but to no avail. At this point, the end of Part One of the poem, the movie has run about 55 minutes, allotting just 32 minutes for the rest of the story. Before the film moves on to the second part of the poem, however, we encounter one of Carewe's most overt departures from Longfellow, an obvious effort to appeal to the British viewer: William Pitt speaks out in Parliament passionately against the mistreatment of the Acadians.

The seventh scene, "New Life in a New Land," opens with the "cumbrous boat" carrying Evangeline and Father Felician, among others, into the bayous. This portion of the film was shot on location in and around St. Martinville, Louisiana, home of what is known as "The Evangeline Oak," perhaps the most photographed tree on the continent. "Ah! how often beneath this oak, returning from labor," Evangeline cries out in II.3, "Thou hast lain down to rest and to dream of me in thy slumbers!" Five years have passed since the deportation, and no one there has seen Gabriel for three years, but he has been seen in St. Louis and in New Orleans, as Evangeline knows, having already missed him in both cities. The movie seems to make more of Baptiste's role than does Longfellow, but the poem gives some warrant in II.1 for his sustained infatuation with her. One of the most effective moments in the movie is drawn from II.2, when the boat carrying Gabriel and the trappers passes the one carrying Evangeline on the opposite side of a narrow ait in the river. Evangeline sings (again an effort at sound in the film) and Gabriel seems to hear her, but she stops, disheartened, at just the wrong instant. The visual take on this tantalizing event in the poem works very effectively.

In the final three scenes, "In Search of Lost Love," "Hope Washes Away," and "Evangeline the Wanderer," Carewe (and Finis Fox, presumably) alters the poem once more by having Evangeline and Basil experience a whitewater accident in which Basil drowns. In some ways, this decision responds to a concern any reader might have with the poem. Longfellow makes a significant change in guides for his heroine when Father Felician is replaced by Basil, who would seem a more appropriate choice for her pursuit of Gabriel into the wilderness. But when autumn finds them at a Jesuit mission in the mountains, Basil returns to his ranch while Evangeline decides to wait for Gabriel to return. A year passes in vain. Longfellow offers an adequate reason for the separation of Evangeline from her guide, but certainly the Hollywood version has greater dramatic force. In the final scene, Carewe makes one more adjustment to the poem, declining to portray Evangeline as a nun, a Sister of Mercy, in favor of having a citizen of Philadelphia describe her as "*a* little sister of mercy." Presumably anxiety over Roman Catholic immigrants from Eastern Europe would account for this small but significant alteration. In Gabriel's last moments Evangeline again sings to him, and then she utters the only words she actually speaks (as opposed to sings) in the film: "O Father, I thank thee."

At this writing a new movie version based on Longfellow's poem in French and English by Topaz Productions in Santa Monica, California, appears to have been shelved and the website* has lapsed. Perhaps a certain degree of irony attaches to the name of a popular Canadian-born actress, Golden Globe Award nominee Evangeline Lilly, who appears in the television series *Lost*.

* *http://www.evangelinethemovie.com/news.html*

6

Reflecting on *Evangeline*

After all of the foregoing and despite my long years of infatuation with the poem, only the most perverse of imps could tempt me to undertake anything like a "definitive" reading of Henry Wadsworth Longfellow's *Evangeline.* I suspect, however, that after generations of being taken too seriously, or perhaps simply of having been too often analyzed, the poem now suffers from not being taken seriously enough. What follows might be regarded as an overly informed reading of the poem, or a set of readings—stabs perhaps—"observations" may be the adequate term. How can I not be alternately helped and haunted by the dozens of images I have examined, or the hundreds of glosses, study questions, and exercises reviewed, or the scores of variations (additions and subtractions) encountered in the poem's dramatic and musical configurations, or the hundred sixty-odd years worth of critical commentaries I've tried to digest?

Narrative and Thematic Structure

Surely somewhere in all that has preceded this chapter I have touched upon the various standard thematic takes on the poem. As an historical poem *Evangeline* may claim status similar to an historical novel, and whether present-day Acadians in Canada or Louisiana or elsewhere are inclined to embrace it or not, the poem and its legend might be justly regarded as a cultural epic. Some Canadian historians might disagree, but F.M. Muhlig's observation made more than a hundred years ago remains largely valid today: "Had the poem of Evangeline never been written, how little would we know or learn of the story of the Acadian people" (7). The poem relates the hard, if not tragic, story of a kind of ethnic cleansing, and it accomplishes that on a personal rather than a broadly generic level. It directly tells of Evangeline's misfortunes and, through her story, of those that befell the Acadian people. In his multi-volume *History of the United States* George Bancroft who, as Secretary of the Navy established the Naval Academy at Annapolis in 1845, relates the story starting from a utopian perspective he may have drawn from Abbé Reynal's account (see page):

> For nearly forty years from the peace of Utrecht [1713] they had been forgotten or neglected, and had prospered in their seclusion. No tax-gatherer counted their folds, no magistrate dwelt in their hamlets. [...] The pastures were covered with their herds and flocks; and dikes, raised by extraordinary efforts of social industry, shut out the rivers and the tide from alluvial marshes of exuberant fertility. [...] Their houses were built in clusters, neatly constructed and comfortably furnished; and around them all kinds of domestic fowls abounded. [...] Happy in their neutrality, the Acadians formed, as it were, one great family. Their morals were of unaffected purity [426].

Using such an idealized portrait as his point of departure, Longfellow offers not a simple plot summary of *Le Grand Dérangement*, but a dramatic rendition of that calamity in the form of a poem both lyrical and narrative in nature.

As Jacques M. Chevalier and others have demonstrated, we also sense something deeply archetypal when we read the poem, something about a lost paradise, a wandering-in-the-wilderness, an exile, and whether Longfellow's idealized portrait of Acadia connects remotely with the place as it actually was in the mid–eighteenth century does not seem altogether relevant. Longfellow does not attempt to recreate historical events except, as indicated in the chapters above, in the general terms an historical novelist might accept. Does the dispersal of the Acadians more closely resemble the Hebrew exodus under Moses, or the wanderings of the Trojans under Aeneas after the fall of Troy? Does Evangeline appear more like Eve, or the Virgin Mary (perhaps the Mater Dolorosa), or the Shulamite woman of *The Song of Solomon*, or Esther, or Ruth? She may well resemble each of these biblical women in various ways.

Newton Arvin posits that *Evangeline* draws its "vitality" not just from "the ancient theme of the wandering but from a peculiarly American footlooseness" (103). The "wandering" or odyssey is an exile, but at the same time a quest. The story is not limited by chronology or geography, but acquires what might be described as psychic or spiritual dimensions. Arvin finds the story and its exilic theme "archetypal." The story "depends," Arvin observes, on its "emotional tone," on its "melancholy": "The pervasive mood of the poem is one of tranquility, mildness, and peace; not the agitation of action and danger so much as the hush of revery" (104). Much of the action, he notes, occurs at night, at sunset or by moonlight. Events appear to have taken place in a distant time, certainly farther back than the ninety or so years it was for Longfellow's first readers, and an atmosphere of "dreamy nostalgia" prevails. So far as action is concerned, the poem stands a pole apart from Byron's immensely popular narrative poems of the previous generation, "The Giaour" (1813), for instance, or "The Corsair" (1814).

Edward Wagenknecht, whose work on Longfellow still may be said to dominate the critical response, makes short shrift of the plot. Having "so far said nothing of the story," Wagenknecht pleads the "extenuation that there is little or no story to tell" (90). Cecil B. Williams finds that "Longfellow did little more than expand Conolly's anecdote," but he adds that "he expanded it at great length" (151). Brian Harding describes the plot as "a distinctively American version of Longfellow's perennial theme: the exile of the modern consciousness from its Edenic state of harmony with nature" (174), and he examines that premise in some detail, but he appears conflicted, referring to it as a "tediously pathetic story" even as he celebrates Longfellow's achievement in giving it "more than sentimental force" in his "rehearsal of the archetypally Romantic theme of the fall from innocent harmony with nature to self-conscious alienation from the natural world" (175). Arvin notes that, significantly, the story ends in the city (103): "And the city, humanly speaking, proves to be quite as benevolent as the river and the prairie have been." Evangeline finds Philadelphia to be "a city of pure friendliness, filled with a Quaker spirit of equality and brotherhood that recalls to her the simple world of her Acadian girlhood" (104). Arvin also remarks on Longfellow's use of embedded episodes "to avert the monotony inherent in so simple a story" (108). Can a "simple" story make a large impact? While Longfellow's poem does not depend entirely on plot and dramatic action for its effect, I have argued implicitly throughout that the story told there, given its folkloric and mythic overtones, exerts huge weight.

The narrative's appeal derives partly from its careful structure and balance, particularly as pertains to its tonal antithesis. Part One begins quietly, even joyously, in the bucolic mode. Arvin notes the "idyllic strain" of the "Vergilian pastoral" (105). Relatively few commentators have reflected on various instances of Longfellow's modulated humor in the first part of the poem, which ends in the chaos of the forced expulsion, the burning of Grand-Pré (houses, barns, and crops), the separation of the young lovers, and the death of Benedict Bellefontaine. Such dire events do tend to overshadow such moments of understated humor as that which occurs near the end of I.1 when we are told that as one of Evangeline's suitors knocked at the door, he "Knew not which beat the louder, his heart or the knocker of iron." Evangeline's "beautiful heifer" (played up in Cheever and Rice's musical comedy version) and the self-important watchdog "Waving his bushy tail" in I.2 also count as playful if not outright comical moments.

Part Two begins quietly as well, but the emotional pitch is subdued and melancholy, never really turbulent even when Evangeline enters the "desert land" and "jagged, deep ravines" of the West, and never truly threatening despite the camps of "savage marauders" and the presence of "the grim, taciturn bear" (presumably the grizzly). The first part boasts the unities of place and time, and serene domesticity is sustained through four of the five cantos; the second part sprawls geographically and chronologically, and to some extent summary exposition and descriptive passages take the place of dramatic narration. Although Basil and other Acadians have established a new home in Louisiana, Evangeline finds her place only at the end of the poem, among the "Lonely and wretched roofs in the crowded lanes of the city" (II.5). Presumably, that is, Evangeline's home in Philadelphia is set apart from its "friendly streets" where René Leblanc lived out his last years. The recurrent characters contribute to the poem's symmetry: not only Evangeline, of course, but also Father Felician, Basil Lajeunesse, and Michael the fiddler play important roles in the second part.

As has been apparent from the foregoing chapters, Longfellow introduces a number of recurring symbols, including moonlight and the lamp, in the process of producing a tightly knit, resonant narrative. One of the most important symbolic clusters, however, has not, from what I can ascertain, been examined: the birds. In some respects *Evangeline* amounts to an amateur ornithologist's or birdwatcher's dream, from the "lordly turkey" and crowing cocks in the first canto to the flocks of wild pigeons in the last. I offer the following canto-by-canto catalog and at the same time promise *not* to reflect on the significance of each bird listed: I.1 turkey, cock (rooster), doves, eagle, swallow; I.2 cocks, pigeons; I.3 magpie; I.4 none, I.5 cock (twice); II.1 none; II.2 pelicans, doves, herons, owl, whooping crane, hummingbirds, mockingbird; II.3 hummingbird, doves, whippoorwill; II.4 swallow, crows; II.5 wild pigeons. Even a casual survey of the fifteen avian species should prompt several observations. For example, domesticated birds predominate in Part One, while they appear rarely in Part Two, even to the point that Longfellow designates as "wild" the ominous pigeons of II.5, connected with the pestilence that falls on Philadelphia. The pigeons in I.2 (ℓ. 165) are "cooing" and appear in the company of crowing roosters and the "voices of children at play," all combining in blended "harmony." No birds appear in the fourth canto of Part One, where the British troops disrupt the betrothal feast. No birds appear in the short opening canto of Part Two, but in the next canto they proliferate, with no fewer than seven species making an appearance, some of them, like the mockingbird (see below), carrying considerable symbolic weight.

I have reflected on the swallows in the preface (page 11). The magpie shows up in René Leblanc's story of the "brazen statue of Justice" (ℓℓ. 306–325), where presumably other birds have "built their nests in the scales of the balance," showing no fear of the statue's symbolic sword flashing above them. The "orphan girl," anticipating Evangeline's fate, "patiently" meets her doom when she is falsely accused of stealing "a necklace of pearls." When a storm brings down the statue, the citizens discover the traditionally thieving magpie's nest inside the statue. Human justice, in effect, is brought into question, and Basil the blacksmith appears to be troubled by the tale. Using an adjective clearly intended to echo that connected with the statue, Evangeline lights "the brazen lamp on the table."

The cocks that appear twice in the last canto of Part One figure in substantially different contexts. Ironically, early in the canto the rooster calls "cheerily" (ℓ. 525) even though the Acadian women are driving their "ponderous wains" to the seashore. Near the end of the canto, as the British soldiers set fire to the fields and village, the cocks suddenly begin to crow, "Thinking day had dawned" (ℓ. 628). Although the pelican figures in Christian iconography as a symbol of Christ, Longfellow draws no such connection with the flocks of pelicans II.2 (ℓ. 758), which appear simply to reflect the exotic world of the Louisiana bayous. Soon, however, we encounter a sort of antithetical pair of birds in the herons, which return "home to their roots in the cedar trees" at sunset (ℓ. 773), and the solitary owl, which greets the moon "with demoniac laughter" (ℓ. 774). Longfellow draws a similar antithetical pair with his mockingbird and whippoorwill (see page 9).

The "mendicant crows" of II.4 (ℓ. 1211) play only a minor role, somewhat comically connected with the squirrels that pillage the granaries at the Indian mission, but the nameless demon lover of Lilinau (pronounced to rhyme with "so"), whose story Longfellow received from H[enry] R[owe] Schoolcraft's *Algic Researches* (1839), his source for *The Song of Hiawatha*, comes across as distinctively birdlike. The "pensive and timid" (155), later "melancholy and taciturn" (156), Lilinau (Leelinau in Schoolcraft's account) pursues a tall, youthful phantom identified by his "bright green nodding plume" (157). As Longfellow tells the story, "she followed his green and waving plume through the forest, / And nevermore returned" (ℓℓ. 1148–1149). The tale fills Evangeline with "pain and indefinite terror" (ℓ. 1159), which Longfellow likens to that of "the cold, poisonous snake" that "creeps into the nest of the swallow" (ℓ. 1160). Schoolcraft's story ends with a party of fishermen some time later spying the "lost daughter" accompanied by her lover: "they saw the green plumes of her lover waving over his forehead, as he glided lightly through the forest of young pines."*

The Poetry of Part Two, Canto Three

I've offered the brief comments above in order to illustrate something of the intricacy and richness of this poem. The longest canto, II.3, runs to 189 lines, divided by textual gaps into six verse paragraphs or sections, and brings Evangeline and Father Felician to the home of Basil the herdsman on Bayou Têche. Because I find this the most moving canto of the poem, in some ways the best with respect to dramatic development, and also the one in which Longfellow writes some of his finest lines (I'm hedging a bit here with my choice of words), I intend to take a close look at it. The second part of the poem begins with the narrator's observation that "Many a weary year had passed since the burning of Grand-Pré." Various readers have wondered whether "many" years means four or five, or perhaps ten or fifteen. In line 682 we are told the "maiden" is "fair" and "young," so while she is no longer the girl of seventeen she was throughout Part One, I'm guessing she is in her early twenties. In the second canto of Part Two Gabriel and his fellow hunters, screened by clumps of palmetto, pass by the boat in which Evangeline and her party lie sleeping. Father Felician has advised her to trust her heart and "what the world calls illusions," and he speaks of their nearness to the Acadian colony in "the Eden of Louisiana." In the soft evening, Evangeline finds herself glowing with love as the mockingbird sings its "delirious music."

Might Longfellow's mockingbird at the end of II.2 be something of a kindred spirit to Keats' nightingale, or are the similarities only coincidental? Like the first-person speaker in the ode, Evangeline is held in a sort of "magic spell" as night falls, but she does not appear haunted by thoughts of mortality as is Keats' speaker-persona. Longfellow's mockingbird, "wildest of singers," seems less domesticated than Keats' nightingale, but equally delusive in nature. Both birds behave rather like Stanley Fish's "self-consuming artifacts."† Keats' speaker must reluctantly concede that unlike the "immortal Bird," he is in fact "born for death." At the poem's end, he is as "forlorn" (the word is derived from the Old English "forelore," or to lose or abandon) as the "faery lands" he mentions at the end of the penultimate stanza. That word brings him back to his "sole" (lone) self. His "fancy," or imagination, "cannot cheat so well" as he

* *In his edition of the* Algic Researches *Mentor L. Williams proposes that the story of the Ojibway maiden "was chiefly Schoolcraft's invention" and is likely connected with "contemporary Indian tales in popular magazines rather than to an authentic Indian source" (159).*

† *I refer here, in passing, to Fish's* Self-Consuming Artifacts: The Experience of Seventeenth-Century Literature *(Berkeley: University of California, 1972).*

had believed it could, and the speaker is left uncertain as the bird's "plaintive anthem fades" whether he has experienced "a vision, or a waking dream," indeed, whether he has been awake or asleep, "sleep" being the last word in the poem. "Ode to a Nightingale" is the only one of the so-called five great odes to end with a question, leaving readers suspended in uncertainty.

Longfellow's mockingbird sings while "Swinging aloft on a willowy spray that hung o'er the water," and we are told that "the whole air and the woods and the waves seemed silent to listen." But the bird's song appears ambiguous: at first "plaintive" and "sad," it suddenly soars "to madness," and Longfellow, perhaps echoing the speaker in Keats' ode in his decision *not* to fly off "charioted by Bacchus and his bards" (that is, leopards), says the mockingbird's song seems "to follow or guide the revel of frenzied Bacchantes" (worshippers of Bacchus, god of wine). Then Evangeline hears single notes "in sorrowful, low lamentation," so perhaps the bird *does* sing in tune with her melancholy. But then the mockingbird gathers up all of his notes (he is gendered male; Keats addresses his nightingale in the second person, so it is gendered neutral) and flings them "abroad in derision." Longfellow then moves into an extended analogy in the epic "as-when" manner, comparing the bird's singing to "a gust of wind" after a storm that shakes the rain from branches "in a crystal shower." The remainder of the analogy connects this simile with a musical "prelude" and with the throbbing hearts of the Acadians as they enter Bayou Têche, "where it flows through the green Opelousas." Through the "amber air" they see smoke rising from what will turn out to be the home of Basil and Gabriel, and they hear a horn and "the distant lowing of cattle." Longfellow's mockingbird, like Keats' nightingale, arouses a sense of longing and anticipation. The music has fled, but the Acadians appear to be pursuing it.

In the first movement of II.3 (*ll.* 887–910) Longfellow introduces the oaks that will figure in what has become one of the most heralded, depicted, and exploited (for tourism's sake) moments in the poem: Evangeline's address or soliloquy to the absent Gabriel beneath what has long been known as The Evangeline Oak in St. Martinville, Louisiana: "Ah! How often beneath this oak, returning from labor, / Thou has lain down to rest, to dream of me in thy slumbers!" (*ll.* 1051–52). The current live oak in question, said to be the third, stands outside the public library, which houses a handsome collection of numerous editions of *Evangeline.** In the first lines of II.3 Longfellow also introduces "Garlands of Spanish moss and of mystic mistletoe," which he

* *One of several photos of the oak is viewable online at http://www.elmada.com/photos/LA/LA01.html. A Google search will also turn up such items as a photograph of the oak in the 1927 flood and the inscription of the historical marker that connects Evangeline and Gabriel with Emmeline Labiche and Louis Arceneaux, the supposed real-life counterparts of Longfellow's characters as described in Felix Voorhies'* Acadian Reminiscences *(1907). See Chapter 2.*

connects with the Druids, effectually unifying this late part of the poem with the third line of the prelude, set in Acadia, where "the murmuring pines and the hemlocks" are said to "Stand like Druids of eld, with voices sad and prophetic." In effect, the oaks of Louisiana are linked with the evergreens of Acadia, but in this context the Druids are connected with "yuletide" and the harvest of mistletoe, obviously a more positive reference. Chevalier and Gheerbrant's *A Dictionary of Symbols* describes mistletoe, particularly when growing in oak, as a symbol of "immortality and regeneration" (662). Inasmuch as they are parasites, students of forestry may object that mistletoe has been somewhat romanticized.

For more than forty lines Longfellow carefully conceals the identity of "the herdsman" whose house stands "secluded and still" by the riverbank, thus constructing one of the several small, low-key dramatic incidents in the poem. In the opening section or verse paragraph of the canto, he carefully devises a small Eden, the focal point of which is Basil's home built of cypress logs and surrounded by "a belt of luxuriant blossoms." At the heart of the garden stand dovecots, "love's perpetual symbol[s]," which have appeared twice before in the poem, most significantly in I.1 where Longfellow tells us a dovecot's "meek and innocent inmates" are "murmuring ever of love." In II.2 he connects the dovecots with the "luxuriant gardens" of Louisiana planters along the Mississippi, whose houses stand "with Negro cabins and dovecots." Longfellow passes up the opportunity here to head off some latter-day criticism of his disinclination to make political or social pronouncements. His *Poems on Slavery* had appeared in 1842. Where, some readers might ask, is "The Slave in the Dismal Swamp," crouching "Like a wild beast in his lair"? (*Complete Poems* 27). I suspect it would be too much of a stretch to suggest that the placement of the dovecots beside the "Negro cabins" carries ironic overtones. In any event, whereas Longfellow connects the dovecots of Part One, in Acadia, with innocence and sustained love, those of Part Two, in Louisiana, he associates with slavery (implicitly) and later with scenes of "endless wooing" but also of "endless contentions of rivals."

The opening section of II.3 concludes with one of Longfellow's many similes,* this one evolved from a simple, familiar metaphor carried to the extension of a conceit. From the rear of the herdsman's house a path runs

> Through the great groves of oak to the skirts of the limitless prairie,
> Into whose sea of flowers the sun was slowly descending.
> Full in his track of light, like ships with shadowy canvas

* *In her "Reader's Supplement" for the Washington Square Press text in its Reader's Enrichment Series (1967) Hortense H. Levisohn notes "at least eighty examples" of simile in the poem (12).*

> Hanging loose from their spars in a motionless calm in the tropics,
> Stood a cluster of trees, with tangled cordage of grapevines.

In the flowery sea of the prairie a mass of trees stands like a fleet of sailing ships. The Spanish moss hangs like a gray ("shadowy") canvas from the limbs, or spars, which are entangled with grapevines and which Longfellow compares to the "cordage," or riggings of the sails. Longfellow attracts the readers' attention here, and elsewhere in the poem, by developing intricate metaphors and images from a rather mundane observation (the "sea of flowers" that constitutes the "limitless prairie"). He begins the second verse paragraph of the canto (*ll.* 911–958) by looking back at his metaphorical construct as he pictures the herdsman (Basil) on his horse with its Spanish saddle on the border of the "woodlands" and the "flowery surf of the prairie." But Longfellow is not yet finished with his prairie-as-ocean conceit. The herdsman, still not identified, raises a horn to his lips, and when he blows it, the "long white horns of the cattle" rise "like flakes of foam on the adverse currents of ocean."

Nearly any random passage from the poem could be selected as evidence that Longfellow was composing in what might almost be called the alliterative tradition of *Beowulf* or of the poet who wrote *Sir Gawain and the Green Knight*: "Then, as the *h*erdsman turned to the *h*ouse, through the *g*ate of the *g*arden / Saw he the forms of the priest and the *m*aiden advancing to *m*eet him," (italics mine). Various sound devices throughout the poem figure so prominently that readers may forget it is not rhymed. After the recognition scene, the embracing, laughter, and weeping, they fall silent and Evangeline is beset by "*d*ark *d*oubts and misgivings" because she has not seen "Ga*b*riel's *b*oat on the *b*ayous."

In his effort to explain, or perhaps to exculpate, his son, Basil's first words in response to Evangeline's weeping are, "Be of good cheer," for Gabriel left just that day. But his next words suggest some annoyance with his son: "Foolish boy! he has left me alone with my herds and my horses." But perhaps he has overstated the circumstances of his son's departure, for Basil then tells her of Gabriel's emotional distress, and he goes so far as to contradict his complaint ("he has left me alone") by saying, "I bethought me, and sent him / Unto the town of Adayes to trade for mules with the Spaniards." Basil's turbulent state of mind is reflected rhetorically in the repetition of certain key words in the following six lines (italics mine):

> Moody and restless grown, and tried and *troubled*, his spirit
> Could no longer endure the calm of this quiet existence.
> Thinking *ever* of *thee*, uncertain and sorrowful *ever*,

> *Ever* silent, or speaking only of *thee* in his *troubles*,
> He at length had become so *tedious* to men and to maidens,
> *Tedious* even to me, that at length I bethought me [...].

The italicized words double up on us as we read, most likely beneath the level of our conscious awareness: troubled/troubles, tedious/tedious. In particular the personal pronoun "thee" and the thrice-repeated "ever" remind us that at least as Basil sees it, his son Gabriel, although he anon refers to him as a "fugitive lover," does reciprocate Evangeline's love. Longfellow employs the repetitive pattern of anadiplosis (a nearly lost rhetorical term) in order to emphasize the word "ever," which occurs at the end of one line and at the beginning of the next.

Nevertheless, one can understand the impatience of some readers and commentators who might agree with Hortense H. Levisohn that Gabriel "seemed successful in avoiding her search for him." Evangeline had heard rumors about Gabriel, Levisohn argues, so "it is perfectly possible that he had heard rumors about her incessant efforts to find him" (15). I suspect our inclination to second guess Gabriel's passion for Evangeline may depend somewhat on how we read his father in this important verse paragraph. As the "good Basil" addresses the lamenting Evangeline, we are told "his voice grew blithe," which is to say lighthearted and playful. Accordingly, when he refers to his son as a "fugitive lover," I do not think we are intended to take his words darkly, but with understood, playfully ironic, quotation marks, just as we are to recognize that his last line, "We will follow him fast, and bring him back to his prison," does *not* indicate that Basil thinks marriage to Evangeline would be tantamount to incarceration.

As if to sustain Basil's efforts to encourage Evangeline's optimism and to cheer her up, the third section of the canto begins with the "glad voices" of the Acadians as they carry Michael the beloved old fiddler into the room on their shoulders. (Longfellow tells us Michael has been living in Basil's home for some time.) Into this melancholy moment in an often quietly melancholy poem Longfellow interjects social noise and gaiety as the "enraptured" Basil "Hailed with hilarious joy his old companions and gossips, / Laughing loud and long, and embracing mothers and daughters." These Acadians, who have accompanied Evangeline and Father Felician in their river and bayou journeys, witness Basil's new wealth and his "patriarchal demeanor" for the first time. Longfellow repeats the phrase "Much they marveled" both to see his new-found prosperity and to hear his advertisement for the wonders of the new land. Basil takes on something of the guise of the land agent or developer here, and he continues in that role into the next verse paragraph.

Here and elsewhere in the poem Longfellow makes us made aware of how quickly he can move the action of the plot and at the same time alter the pathos of his narrative. The fourth section abruptly shifts emotional gears: "Over the joyous feast the sudden darkness descended." The heavy sounds amount to a sort of adumbration as the joy is suddenly deadened. But just as quickly, Longfellow lightens the mood: "All was silent without, and, illuming the landscape with silver, / Fair rose the dewy moon and the myriad stars; but within doors, / Brighter than these, shone the faces of friends in the glimmering lamplight." As readers we have connected the outer world, particularly the world of silence and silvery moonlight, with Evangeline, at least since the often-quoted (and illustrated) passage in I.3 where the lovers whisper together and watch the moon rise "Over the pallid sea and the silvery mists of the meadows. / Silently one by one, in the infinite meadows of heaven, / Blossomed the lovely stars, the forget-me-nots of the angels." Clearly the lines in II.3 echo those in I.3, and some readers might even recall that I.3 ends with Evangeline extinguishing her lamp as Gabriel watches below. Moreover, as she "serenely" sees the moon pass with its "sailing shade of clouds" in I.3, Evangeline feels a "sadness" come over her soul, and the canto ends with one of the most important scriptural references in the poem: "As out of Abraham's tent young Ishmael wandered with Hagar!" The exclamation mark could well be Longfellow's way of admonishing his readers to consult their Bibles, where they will find in Genesis 21:9–21 that Hagar and her son are being sent out to wander in the wilderness. My supposition, however, may be expecting too much even of an attentive reader in Longfellow's day.

In any event, we next encounter in II.3 a transition from the lovely but haunted outside into the communal warmth and pleasure of Basil's parlor, where wine flows "in endless profusion" and where the "ci-devant blacksmith" repeats his welcome "to a home, that is better perchance than the old one!" Longfellow chooses anaphora, common to oratory, as his rhetorical tool: "Here no hungry winter [...] / Here no stony ground [...] / Here, too, numberless herds run wild [...] / Here, too, lands may be had for the asking [...]." In Louisiana, as in Canada, Basil waxes political, lashing out against "King George of England" as he had at the church in Grand-Pré. When the former blacksmith thumps the table with "his huge, brown hand," Longfellow indulges in another understated moment of humor in the poem, as Father Felician, "astounded," pauses "with a pinch of snuff halfway to his nostrils."

His guests' startled reaction to Basil's wrath apparently calms him down, for his next words are "milder and gayer," even though he warns them about "the fever," which might well compromise the appeal of his Chamber of Commerce inducements to settle. Basil's warning also foreshadows the yellow fever that will take Gabriel's life in the last canto. The possibly awkward moment, however, is averted when neighboring Creoles and Acadian planters show up. Promptly, old friends are reacquainted and new friends are made, "Drawn by the gentle bond of a common country together." In effect, Longfellow offers us the conventional immigrant's dream: free, fertile land with ample wild game and timber for building; independence from outside influences; and the welcome of already settled colonists. This section of the canto may appear hackneyed to readers of the twenty-first century, but for readers of this poem when it appeared on the first of November in 1847, only nine months had elapsed since the signing of the treaty with Mexico that ended hostilities in California; and the Treaty of Guadalupe Hidalgo, which ceded California, Nevada, New Mexico, and most of Arizona to the United States, lay three months ahead. The Oregon Territory would be officially organized in 1848. Many of Longfellow's readers doubtless shared in the settlers' enthusiasm voiced by Basil and his Acadian neighbors. The Acadians promptly celebrate the conviviality of the moment with the return of Michael the fiddler, who draws them into the "Whirl of the dizzy dance."

In the fifth verse paragraph of the canto Longfellow demonstrates again his tendency to generate a sort of pendulum-like oscillation in events and in the mood or emotional pitch. The priest and the herdsman converse while Evangeline stands "like one entranced," as in the music she hears "the sound of the sea" and an "irrepressible sadness" comes over her, reminding us again of the prelude and of the passage on I.3, when she entered the garden alone. The next dozen lines, as in I.3, are suffused with silver moonlight and silence. On the river, Longfellow writes, a "tremulous gleam of the moonlight" falls "Like the sweet thoughts of love on a darkened and devious spirit." Longfellow's diction here (not simply "moonlight" but a "tremulous gleam") and the ominously worded simile verge on paradox. We experience considerable tension between "sweet thoughts of love," on one hand, and "darkened and devious spirit," on the other. We might expect that Evangeline's spirit would be "darkened," but that it would be somehow "devious" seems unlikely; presumably, then, the spirit embodied in this simile is not hers. We may not recall Longfellow's description of the Acadians being lost in "sluggish and devious waters" from II.2 (ℓ. 767), but we almost certainly recall the "devious spirit" of line 1030 when Longfellow leads Evangeline into the West early in IV.1 where the Nebraska, which early explorers called the North Platte, follows a "devious course" (ℓ. 1083).* Nevertheless, the language is burdened with foreboding.

* *In any event, Longfellow's geography at the start of the fourth canto is erroneous, as the North Platte does not run through the Wind River Mountains of Wyoming.*

The image cluster with which we might associate Evangeline (silence, the color silver, and moonlight) reasserts itself. In the present case, the moonlight "inundate[s] her soul" with "indefinable longings" as she passes under the oak trees along a path that leads her "to the edge of the measureless prairie," yet another foreshadowing image: "Silent it lay, with a silvery haze upon it." Overhead, again in language that echoes that of I.3, where stars are described as "forget-me-nots of the angels," the stars appear as "the thoughts of God in the heavens." In I.3 the stars are seen as blossoming in the "infinite meadows of heaven"; in II.3 fireflies gleam and float away in "infinite numbers." Longfellow takes advantage of the moment to editorialize, subtly pointing out that humankind has "ceased to marvel and worship" except when dazzled by some extraordinary event like a blazing comet (Longfellow may have been thinking of Halley's Comet, which had appeared in 1835). He capitalizes on his point by making another scriptural reference, this one to Daniel 5:25–28, where Daniel tells Belshazzar that his kingdom will be divided and given to the Medes and the Persians. Evangeline calls out to Gabriel as she did while standing alone by the church cemetery near the end of I.4, but she speaks here at much greater length. The seven plus lines constitute her longest speaking part in the poem, and they assume the form of a small soliloquy, providing rare insight into her own capacity to vocalize her inner feelings. In his effort to suggest the passion of her speech, Longfellow again employs anaphora: "Ah! how often thy feet have trod this path [...] / Ah! how often thine eyes have looked [...] / Ah! how often beneath his oak [...]."

As if in answer to her lament, a whippoorwill suddenly sounds its note "Like a flute in the woods." This avian moment suggests comparison with the mockingbird's song at the end of II.2, but this bird does not end its song in "derision." The song of the whippoorwill fades "Farther and farther away," recalling again Keats' nightingale, and it ends in "silence." At that point, in one of the many instances of personification in the poem that verges on what John Ruskin would later (in 1856) dub the "pathetic fallacy," the oaks seem to whisper "Patience!" and the "moonlit meadow" sighs and responds, "Tomorrow!" The theme of patience has echoed throughout the poem, from the last lines of the prelude and from the watchdog and cows of I.2 to Father Felician's advice at the end of II.1, where we encounter a voice that mingles with "the funeral dirge of the ocean" to whisper "Despair not!" The Jesuit priest at the Indian mission in II.4 will also advise patience when he tells Evangeline to consider the symbolic compass flower, and the poem proper (minus the epilogue) refers in the last lines to the "constant anguish of patience." This poem provides one of literature's most striking examples of how the repetition of a single word, usually an abstract noun, establishes thematic focus.

In the final section of II.3 Longfellow propels the pendulum in a counter movement as the bright sun replaces the "calm and magical moonlight." At least as early as the 1916 Riverside Literature Series text of the poem, line 1060 has been glossed as an allusion to John 12:3. The flowers that "Poured out their souls in odors, that were their prayers and confessions" in the previous verse paragraph are depicted in this line as follows: "[...] all the flowers of the garden / Bathed his [the sun's] shining feet with their tears, and anointed his tresses / With the delicious balm that they bore in their vases of crystal." John 12.3 refers to Mary Magdalene and reads in part, "Then took Mary a pound of ointment of spikenard very costly, and anointed the feet of Jesus, and wiped his feet with her hair." Significantly, Longfellow shifts his frame of reference from the Old Testament in the previous section to the New Testament, where the image is more optimistic. He follows with Father Felician's playful references to Gabriel as the Prodigal Son out of Luke 15:11–24 and to Evangeline as a Foolish Virgin, one of the five "who slept when the bridegroom was coming" out of Matthew 25:1–12. Allusions of various sorts—historical, mythological, classical, folkloric—appear throughout the poem, but scriptural references predominate, with the 1962 Riverside Literature Series text accounting for no fewer than fifteen.

At this crucial juncture Evangeline changes her guide from the aged Father Felician to the younger and more robust Basil Lajeunesse, and more significantly, she heads toward the frontier with just one companion, whereas before she has been traveling with several other Acadian exiles. How swiftly Longfellow alters the emotional pitch of his poem is implied in the following five lines:

> Thus beginning their journey with morning, and sunshine, and gladness,
> Swiftly they followed the flight of him who was speeding before them,
> Blown by the blast of fate like a dead leaf over the desert.
> Not that day, or the next, nor yet the day that succeeded,
> Found they trace of his course, in lake or forest or river [...].

In just three lines we move from sunshine and gladness to the simile of "a dead leaf over the desert." Longfellow collapses time and distance in the next two lines. About 150 miles separate Basil's home on Bayou Têche from the town of Adayes, located to the north of present-day Natchitoches. At ten to fifteen miles per day about two weeks would have elapsed before they arrived "Weary and worn" only to learn "from the garrulous landlord" that Gabriel had left just a day earlier with other hunters to take "the road of the prairies."

Evangeline and Other Characters

Evangeline tells a story of love and loss, and Longfellow imposes thematic statements throughout. It tells of "affection that hopes, and endures, and is patient," and it celebrates "the beauty and strength of woman's devotion," as we are informed at the end of the Prelude. We should probably note, too, that he uses "woman's" generically; that is, Longfellow asserts his concern not simply with one particular woman's devotion, but with that of women in general, as represented by Evangeline. As Brian Harding observes, Longfellow "wrote most feelingly when his theme was the frailty and the evanescence of human happiness." He concludes that in this "tale of woman's constancy Longfellow found an opportunity to explore the theme of loss" (176). Could one conclude that the reference to "woman's devotion" makes the poem necessarily, in some ways, a feminist text, whether feminists have embraced it or not (from what I can tell, as in my prefatory chapter, "not")? After all, this poem takes its point of departure from the counter-conventional premise that the woman pursues the man, who weakly yields to his own "moody and restless" frustration. We might think of Evangeline in epic terms as the anti–Penelope, the woman who does *not* stay at home weaving while her beloved wanders a lonely exile in the dangerous world. They share the strength of their devotion, but they express it quite differently.

Another question comes to mind: In 1847, or in 1897, or in 1947, or in 2007 would this poem have been apprehended in the same way by both the young men and the young women who encountered it in school? It seems unlikely. As I imagine the matter—and to some extent as I remember it—women, or girls, tended to identify with or to admire Evangeline. But perhaps in more recent decades they have interrogated her. A better sort of question than most of those generated by the school text editors (see Chapter 3) might have been: What choices did Evangeline have to make? Can you defend her against the charge of being simply a passive conformist? Where might she have opted to act in some ways other than she did? Does Longfellow, perhaps unintentionally, critique the patriarchal culture in which Evangeline and his own contemporaries lived? Does Longfellow suggest Gabriel's motives for behaving as he does? Why does Gabriel have so limited a voice and presence in the poem?

Longfellow's selection of names for his characters resonates, conceivably to the point of suggesting allegory or archetype. Scholars have commented on Longfellow's fabrication of the name "Evangeline," perhaps from "Eve" and "angel" or more likely from "evangel," an alternative word for the gospel or "good news." Longfellow's diary entry for 7 December 1845, indicates that he also considered naming her "Gabrielle" or "Celestine" (*Life* II, 26). Consistent with the implications of "Evangeline," Longfellow associates his heroine not only with affection and patience, but from the outset with "celestial brightness" and "ethereal beauty"; near the end of the fourth canto, Part One, he tells us that "from the fields of her soul a fragrance celestial ascended"; at the end of the poem we see her with "celestial light" encircling her head like a nimbus or halo, as if she has achieved sainthood. She is explicitly connected with Saint Eulalie at the end of the first canto (see page 5). Saints Eulalia of Mérida and of Barcelona were virgins of twelve to fourteen years of age during the third century A.D. Their similar stories have fostered some doubt as to whether they are one and the same: they were gruesomely tortured for refusing to recognize the pagan deities, and at their deaths a white dove flew from their mouths. In II.1 the Acadians who urge Evangeline to marry Baptiste LeBlanc connect her with Saint Catherine of Siena, who vowed to lead a single life. In short, from one perspective Longfellow offers us something of a saint's life; one may feel tempted to consult the Roman Catholic calendar (in vain) for her saint's day.

Less explicitly stated than her putative sainthood but nevertheless evident are Evangeline's courage and daring. Not a Longfellow fan, Margaret Fuller appears to have left no record of her response to the poem, but in *Women and the Nineteenth Century*, published just two years before *Evangeline* went to press, she declares herself a champion of women's "self-dependence" (40) and expresses her "faith" in the "feminine side, the side of love, of beauty, of holiness" (41–42; see page 3). At the end of I.4 Longfellow showers his heroine with traditionally maternal traits: "Charity, meekness, love, and hope, and forgiveness, and patience," added to which she is described as being notably "forgetful of self."

And what about Evangeline's mother? Because Longfellow never mentions her in the poem, we might assume that she died in giving birth to her only child. Perhaps Benedict Bellefontaine shares that unfortunate fate with his longtime friend Basil Lajeunesse, whose wife also is never mentioned. As Longfellow describes her, Evangeline represents the dutiful daughter, and we are told she "governed his household." Although traditional Freudian and Jungian psychoanalytical approaches to literary texts have fallen into disfavor, I suspect readers still inclined in those directions will detect aspects of the Electra complex. After smiling and advising the pallid Gabriel to "be of good cheer" and assuring him that nothing can harm them if they truly love each other, Evangeline turns to her aged father and "with a smile and a sigh, she clasped his neck and embraced him, / Speaking words of endearment where words of comfort availed not" (I.5). The Freudian/Jungian reader might observe that while Evangeline also "clasped" Gabriel, it was only by the hands (she also lays her head on his shoulder). The crucial point such a reading might suggest, however, would be that Evangeline may be exercising a choice here: Might she have elected to join Gabriel and to leave her father to the care of his Acadian friends and Father Felician? The text of the poem leaves the matter open: "So unto separate ships were Basil and

Gabriel carried, / While in despair on the shore Evangeline stood with her father." The 1929 Del Rio film, as indicated in Chapter 5, perhaps responding to complaints of her passivity at this point in the poem, or of her unwillingness to abandon her father, portrays Evangeline throwing herself into the surf in pursuit of Gabriel.

Longfellow may not have nurtured conscious intentions along the lines I've intimated here, but if one grants the Freudian/Jungian hypotheses concerning this "feminine Oedipus complex," Evangeline's apparent decision to stay with her father acquires a different nuance. Implicitly, her feelings for Gabriel are conflicted. Her father's death, in effect, frees Evangeline to pursue an appropriate male, but the complex bars her from ever experiencing a normal heterosexual relationship. I mention all of this only as an intriguing avenue for investigation. Longfellow is most often regarded as the father of daughters, but at the time he was finishing this poem his son Charley was just turning three and his daughter Fanny was a newborn (she would die within a year). The three famous daughters of "The Children's Hour," "Grave Alice, and laughing Allegra, / And Edith with golden hair" (*Complete Poems* 248), were not born until between 1850 and 1855. In short, I do not suppose that the poem has much to offer along the lines of biographical interpretation.

Evangeline appears to have no connections with an older woman, either friend or relative, nor does she appear to have any girlfriends among the Acadians. Only her meeting with the widowed Shawnee woman in II.4 connects Evangeline with another of her own gender. Clearly Longfellow intends for the Shawnee widow to be a kindred spirit, as each of the women may claim to exemplify "patience as great as her sorrow." Evangeline responds to this woman's story with a mixture of pity and compassion, but at the same time she is "pleased" to share her suffering; in short, she feels the sort of empathy that will stand her in good stead when she takes religious orders. Most of the dramatic adaptations (see Chapter 5) remedy the deficit of female companionship in one way or another.

The etymological origins of Evangeline's father's name, Benedict, should be obvious even to the reader who is not, as Longfellow was, a foreign language professor at Harvard. His name indicates "good words," and his surname also suggests benevolence: Bellefontaine, the good, possibly "noble," fountain or source. This sort of elementary name symbolism would not be relevant, of course, if Longfellow had not created characters consistent with their nomenclature. Evangeline obviously fulfills the promise of all the abstract nouns applied to her. Benedict Bellefontaine, "the wealthiest farmer of Grand-Pré," dwells on "goodly acres" and despite his "seventy winters" is stalwart and "stately in form" (I.1). He is "at peace with God and the world" and he is, importantly, a close friend of Basil the blacksmith, who is "honored of all men." When the blacksmith brings dire news of the British fleet, the "jovial farmer," well aware of the ping-pong game England and France have conducted over several generations, argues in favor of "some friendlier purpose" (I.2). He is not simply naïve. When Father Felician simultaneously greets and blesses the devastated farmer in I.5, he puns on his name as he, Longfellow, and presumably the readers are well aware: "*Benedicite!*" murmurs the priest. Thirty lines later Benedict has died and the life he knew burns in the distance, ironically providing "funeral torches" for his hasty seaside burial. The death of "good Benedict" (I.4) at the conclusion of the first part of the poem constitutes the end of a certain innocent, optimistic confidence in goodness and well-being.

If the aura Longfellow creates at the end of Part One seems strangely familiar, it may owe to that greater epic concerning a way of life gone up in flames and of the exile that follows, Virgil's *Aeneid*. When Troy burns and Aeneas pursues his new destiny to found the empire that will be Rome, he parts with the old culture, first losing his wife Creusa as the fire rages (a separation reminiscent of that involving Evangeline and Gabriel) and later losing his father Anchises. The new world will be built elsewhere: in Italy for the Trojans, in Louisiana for the Acadians. Longfellow, in effect, inverts the conditions of *The Aeneid*, making not Aeneas-Gabriel the protagonist of his pocket epic, but Creusa-Evangeline. I am not inclined to push this nexus much further, and I would not claim to be the first to propose it. Certainly Longfellow's use of various epic devices, including the dactylic hexameter, extended simile, and an apostrophe to the Muse in II.1, encourages such speculations. In I.5, for example, an epic simile hints at the eventual pursuit of Gabriel into the American West:

> Then rose a sound of dread, such as startles the sleeping encampments
> Far in the western prairies or forests that skirt the Nebraska,
> When the wild horses affrighted sweep by with the speed of the whirlwind,
> Or the loud bellowing herds of buffaloes rush to the river.
> Such was the sound that arose on the night, as the herds and the horses
> Broke through their folds and fences, and madly rushed o'er the meadows.

Like Aeneas with Dido and like Penelope with the suitors, Evangeline will be tempted by another (the old notary's son Baptiste Leblanc), but she will resist. The eventual destinies of Aeneas and of Evangeline diverge considerably and yet both—as literary characters—help to define their cultures.

Edward Wagenknecht traces the name of Basil Lejeunesse to John C. Frémont's *Narratives of Exploration and Adventure* (shortened modern title), which Longfellow mentions having read in 1846 (*Life* II, 65). Frémont refers to Lajeunesse, later killed by Indians, as "my favorite man" (142). The onomastics of the matter may be a bit contrived, but I speculate that Longfellow seized upon the name partly because of its meaning in French, "youth," which fits Gabriel admirably; moreover, I suspect he took his earlier name for Evangeline (Gabrielle) as the source for the silent lover's given name. The possible connection of his name with that of the archangel, perhaps as he is portrayed in the fourth book of *Paradise Lost*, may or may not be coincidental, but traditionally, as in Milton's epic, Gabriel is the guardian of Eden (Acadia). As with Evangeline, Longfellow makes no mention of Gabriel's mother, a circumstance that would likely have contributed to the close friendship of the young lovers' fathers. As indicated in Chapter 4, Basil Lejeunesse emerges as a character considerably transformed by his experiences in Louisiana, recreating himself from blacksmith to "herdsman" (cowboy or rancher). Although we are given no hints as to the sort of man his son might have become had all gone well in Acadia—most likely he would have taken over his father-in-law's "goodly acres"—he becomes a coureur de bois, or trapper, after he leaves the "Eden of Louisiana" for the Ozarks and points west and north.

The old notary, René Leblanc, as commentators have noted from the outset, is the only historical personage in the poem except for the British Colonel Winslow. René, as film producers appear to have seen his role, balances the free-spirited Michael the fiddler, first seen seated by the cider press and described as a man possessing "the gayest of hearts and of waistcoats" (I.4). In Longfellow's day as in the period dealt with in the poem, cider was pretty much "hard cider" by definition. Bent with age, René possesses "a look of wisdom supernal." As the father of twenty children and the grandfather of more than a hundred, he represents male fertility; he is "beloved by all, and most of all by the children." His stories of the werewolf and of "the white Létiche" (III.1) parallel the Shawnee woman's tales of the supernatural Mowis and Lilinau in Part Two. He is also connected with Acadian history, having been imprisoned for siding with the English, probably in King George's War (1744–48). Like Benedict Bellefontaine, René tends to be less suspicious of the motives of the British fleet than is Basil the blacksmith. His position as notary also establishes René as a character involved with serious legal and commercial matters (the world of *negotium*), whereas Michael, "Borne aloft on his comrades' arms" in Part Two, represents pleasure and entertainment (the world of *otium*). Unless intended ironically, I do not suppose Longfellow suggests any association with the archangel in Michael's case. The fact that the Acadians, eventually to become the Cajuns, forget about other cares and give themselves to the "maddening / Whirl of the dizzy dance" of the "Dreamlike" music implies his role of helping them to escape from unhappy memories of their lost homeland (II.3).

The parish priest, Father Felician, whose name connotes happiness or felicity, is the first person we meet, just 43 lines into the poem, and he stays with us until the end of the third canto of Part Two. Longfellow uses qualifiers like "solemnly" and "reverend" in the initial encounter, which features children kissing the priest's extended hand and "matrons and maidens" hailing him "with words of affectionate welcome" (I.1). Father Felician moves slowly, and as we learn later, he is at least in his sixties. At the betrothal feast the priest sits next to the notary, Evangeline's father sits beside Basil the blacksmith, and the "jolly" fiddler sits apart and sings, his face flushed with cider. The pairing of the notary with the priest likely reflects their involvement in the most serious affairs of the community. When the blacksmith speaks out defiantly against the British in I.4, Father Felician restores order with "a gesture" of his "reverend hand." His lessons for the congregation are, of course, conventionally Christian ones of "love and forgiveness."

Throughout the poem Father Felician's name echoes ironically as he often utters his compassionate and consolatory words with a "solemn" and "mournful" (I.4) tone of voice. In I.5 while the stars overhead are "unperturbed by the wrongs and sorrows of mortals," Father Felician feels "the awful presence of sorrow" and sits beside Evangeline to weep with her. The priest concludes Part One by conducting "the service of sorrow" over Benedict Bellefontaine's seaside grave as the ocean seems to respond in terms formerly connected with him—"mournful" and "solemnly." In Part Two the priest plays the role of Evangeline's "friend and father confessor," advising her that "affection never was wasted" and imposing values Longfellow promotes in the poem: "Sorrow and silence are strong" and "patient endurance is godlike." He associates love and affection with "labor" and "work," and Longfellow tells us that Evangeline (as if she had read and taken to heart Longfellow's signature poem, "A Psalm of Life," published nine years earlier) "labored and waited." When Evangeline heads out in pursuit of Gabriel at the end of II.3 she parts from Father Felician, who presumably stays with the Acadian community in Louisiana, and takes the more rugged Basil as her guide. The Jesuit priest they meet at the Indian mission is not named, but his advice to her parallels that of Father Felician: "Patience!" He warns her that the "blossoms of passion" merely "beguile us" and "lead us astray"; only the humble compass flower can offer proper direction. But years pass, and Evangeline finds only "disappointment" (II.4).

Surely the most thoroughly transformed character in the poem turns out to be Evangeline herself. At the end of I.1 we see her, betrothed at age seventeen, as "a woman now, with the heart and hopes of a woman." By the end of II.4 she is "Faded" and "old," and "Each succeeding year" has stolen "something away from her beauty, / Leaving behind it, broader and deeper, the gloom and the shadow." We are told that "faint streaks of gray" now fall over her forehead. In II.5, although Evangeline has not forgotten Gabriel, he has become an "image" in her heart "Clothed in the beauty of love and youth." In effect, he has become an idealized memory, "not changed," Longfellow writes, but "transfigured." Meanwhile, Evangeline has settled in Philadelphia, where we learn that René Leblanc died accompanied by just one of his many descendants. Her "life of trial and sorrow" has taught her the lessons that have reverberated throughout the poem: "Patience and abnegation of self, and devotion to others." Her affection has not been "wasted," as Father Felician admonished, but "diffused," and she has become a Sister of Mercy. Longfellow distributes intimations of her saintly nature throughout the poem, and she now appears on the verge of that aforementioned sainthood itself as the "celestial brightness" that encircles her forehead is "Such as the artist paints o'er the brows of saints and apostles."

* * *

Critics and scholars have never fully agreed on just what manner of beast *Evangeline* might be generically. Is it a miniature epic? Newton Arvin denies epic status to the poem but suggests only that it is some "minor poetic form" (107). Guida M. Jackson, however, includes the poem in her *Encyclopedia of Literary Epics* (1996), where she curiously errs by twenty years in dating *Le Grand Dérangement* to 1735. Edward Wagenknecht most likely draws on Longfellow's journal entry for November 28, 1845 in calling it an "idyll," a designation that appears dismissive, at least from a 21st-century perspective; moreover, Longfellow had at that date hardly begun his writing. In fact, a year later he had just started work on Part Two of what by that time he might have come to regard as something greater than an "idyll." Critics have likened the Acadians' expulsion and Evangeline's journey to an exile, odyssey (very commonly), and exodus; Evangeline's has even been called a "sentimental journey" (Harding 174). Surprisingly few commentators have been drawn to the features of the quest motif, although the term has come up over the years, as in the outline for the Kingsley-Palmer text (see page 83).

Although I would not presume to attempt a rigorous analysis based on Joseph Campbell's *The Hero with a Thousand Faces* (1949, 2nd edition 1968), his commentary on the "monomyth" of "the destiny of Everyman" (33), adjusted for the heroine Evangeline, applies rather well. This quest-epic, or perhaps quest-idyll, at least follows the general outline of Campbell's "hero," beginning with his now familiar definition, which might (or might not) need to be refined to address the "heroine": "A hero ventures forth from the world of common day into a region of supernatural wonder: fabulous forces are there encountered and a decisive victory is won: the hero comes back from this mysterious adventure with the power to bestow boons on his fellow man" (28). Although *Evangeline* does not fully conform to Campbell's premises which, despite his observations on Demeter, seem narrowly male-centered, most of Part One of the poem is devoted to establishing what Campbell calls "the world of common day," and II.4, while it may not open readers to a "region of supernatural wonder," clearly introduces us to a realm of the exotic other, of "Billowing bays of grass ever rolling in shadow and sunshine, / Bright with luxuriant clusters of roses and purple amphoras." The "fabulous forces" include herds of buffalo and elk, wolves, vultures, "riderless horses," and "the grim, taciturn bear." Evangeline enters, too, though without elaboration, the world of "savage marauders." Indians guide her to the camp of the Shawnee widow whose stories of the Mowis and "the fair Lilinau" draw a "mysterious horror" into her mind. Does Evangeline win a "decisive victory" over the "fabulous forces," including those of the British forces in Part One? Perhaps her survival and her commitment to the values with which Longfellow connects her provide victory enough. One could certainly contend that her return to civilization in the form of "the friendly streets of the city" of Philadelphia in II.5 constitutes a return journey, and her new role as a Sister of Mercy indicates that she has indeed acquired "the power to bestow boons on [her] fellow man."

In the first canto of Part Two Father Felician reminds Evangeline that "affection never was wasted," that "Sorrow and silence are strong," and that "patient endurance is godlike." At the end of the poem a now aged Evangeline "meekly" bows her head and murmurs, "Father, I thank thee!" In some respects she acquires the "paradise within" that Milton's Michael offers to Adam and Eve near the end of *Paradise Lost*, and she achieves that end by exercising the virtues he commends: "only add / Deeds to thy knowledge answerable, add faith, / Add virtue, patience, temperance, add love, / By name to come called charity, the soul / Of all the rest."

Bibliography

Primary Sources (Editions of the Longfellow Poem)

Evangeline. Anonymous editor. London: Kent and Richards, 1848. Introduction supposedly by Longfellow.

Evangeline. Anonymous illustrator. Decorated with Leaves from the Acadian Forests. Boston: Houghton Mifflin, 1887.

Evangeline. Prose version by Carolyn Sherwin Bailey. Springfield, MA: Milton Bradley, 1929.

Evangeline. Illustrations by Jane E. Benham, Birket Foster and John Gilbert. London: David Bogue, 1849; Boston: Ticknor and Fields, 1850; New York: John B. Alden, 1892.

Evangeline. Edited by Claude Towne Benjamin. New York: Maynard, Merrill, 1893. Maynard's English Classic Series; revised in 1920 and reprinted in Merrill's English Texts.

Evangeline. Illustrated by Howard Chandler Christy. Indianapolis: Bobbs-Merrill, 1905.

Evangeline. Edited by W.F. Conover. Chicago: A. Flanagan, 1899.

Evangeline. Edited by Jane M. Cutts. Farmington, ME: D. H. Knowlton, 1911.

Evangeline. Illustrated by F.O.C. Darley. Boston: Ticknor and Fields, 1866; Boston: Houghton Mifflin, 1883, 1893; Boston: Houghton Mifflin, 1894, features the cruder 1866 designs.

Evangeline. Edited by A.J. Demarest. Philadelphia: Christopher Sower, 1911.

Evangeline. Illustrated by Frank Dicksee. London: Cassell, Petter, Galpin, 1882; New York: A.L. Burt, 1900; New York: Grossett and Dunlap, 192_.

Evangeline. Illustrated by Arthur Dixon. London: Ernest Nister, n.d.; New York: E.P. Dutton, n.d. [1907].

Evangeline.Illustrated by John Gilbert. London: George Routledge, 1853, 1856; New York: Grossett and Dunlap, 192_.

Evangeline. Edited by Edward Everett Hale. New York: Newson, 1897.

Evangeline. Edited by Arthur L. Hamilton. San Francisco: Whitaker and Ray, 1903.

Evangeline. Illustrated by H. Hirschauer, C.S. White, and Louis Meynelle. Boston: Samuel E. Cassino, 1893.

Evangeline. Introduction by Howard Mumford Jones; suggestions for reading and discussion by Harriett Tippett. Boston: Houghton Mifflin, 1962. This volume might be regarded as heir to the Riverside Literature Series, #1, edited by H.E. Scudder. Line numbers for the poem indicated in this book refer to this 1962 edition.

Evangeline. Edited by Maud Elma Kingsley and Frank Herbert Palmer. Boston: Palmer, 1909.

Evangeline. Edited by Agnes Lathe. Boston: Benjamin H. Sanborn, 1899.

Evangeline. Textual notes by Hortense H. Levisohn. New York: Washington Square, 1967.

Evangeline. Minnehaha Edition. Chicago: Smith-Andrews, 1895; Chicago: M.A. Donohue, n.d. (inscribed "Christmas 1907").

Evangeline. Edited by William Moyers. Mount Vernon, NY: Peter Pauper, 1949.

Evangeline. Illustrated by John R. Neill. Chicago: Reilly and Britton, 1909.

Evangeline. Illustrated by Violet Oakley and Jessie Willcox Smith. Boston: Houghton Mifflin, 1897.

Evangeline. Edited by Françoise Paradis. Special Commemorative Edition. Illustrations by E.A. Abbey, C.S. Reinhart, Granville Perkins, et al. Coral Springs, FL: Llumina Press, 2004.

Evangeline. Edited by Eliza Robins. London: H.G. Clarke, 1848. Listed as an "unauthorized" edition in *The National Union Catalog of Pre–1956 Imprints*, Vol. 340, 223.

Evangeline. Edited by H[orace] E. Scudder. Boston: Houghton Mifflin, 1883. Citations from the poem refer to this text, #1 in the Riverside Literature Series, as reissued in 1962.

Evangeline. Edited by Lewis B. Semple. New York: Macmillan, 1900.

Evangeline. Illustrated by Howard Simon. New York: Duell, Sloan and Pearce, 1966.

Evangeline. Edited by Lucy Adella Stone. Chicago: Sloan, 1914.

Evangeline. Edited by Eva March Tappan and Margaret Ashmun. Boston: Houghton Mifflin, 1916.

Evangeline. Edited by E.O. Vaile. Oak Park, IL: Intelligence and Week's Current, 1899.

Secondary Sources

Ancelet, Barry Jean. "Elements of Folklore, History, and Literature in Longfellow's *Evangeline*." *Revue de Louisiane/Louisiana Review* 11.2 (1982): 118–126.

Arvin, Newton. *Longfellow: His Life and Work*. Boston: Atlantic, Little, Brown, 1963.

Banner, Lois W. *American Beauty*. New York: Knopf, 1983.

Baym, Nina. *Feminism and American Literary History*. New Brunswick: Rutgers University Press, 1992.

Bordman, Gerald. *The Oxford Companion to American Theater*. New York: Oxford, 1984.

Brasseaux, Carl A. *In Search of Evangeline: Birth and Evolution of the Evangeline Myth*. Thibodaux, LA: Blue Heron, 1988.

Briggs, Harold E. and Ernestine Briggs. "The Early Theater on the Northern Plains." *Mississippi Valley Historical Review* 37.2 (September 1950): 231–264.

Broadhurst, Thomas W. *Evangeline: A Play in Twelve Tableaux*. New York: Samuel French, 1926.

Calhoun, Charles C. *Longfellow: A Rediscovered Life*. Boston: Beacon, 2004.

Chevalier, Jacques M. *Semiotics, Romanticism and the Scriptures*. Berlin: Mouton de Gruyter, 1990.

Cremin, Lawrence A. *American Education: The Metropolitan Experience, 1876–1980*. New York: Harper & Row, 1988.

Cuban, Larry. *How Teachers Taught: Constancy and Change in American Classrooms, 1880–1990*. 2nd edition. New York: Teachers College Press, 1993. Information on the historical context of the era is drawn largely from R. Freeman Butts and Lawrence A. Cremin's *A History of Education in American Culture.* New York: Holt, Rinehart and Winston, 1953.

Day, Martin S. *History of English Literature, 1660–1837.* Garden City, NY: Doubleday, 1963.

Derbyshire, John. "Longfellow and the Fate of Modern Poetry." *New Criterion* 19.4 (December 2000): 12–20.

Dexter, Edwin Grant. *A History of Education in the United States.* New York: Burt Franklin, 1971; reprint of 1906 edition.

Eliot, T.S. "The Metaphysical Poets." In *Selected Prose*, edited by Frank Kermode, 59–67. New York: Harcourt Brace and Farrar, Straus & Giroux, 1975.

Emerson, Ralph Waldo. *Selected Lectures of Ralph Waldo Emerson.* Edited by Ronald A. Bosco and Joel Myerson. Athens: University of Georgia Press, 2005.

Epstein, Joseph. "Who Killed Poetry?" *Commentary* 86 (August 1988): 13–20.

Evangeline [motion picture]. Dir. Edwin Carewe. Perf. Dolores Del Rio and Roland Drew. United Artists. 1929; DVD restored 2001.

Evans, James Allan. "Longfellow's Evangeline and the Cult of Acadia." *Contemporary Review* 280 (February 2000): 104–112.

Fox, Finis. *The Romance of Evangeline.* New York: A.L. Burt, 1929.

Frye, Northrup, Sheridan Baker and George Perkins. *The Harper Handbook to Literature.* New York: Harper & Row, 1985.

Fryer, Judith. *The Faces of Eve.* New York: Oxford, 1976.

Fuller, Margaret. *Essays on American Life and Letters.* Edited by Joel Myerson. New Haven: College & University, 1978. Includes full text of *Woman in the Nineteenth Century.*

_____. *Woman in the Nineteenth Century.* New York: Norton, 1978.

Fussell, Paul. "Sentimentality." In *Princeton Encyclopedia of Poetry and Poetics*, enlarged edition, edited by Alex Preminger, 763–764. Princeton, NJ: Princeton University Press, 1974.

Gagné, Marc. *Évangéline et Gabriel: Poème Dramatique.* Québec: Le Loup de Goutièrre, 1994.

Gilbert, Sandra M. and Susan N. Gubar. *The Madwoman in the Attic.* New Haven: Yale University Press, 1979.

Gioia, Dana. "Can Poetry Matter?" *Atlantic Monthly* 267 (May 1991): 94–98, 100, 102–106.

_____. *Can Poetry Matter?: Essays on Poetry and American Culture.* Saint Paul: Graywolf, 1992. 1–24.

_____. "Longfellow in the Aftermath of Modernism." In *The Columbia History of American Poetry*, edited by Jay Parini and Brett C. Millier, 64–96. New York: MJF Books, 1993.

Goldsmith, Oliver. "The Deserted Village." In *Norton Anthology of English Literature* Volume C, edited by Lawrence Lipking and James Noggle, 2877–2886. New York: Norton, 2006.

Goodwin, John Cheever, and Edward Everett Rice. *Evangeline: Opéra Bouffe.* Boston: Louis P. Goullard, 1877.

Gorman, Herbert S. *A Victorian American: Henry Wadsworth Longfellow.* Port Washington, NY: Kennikat, 1967; reprint of 1926 edition.

Haralson, Eric. "Mars in Petticoats: Longfellow and Sentimental Masculinity." *Nineteenth-Century Literature* 51.3 (December 1996): 327–355.

Harrington, Joseph. "Why American Poetry is Not American Literature." *American Literary History* 8 (Fall 1996): 496–515.

Haufe, Simon. *Dictionary of British Book Illustrators and Caricaturists, 1800–1914.* Woodbridge: Antique Collectors Club, 1981

Hawthorne, Nathaniel. Anonymous review of *Evangeline*. Hubert H. Hoeltje. "Hawthorne's Review of *Evangeline*." *New England Quarterly* 23.2 (June 1950): 232–235.

_____. *The Letters, 1843–1853*. Centenary Edition, XVI. Edited by Thomas Woodson, L. Neal Smith, and Norman Holmes Pearson. Columbus: Ohio State University Press, 1985.

Hershfield, Joanne. *The Invention of Dolores del Rio*. Minneapolis: University of Minnesota Press 2000.

Hewitt, Barnard. *Theatre U.S.A., 1665 to 1957*. New York: McGraw-Hill, 1959.

Higginson, Thomas Wentworth. *Henry Wadsworth Longfellow*. Boston: Houghton Mifflin, 1902.

Hirsh, Edward. *Henry Wadsworth Longfellow*. University of Minnesota Pamplets of American Writers, #35. Minneapolis: University of Minnesota Press, 1964.

Hodnett, Edward. *Five Centuries of English Book Illustration*. Aldershot: Scolar, 1988.

Irmscher, Christoph. *Longfellow Redux*. Urbana: University of Illinois Press, 2006.

Jarrell, Randall. *No Other Book: Selected Essays*. Edited by Brad Leithauser. New York: HarperCollins, 1999.

Johnston, A.J.B. "Imagining Paradise: The Visual Depiction of Pre-Deportation Acadia 1850–2000." *Journal of Canadian Studies* 38.2 (Spring 2004) 105–128.

Jones, Howard Mumford. "Evangeline: An American Idyll." *Evangeline*. Boston: Houghton Mifflin, 1962. Includes notes and Suggestions for Reading and Discussion by Harriett Tippett.

Kleinzahler, August. "Poetry's Decay." *Harper's Magazine* 284 (May 1992): 35–36, 38.

Kreymborg, Alfred. *Our Singing Strength: An Outline of American Poetry (1620–1930)*. New York: Coward-McCann, 1929.

Leroux, Xavier. *Évangéline: Légende Acadienne en Quatre Actes*. Paris: Choudens, 1895.

Lewisohn, Ludwig. *Expression in America*. New York: Harper & Brothers, 1932.

Longfellow, Henry Wadsworth. *The Letters of Henry Wadsworth Longfellow* III. Edited by Andrew Hilen. Cambridge, MA: Harvard University Press, 1972.

Longfellow, Samuel. *Life of Henry Wadsworth Longfellow*. Three volumes, including extracts from journals and correspondence. Boston: Houghton Mifflin, 1891.

Lowell, James Russell. "A Fable for Critics." In *The Complete Poetical Works of James Russell Lowell* Cambridge Edition, 113–148. Boston: Houghton Mifflin, 1896.

Luening, Otto. *Evangeline: Opera in 3 Acts*. New York: C.F. Peters, 1974. Libretto & music.

_____. *The Odyssey of an American Composer*. New York: Scribner, 1980.

Mahony, Bertha E., Louise P. Latimer, and Beulah Folmsbee. *Illustrators of Children's Books, 1744–1945*. Boston: Horn Book, 1947, 1961.

Maillet, Antonine. *Evangeline the Second*. Translated by Luis de Cespedes. Toronto: Simon & Pierre, 1987.

Mayorga, Margaret G. *A Short History of the American Drama*. New York: Dodd and Mead, 1932.

Meserve, Walter J. *Heralds of Promise: The Drama of the American People During the Age of Jackson, 1829–1849*. New York: Greenwood, 1986.

Muhlig, F.M. *The "Evangeline" Book*. Chicago: A. Flanagan, 1898.

Murphy, Brenda. *American Realism and American Drama, 1880–1940*. Cambridge: Cambridge University Press, 1987.

Odell, George C.D. *Annals of the New York Stage*. Vols. X–XIV. New York: Columbia University Press, 1938.

Onderdonk, James L. *History of American Verse (1610–1897).* New York: Johnson Reprint, 1901, 1969.

O'Reilly, Mary. *Evangeline Entertainment.* Chicago: A. Flanagan, 1905.

Parrington, Vernon Louis. *Main Currents in American Thought* Volume II, *The Romantic Revolution in America, 1800–1860.* New York: Harcourt Brace, 1927.

Peck, George Washington. "Evangeline," *American Review* (February 1848): 1–15.

Poe, Edgar Allan. *Essays and Reviews.* New York: Literary Classics of the United States, 1984.

Porter, Noah. *Evangeline: The Place, the Story and the Poem.* New York: Cassell, Petter, Galpin, 1882.

Pound, Ezra. *ABC of Reading.* New York: New Directions, 1934, 1960.

Price, Olive M. "Evangeline," *Short Plays from American History and Literature.* New York: Samuel French, 1925.

Rainey, Sue. *Creating Picturesque America.* Nashville: Vanderbilt University Press, 1994.

Ray, Gordon N. *The Illustrator and the Book in England from 1790 to 1914.* New York: Oxford, 1916.

Reid, Forrest. *Illustrators of the Eighteen Sixties.* London: Faber and Gwyer, 1928; New York: Dover, 1975.

Review of *Evangeline: A Play in Four Acts* Adap. Thomas W. Broadhurst, *New York Times Theater Reviews.* 5 Oct. 1913, sec. 3: 17.

Richardson, Charles F. *American Literature, 1607–1885.* New York: G.P. Putnam's, 1892.

Rust, Richard Dilworth. "Henry Wadsworth Longfellow." In *Fifteen American Authors Before 1900,* edited by Robert A. Rees and Earl N. Harberts, 263–283. Madison: University of Wisconsin Press, 1971.

Santayana, George. "The Genteel Tradition in American Philosophy." *Winds of Doctrine: Studies in Contemporary Opinion.* London: J.M. Dent, 1913.

Schwartz, Delmore. *Selected Essays of Delmore Schwartz.* Edited by Donald A. Dike and David H. Zucker. Chicago: University of Chicago Press, 1970.

Seelye, John. "Attic Shape: Dusting Off *Evangeline.*" *Virginia Quarterly Review 60.1* (Winter 1984): 21–44.

Stedman, E[dmund] C[larence]. *Poets of America.* Boston: Houghton Mifflin, 1885.

Thomson, Jay Earle. *The Land of Evangeline: Silent Reading.* Boston: D.C. Heath, 1924.

Toll, Robert C. *On with the Show: The First Century of Show Business in America.* New York: Oxford, 1976.

Traver, Robert. *Evangeline:* A *Legitimate Spectacular Drama in Five Acts.* Albany, MO: Freeman Print, 1878.

Usmiani, Renate. "Preface: Evangeline the Second: Antonine Maillet's Archetype of Acadian Womanhood." In *Evangeline the Second,* translated by Luis de Cespedes, 11–17. Toronto: Simon & Pierre, 1987.

Van O'Connor, William. "The Writer and the University." *Texas Quarterly* 3 (Spring 1960): 51–63.

Voorhies, Felix. *Acadian Reminiscences.* New Iberia, LA: Frank. J. Dauterive, 1907.

Wagenknecht, Edward. *Henry Wadsworth Longfellow: His Poetry and Prose.* New York: Ungar, 1986.

_____. *Henry Wadsworth Longfellow: Portrait of an American Humanist.* New York: Oxford, 1966.

_____. *Longfellow: A Full-Length Portrait.* New York: Longmans Green, 1955.

Warhol, Robyn R. and Diane Price Herndl. *Feminisms.* New Brunswick: Rutgers University Press, 1991.

Wasserstrom, William. *Heiress of All the Ages.* Minneapolis: University of Minnesota Press, 1959.

Weitenkampf, Frank. *The Illustrated Book.* Cambridge: Harvard University Press, 1938.
Welter, Barbara. *Dimity Convictions: The American Woman in the Nineteenth Century.* Athens: Ohio University Press, 1976.
Whitman, Walt. *Prose Works* 1892, Volume 1, Specimen Days. Edited by Floyd Stovall. New York: New York University Press, 1963.
Williams, Cecil B. *Henry Wadsworth Longfellow.* New York: Twayne, 1964.
Williams, William Carlos. *Collected Poems,* II. Edited by Christopher MacGowan. New York: New Directions, 1986.

Index

Abbey, E.A. 51, 111–113, 130, 143
Abraham 6, 185
Acker, Kathy 43, 57
Adam 196
Adayes 83, 183, 188
Aeneas 176
Agassiz, Louis 37
Alcott, Louisa May 20
Anclet, Barry Jean 167
Anglo-Saxon 30, 84
Aphrodite 139
Apollo 38
Appleton, Jean 146
Arceneaux, Louis 181
Arvin, Newton 49, 59, 66, 144, 176–177, 195
Ashmun, Margaret 3–4, 62, 64, 85–87, 88, 89
Atchafalaya River 83, 118, 133, 138, 153, 183
Austin, George Lowell 21

Bacchantes, Bacchus 160, 181
Bailey, Carolyn Sherwin 143, 170
Bancroft, George 176
Banner, Lois W. 94, 96, 101, 108, 115
Banvard, John 37
Barras, Charles M. 156
Barthes, Roland 13, 55
Barton, Clara 40
Bateman, Sidney Frances 145–146
Baum, Frank 114
Baym, Nina 58–59
Benham, Jane 15, 94, 95–101, 104–105, 108, 115, 117, 119, 121, 125–126, 129
Benjamin, Claude Towne 63, 67–70, 71, 72, 90
Berlin, Irving 162
Blake, William 95
Blockley, John J. 161
Boston 74, 93, 111, 138
Bowdoin College 17, 18, 21, 30, 59, 64
Brasseaux, Carl A. 42–43
Bridgman, Laura 2
Briggs, Ernestine 147
Briggs, Harold 147
Broadhurst, Thomas 146–148, 151–155, 169, 170
Bronson, Walter C. 68
Brontë, Charlotte 19, 39
Brooks, Van Wyck 48
Browning, Elizabeth Barrett 84
Browning, Robert 6
Bryant, William Cullen 41, 52, 110
Bunce, Oliver Bell 110
Byron, George Gordon, Lord; Byronic 9, 17, 35, 54, 177

Cain, Noble 162
Cajun 92, 139, 167, 193
Calhoun, Charles C. 30, 32–33, 43, 45, 51, 92
Campbell, Joseph 195–196
Carewe, Edwin 143, 171–174
Carlson, Marian R. 51
Carlyle, Thomas 18
Carter, George 161
Catholicism *see* Roman Catholicism
Chevalier, Jacques M. 55, 176, 182
Christy, Howard Chandler 95, 115, 117–118, 120, 125, 130, 141
Civil War 20, 39, 40, 63, 110, 150, 161
Clough, Arthur Hugh 65

Cole, Thomas 138
Coleridge, Samuel Taylor 48
Conolly, H.L. 38, 65, 177
Conover, W.F. 7, 63, 77–81, 86–87
Conrad, Mary S. 169
Cooper, Miriam 85, 88, 90, 142–143, 145, 170–171, 172
Craigie House 19, 64
Cremin, Lawrence A. 92
Cuban, Larry 63
Curtis, George William 68
Cutts, Jane M. 55, 59, 89
Cyr, Don 51

Dalziel, Edward 95
Dalziel, George 95
Dana, Henry Wadsworth Longfellow 50
Daniel 187
Dante 20, 30
Darley, F.O.C. 94–95, 99, 101–105, 121–124, 126, 130–135, 136, 138, 141
Davidson, William D. 90, 168–169
Day, Martin S. 35
Del Rio, Dolores 6, 85, 142–143, 145, 162, 171–172, 191
Demarest, A.J. 84, 89
Demeter 196
Derbyshire, John 31–32, 34, 35
Dewey, John 63
Dexter, Edwin Grant 40
Dickens, Charles 18, 19, 44
Dickinson, Emily 22, 58
Dicksee, Frank 61, 95, 99, 105–111, 113, 125–126, 127–128, 131–136, 143
Dixon, Arthur 94
Donne, John 26–27, 29, 166
Douglas, Ann 13
Drew, Roland 171
Druids 38, 66, 73, 85, 136, 182
Durand, Asher 138

Earhart, Will 162
Electra 190
Eliot, George 20, 21
Eliot, T.S. 26, 27, 29, 30, 71
Emerson, Ralph Waldo 15, 19, 34, 37, 138
Epstein, Joseph 23, 25–26
Esther 176
Evangeline Trail Tourism Association 42
Evans, James Allen 42, 56
Eve 54, 176, 189, 196

Faed, James 65, 99
Faed, Thomas 65, 99, 119, 161
Farina, Mimi 167
Faulkner, William 53, 92
Fish, Stanley 180
Ford, John 30
Formalism *see* New Formalism
Forsyth, Malcolm 162
Foster, Birket 15, 93, 94, 95, 97, 99, 105, 136–141
Fox, Finis 143, 172, 173
Fox, William 143
Freiligrath, Ferdinand 45
Frémont, John C. 19, 36, 192–193
Freud, Sigmund 30, 190–191
Freytag's Pyramid 149
Frost, Robert 24, 27
Fry, William Henry 160
Frye, Northrup 57
Fryer, Judith 2
Fuller, Margaret 2–3, 19, 40, 43–45, 190
Furst, William 154–155
Fussell, Paul 57

Gabriel, Virginia 161
Gagné, Marc 164–166, 170
Gale, Robert L. 51
Garcia, Jerry 167
Gauthier, Mary 167
George, Graham 163
George II (King of England) 185
Gheerbrant, Alain 182
Gibson, Charles Dana 115, 117, 118–119
Gilbert, John 15, 94, 95, 99–101, 105, 106, 108, 123–130, 141
Gilbert, Sandra 75
Giles, Henry L. 15, 39
Gioia, Dana 23–24, 29–31, 32, 35, 52–54, 55
Goethe 4, 18, 44, 53
Goldsmith, Oliver 39, 67
Goodwin, John Cheever 21, 145–146, 156, 161, 170, 177
Gorman, Herbert S. 15
Gregory, Horace 50–51
Grierson, Herbert J. 29
Griffith, D.W. 170
Gubar, Susan 75
Guggenheim Foundation 25, 162
Guirard, Leona "Tootie" 167

Hagar 6, 185
Hale, Edward Everett 63, 70–74, 77, 78, 81, 84, 86, 88
Haliburton, Thomas C. 61, 64, 74
Halley's Comet 187
Hamilton, Arthur 84, 89
Haralson, Eric L. 24, 33, 34
Harding, Brian 177, 189, 195
Hardy, Thomas 21, 57
Harper, Frances E.W. 52
Harrington, John 27, 28

Harris, Emmylou 16, 167
Harvard University v, 18, 20, 21, 25, 26, 30, 44, 59, 64, 69, 70, 91, 191
Haufe, Simon 95
Hawthorne, Manning 50
Hawthorne, Nathaniel 13, 17, 18, 19, 38, 40, 44–45, 46, 50, 65, 75, 98
Hays, William Shakespeare 161
Hemingway, Ernest 32, 91
Herbert, George 29
Herbin, John Frederic 42
Herndl, Diane Price 14
Herrick, Robert 26, 29
Hershfield, Joanne 171
Hidalgo, David 167
Higginson, Thomas Wentworth 58
Hilen, Andrew 51
H[ines], F[red] 114
Hirschauer, H. 108, 110
Hirsh, Edward L. 49
Hodnett, Edward 99
Holmes, Oliver Wendell 20, 46, 66
Homer, Homeric 37, 56, 65, 67
Howe, Samuel G. 2, 38, 46
Howells, William Dean 21, 144
Hudson River School 138
Hughes, Libby 51

Irmscher, Christoph 23, 29–30, 32–33, 51
Irving, Washington 18
Irwin, Selden 146–147, 150
Ishmael 74, 185

Jackson, Guida M. 195
James, Henry 3, 21
James, William 34
Jarrell, Randall 24, 26–27
Jesuit 11, 12, 154, 174, 187, 194
Johnson, Charles Howard 94
Johnston, A.J.B. 170
Jolson, Al 162
Jones, Howard Mumford 81, 91–92
Jonson, Ben 29, 54
Jungian 190–191

Keats, John 80, 180–181, 187
King George's War 193
Kingsley, Maud Elma 7, 63, 82–84, 89
Kleinzahler, August 24–25
Kreymborg, Alfred 48

Labiche, Emmeline 167, 181
Lathe, Agnes 63, 74–76, 77, 78, 81
Lermontov, Mikhail 54
Leroux, Xavier 161, 164, 170
Létiche 193
Levisohn, Hortense H. 182, 184
Lewisohn, Ludwig 48, 49
Lilinau 11, 73, 119, 150, 154, 155, 164, 170, 179, 193, 196
Lilly, Evangeline 174
Longfellow, Alice Mary (daughter) 19, 41, 64
Longfellow, Anne Allegra (daughter) 20, 97
Longfellow, Brenda 50
Longfellow, Charles "Charley" Appleton (son) 19, 20
Longfellow, Edith (daughter) 19
Longfellow, Ernest Wadsworth (son) 19
Longfellow, Frances "Fanny" (daughter) 19, 38
Longfellow, Frances "Fanny" Appleton (second wife) 18, 19, 20
Longfellow, Layne 51
Longfellow, Mary Storer Potter (first wife) 18
Longfellow, Samuel (brother) 22, 38, 45, 50, 65, 97
Longfellow, Stephen (father) 17
Longfellow, Stephen, Jr. (brother) 17
Longfellow, Zilpah (mother) 17
Longfellow-Evangeline State Park 42
Lovejoy, Elijah 18
Lowell, James Russell 41, 43–44, 46
Lowell, Robert 44
Lowes, John Livingston 48
Luening, Otto 162–164, 170, 172

Mahony, Bertha E. 94
Maillet, Antonine 56, 156
Maine Memory Network 16
Manifest Destiny 18, 37
Mann, Horace 40
Matthews, Brander 47–48
Mayorga, Margaret 156
McClatchy, J.D. 31, 50
McCord Museum of Canadian History 16
McCrie, George 68
McGuffey, William Holmes 62
McGuffey's Sixth Eclectic Reader 168
Merrill, James 44
Meserve, Walter I. 144, 147
Meynelle, Louis 108, 110
Micmacs 88
Milton, John 41, 56, 67, 71, 193, 196
Mississippi River 37, 48, 57, 83, 133, 136, 150, 182
Modernism 26, 27, 29, 30, 53, 71
Monteiro, George 50
Moses 176
Motley, John Lothrop 38
Mowis 10, 73, 150, 193, 196

Moyers, William 142–143
Muhlig, F.M. 63, 76–77, 87–88, 168, 175
Murphy, Brenda 145

Nebraska River 186, 192
Neill, John R. 95, 114–116, 118, 126–128, 130
New Critics 27, 29, 48, 55, 68, 73
New Formalism 23, 35, 56, 88
Nicco, Carlo 141–142
Nietzsche, Friedrich 23
Nightingale, Florence 40
Niobara River 86
Norris, Mary Harriott 74
Norton, Andrews 45
Norton, Charles Eliot 69

Oakley, Violet 123–124
O'Connor, William Van 24
Odysseus 13, 90
Ohio River 83, 133, 136
Olivier, André 43
Onderdonk, James L. 48
O'Reilly, Mary 89, 168–170
O'Sullivan, John L. 18, 37
Ozark Mountains 77, 106, 130, 136, 164, 169, 193

Palmer, Frank Herbert 7, 63, 82–84, 89
Paradis, Françoise 51, 112–113
Parini, Jay 24
Parkman, Francis 19, 77
Parrington, Vernon Louis 34, 48
Peace of Utrecht 61, 176
Pearl, Michael 30
Pearson, P.H. 89
Peck, George Washington 46, 47, 66
Penelope 6, 59, 189, 192
Percival, William 160
Perez, Louis 167
Perkins, Granville 112, 135
Persephone 12
Pitt, William 173
Plaquemine (Bayou) 10, 83, 133
Plato, Platonic 24, 90
Poe, Edgar Allan 13, 18, 19, 43–45, 52, 53, 58, 144
Pope, Alexander 71, 84
Porter, Noah 61, 99
Postmodernism 43, 57, 112
Pound, Ezra 24, 26, 27, 30, 53, 55, 81, 82
Pre-Raphaelites 95, 105–106
Price, Olive 90, 168–170
Pyle, Howard 124

Quaker 151, 154, 162, 177

Rainey, Sue 110
Rainforth, Maria 146–147
Ray, Gordon N. 95
Reinhart, C.S. 112
Revolutionary War 12, 17, 92
Reynal, Abbé Guillaume Thomas François 61, 78, 176
Rice, Edward Everett 146, 156, 161, 170, 177
Richards, Edouard 78
Richardson, Charles F. 33–34, 44, 46
Robertson, E.S. 69
Robertson, Robbie 167
Robins, Eliza 62, 65, 78
Roman Catholicism 39–40, 65, 66, 81, 151, 165, 174, 190
Roscoe, Albert 171
Rose, Billy 162
Rossetti, William Michael 68
Ruskin, John 187
Rust, Richard Dilworth 48, 49, 50, 60
Ruth 54, 59, 176

Saint Catherine of Siena 190
Saint Eulalie 5, 163, 190
St. Martin Parish Library, St. Martinville v, 13, 42–43, 83, 113, 162, 164, 173, 181
Santayana, George 34
Schoolcraft, H.R. 67, 179–180
Schubert, Franz 17–18, 169
Schwartz, Delmore 25–26, 28
Scott, Sir Walter 67, 72
Scudder, Horace E. 41, 46, 55, 62, 63, 64–67, 68, 72, 73–74, 78, 80, 81, 84, 85, 88
Seeley, John 28–29, 31, 50, 53, 54, 55, 57, 58, 85
Semple, Lewis B. 3, 48, 62, 63–64, 74, 84–85, 89
Seven Years War 172
Sévigné, Marie de 39
Shakespeare 24, 29, 30
Shawnee 10, 12, 89, 119, 150, 191, 193, 196
Shelley, Percy Bysshe 18, 69, 70
Shulamite Woman 176
Sidney, Sir Philip 26
Sieper, Ernst 89
Simon, Howard 142–143
Sisters of Mercy 1, 12, 40, 75, 97, 111, 117, 151, 166, 174, 195, 196
Sloan, Lucy Adella 4, 7, 90
Smith, Elizabeth Oakes 52
Smith, Jesse Willcox 124, 127
Song of Solomon, Song of Songs 9, 176
Spenser, Edmund 9, 10, 54
Stedman, E.C. 14, 41, 58, 67–68
Stevens, Wallace 26, 32, 37

Stevenson, Robert Louis 21
Stowe, Harriet Beecher 19, 41, 54
Sumner, Charles 37, 45
Sumner, Horace 3

Tappan, Eva March 62, 64, 85–87, 88,89
Taranto, Paul 164, 170
Taylor, Walter Fuller 48
Têche Bayou 42, 106, 162, 164, 169, 180, 181, 188
Tennyson, Alfred, Lord 19, 59, 67
Thomas, J.R. 160
Thomson, Jay Earle 64, 87–89, 90
Tippett, Hariett 14, 91
Traver, Robert 146–152, 169, 170
Treaty of Ghent 17
Treaty of Guadalupe Hidalgo 37, 186

Uncle Tom's Cabin 12, 13, 19, 41, 54, 147
Usmiani, Renate 156

Vaile, E.O. 63, 81–82, 84
Vaudeville 21
Virgil (Vergil) 65, 177, 192
Voorhies, Felix 42, 167, 181

Wachita (Lake) 83, 153
Wagenknecht, Edward 39, 49, 51, 177, 192, 195
Wallowa River 86
Walsh, Raoul 170
Warhol, Robyn R. 14
Wasserstrom, William 4, 94, 96, 106, 118–119
Wax, Jamie 164, 170
Weills, Charles Raymond 161–162
Weills, William Edgar 161–162
Weitenkampf, Frank 118, 141
Welter, Barbara 1–2, 4
Whipple, E.P. 68, 69
White, C.S. 108, 110
Whitman, Walt 20, 21, 34, 49, 58, 59, 71, 138
Whittier, John Greenleaf 19, 45, 47, 52
Wigglesworth, Michael 39
Wilde, Oscar 21
Williams, Cecil B. 49, 177
Williams, Mentor L. 180
Williams, William Carlos 24, 31, 80
Wordsworth, William 26, 48

Yeats, William Butler 22, 54
Young, Brigham 19, 37
Young, Charlotte 161

www.ingramcontent.com/pod-product-compliance
Lightning Source LLC
Chambersburg PA
CBHW032057300426
44116CB00007B/783

* 9 7 8 0 7 8 6 4 4 2 1 7 1 *